LEGENDARY LOCALS

OF

ALBUQUERQUE

NEW MEXICO

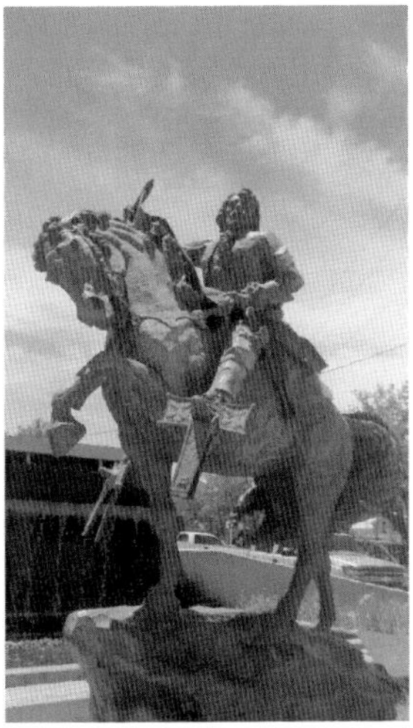

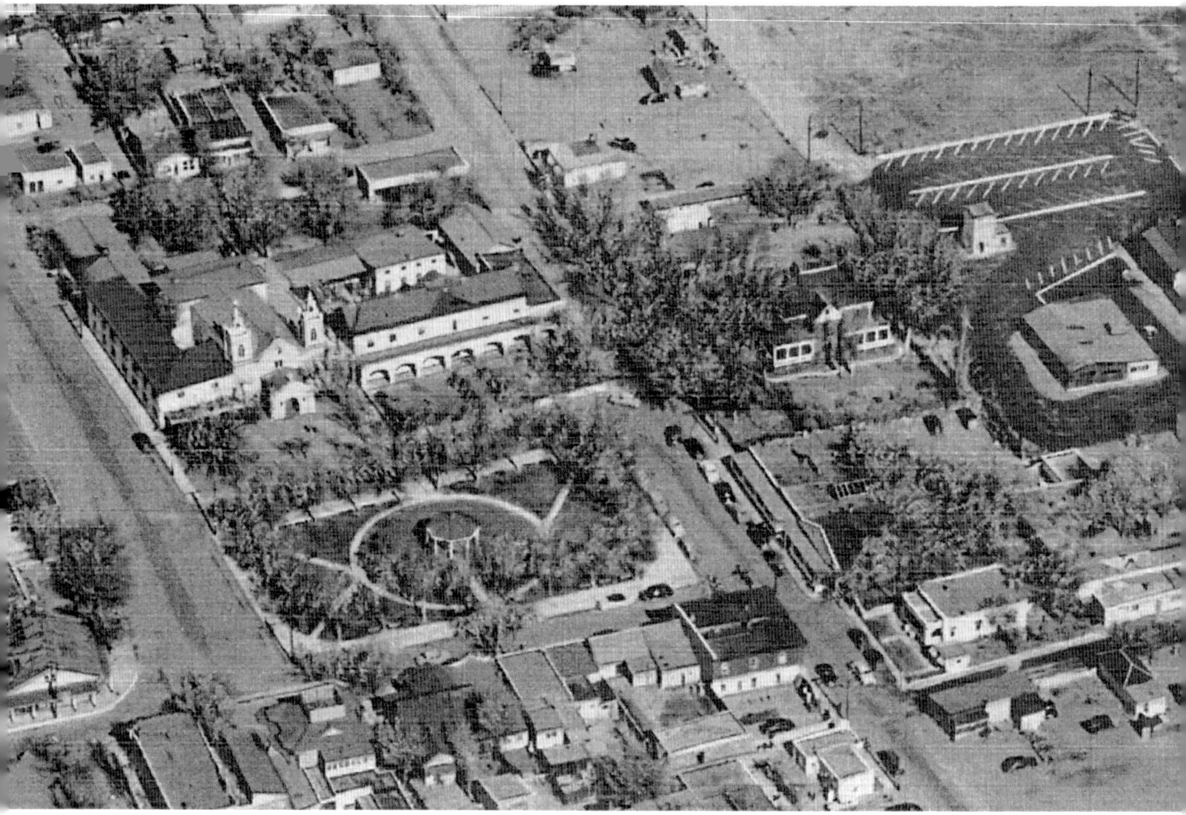

Albuquerque's Old Town Plaza, c. 1950
Long the center of Albuquerque, Old Town Plaza is shown in an aerial photograph, looking northeast. (Author's collection.)

Page 1: Gov. Francisco Cuervo y Valdés
Francisco Cuervo y Valdés is considered to be Alburquerque's founding father. See page 11 for more information. (Author's collection.)

LEGENDARY LOCALS

OF

ALBUQUERQUE
NEW MEXICO

RICHARD MELZER

LEGENDARY LOCALS

ISBN 978-1-4671-0197-4

Legendary Locals is an imprint of Arcadia Publishing
Charleston, South Carolina

Printed in the United States of America

Library of Congress Control Number: 2014948990

For all general information, please contact Arcadia Publishing:
Telephone 843-853-2070
Fax 843-853-0044
E-mail sales@arcadiapublishing.com
For customer service and orders:
Toll-Free 1-888-313-2665

Visit us on the Internet at www.arcadiapublishing.com

Dedication
To Kam, my diamond in the desert, my beacon in the night

On the Front Cover: Clockwise from top left:
Richard Mullane, astronaut (Author's collection; see page 116), Maria Chiwiwi, pottery artist (Courtesy of Albuquerque Museum, PA1990-013-274; see page 66), Don Perkins, football player (Author's collection; see page 121), Johnny Tapia, boxer (Author's collection; see page 124), Vivian Vance (Courtesy of Albuquerque Museum, PA1978-153-Vance; see page 81), Pete V. Domenici, senator (Author's collection; see page 21), Joe S. Sando, historian (Author's collection; see page 59), Carrie Tingley, governor (Courtesy of Albuquerque Museum, PA1994-020-001; see page 17), Dennis Chavez, senator (Author's collection; see page 19).

On the Back Cover: From left to right:
Clyde Tingley, governor (Courtesy of the Albuquerque Museum; see page 16), J.L. Dodson, automobile pioneer (Courtesy of the Albuquerque Museum, PA 1990-013-240; see page 111).

CONTENTS

ACKNOWLEDGMENTS

Every new book presents its own set of unique challenges and joys. The greatest challenge in writing this book was to decide who should be included in this "who's who" of Albuquerque history. A great pleasure has been to discuss this dilemma with some of the city's most dedicated historians, including the following: Ed Boles; Don Bullis; Ann Carson; Henrietta Christmas of the New Mexico Genealogical Society; Gary Herron; Chuck Hornung; Van Dorn Hooker; Ted Jojola of the University of New Mexico's School of Architecture and Planning; Carleen Lazzell; Margaret Espinosa McDonald; Mo Palmer; Joe and Rita Powdrell; Dick Ruddy and Diane Schaller of Historic Albuquerque Incorporated; Susan Schwartz at Fairview Cemetery; Francisco Sisneros at the Hispanic Genealogical Research Center; John Taylor; Nancy Tucker; and Carlos Vásquez of the National Hispanic Cultural Center.

The following people have been helpful in the gathering of rare images: Rigo Chavez of the Albuquerque Public Schools; Jennifer DeMerritt; Leba Freed at the Wheels Museum; Daniel Kosharek at the Photo Archives of the Museum of New Mexico; Gayle McCutchen at the Vietnam Veterans Memorial; Eileen Price at the University of New Mexico's Center for Southwest Research; Paul Rhetts at Rio Grande Books; Nona Browne at the Menaul Historical Library of the Southwest; Edie Steinhoff of the Public Information Office at New Mexico Tech; Judy Basen Weinreb of the Israel C. Carmel Archives at Congregation Albert; Brother Charles T. Schreiner and Brandon Thompson of the Good Shepherd Center; and especially Glenn Fye at the Albuquerque Museum. Don Bullis, John Taylor, and Rena Chávez Melzer read the entire manuscript, making terrific suggestions and vital corrections. Special thanks to Baldwin G. Burr, who lent masterful technical skills, long hours, and endless patience.

The project's chief joy was meeting many of the outstanding men and women (or their descendants) included in this book. Without exception, they could not have been more generous with their time, stories, and photographs. It is no wonder why they must be counted among the greatest citizens of our great city.

Finally, I feel compelled to apologize to the many worthy Albuquerqueans who I did not include in this book of legendary citizens. Space, not value, precludes their inclusion. In the best of worlds, this book would be twice as long or, better yet, composed of several volumes.

Unless otherwise noted, all images are from the author's private collection.

INTRODUCTION

How is it possible to capture the heart, soul, and spirit of a place and its people? In the case of Albuquerque, New Mexico, talented people have written songs (like Jim Glaser's "The Lights of Albuquerque"), poems (Margaret Randall's "Favorite Places"), and novels (Rudolfo Anaya's *Alburquerque* [1992]). Artists like Betty Sabo have painted pictures and created sculptures. Sandra Fye, Carleen Lazzell, and Mo Palmer have used historic photographs to depict the city's past. Oral histories have been collected. Marc Simmons and Robert Turner Wood have written first-rate narratives. The Albuquerque Museum has created one exceptional exhibit after another. The Albuquerque Historical Society and local genealogical groups have offered lectures and printed valuable publications.

Another way to portray a dynamic community like Albuquerque is to consider its legendary residents: men and women, young and old, popular and controversial. Individually, each has made major contributions of one kind or another. Collectively, they have molded the city, its unique character, and its endless charm. Historians have long abandoned the notion that history is driven by heroic leaders alone. But, the importance of individuals in larger movements and historical periods cannot be denied.

The purpose of this slim volume is to add another dimension to the portrait of the city of Albuquerque by focusing on dozens of its leading residents, past and present. To be included, a person must have significantly contributed to Albuquerque's character, development, and deserved reputation. These legendary residents are much like the specially shaped balloons in a mass ascension at Albuquerque's annual International Balloon Fiesta. The ascension as a whole (representing the city's population as a whole) is awe-inspiring, but the balloons (our legendary locals) make each ascension even more impressive and interesting for the thousands who come from far and near to observe the spectacular event.

CHAPTER ONE

Founders, Politicians, and Diplomats

Albuquerque was founded by Spanish settlers under the leadership of Capt. Martin Hurtado in 1706. It was named for the Duke of Alburquerque (with an extra "r"), the viceroy of New Spain from 1702 to 1711. As a royal *villa* (town), Alburquerque was governed by an *alcalde mayor* (with extensive local executive, legislative, and judicial powers) chosen by the Spanish governors of New Mexico. By 1776, the villa's population had grown to 763.

New Mexico was conquered by the United States during the Mexican War (1846–1848). Enjoying its first taste of democracy, Albuquerque (by common usage now without its extra "r") was incorporated as a city in 1885, with an elected mayor and city board. Its earliest ordinances included stiff licensing for businesses, dogs, and saloons. It also included some strange requests, like an appeal for the prohibition of naked men bathing in the Rio Grande, a practice that was considered "rather unpleasant for residents and promenades in the vicinity."

In 1917, like many municipalities in the United States, Albuquerque adopted a commission-manager form of city government in which the commission's chairman held considerable power. Clyde Tingley held this mayoral-like position for many years in the 1920s and 1930s and was often (mistakenly) referred to as Albuquerque's "mayor." The city returned to a mayoral system of government in 1974, electing Harry Kinney as its first true mayor in almost 60 years. Since then, Albuquerque has had seven mayors: five Democrats and two Republicans.

Albuquerque's population of 545,852 in the 2010 census makes it by far the largest city in New Mexico. With a quarter of the state's total population, Albuquerque and its surrounding area became a new congressional district in 1969. It has elected three Republicans and two Democrats as its representatives in the US Congress. Of the state's US senators, six have called Albuquerque home, and seven of the city's residents have served as governor since statehood was achieved in 1912.

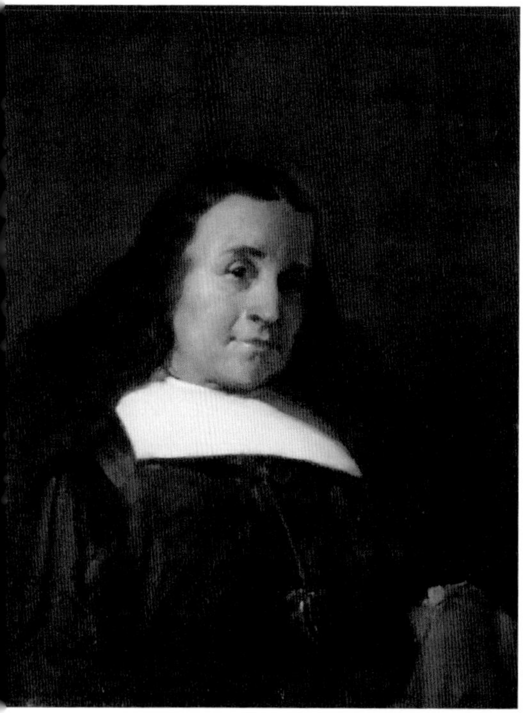

Dukes of Alburquerque

Francisco Fernández de la Cueva (1666–1724) was the 10th Duke of Alburquerque when he served as the 42nd viceroy of New Spain from 1702 to 1711. Arriving in New Spain when he was 35 years old, de la Cueva (above) became the youngest viceroy in the Spanish colony's 286-year history. During his time in office, two *villas* were founded: Alburquerque and San Francisco de Cuellar (now Chihuahua). Beltrán Osorio y Diez de Rivera (1918–1994) was the 18th Duke of Alburquerque, Spain. He visited Albuquerque in 1956 (below) to help celebrate the city's 250th anniversary. His gift was a valuable 17th-century *repostero* (tapestry), now at the Albuquerque Museum. The duke was a racehorse jockey, although many consider him to have been one of the worst jockeys in racing history; he seldom finished a race and was often injured while trying. (Left, painting by Gerald Cassidy, courtesy of the Museum of New Mexico, 008780; below, courtesy of Albuquerque Museum, PA1994-012-004.)

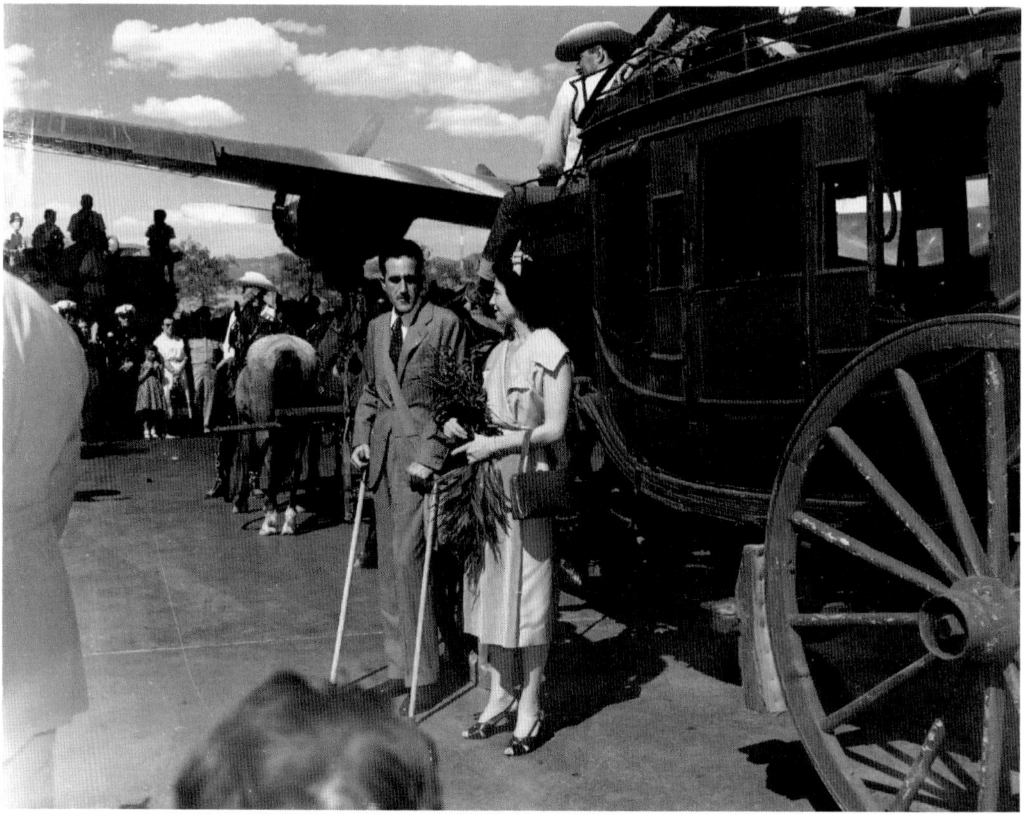

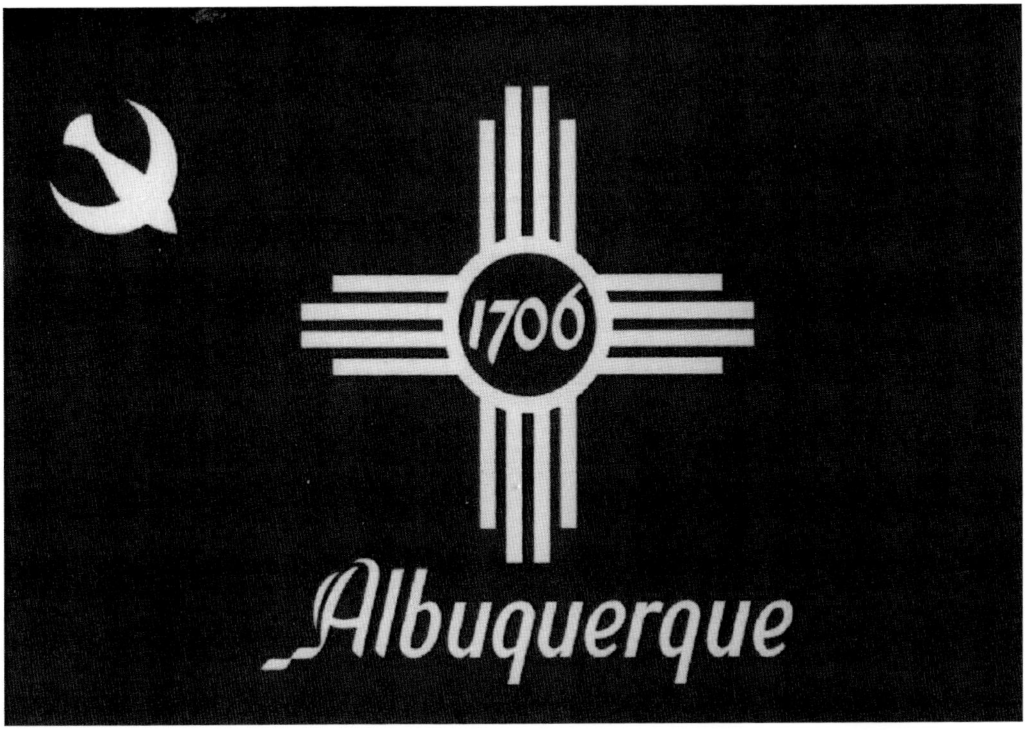

Gov. Francisco Cuervo y Valdés (c. 1678–1707)

Gov. Francisco Cuervo y Valdés is considered Alburquerque's founding father, because the villa was established during his term in office. Although he likely exaggerated the numbers, his report to the viceroy of New Spain told of 35 families, including 252 men, women, and children, who had settled on a "good place" with abundant "land, water, pasture, and firewood." The new town in the Rio Abajo was officially founded on April 23, 1706. Appropriately, Cuervo's bronze statue is located at the northern gateway to Albuquerque's Old Town Plaza, at Rio Grande Boulevard and Romero Street. The 12-foot, 6-inch, $100,000 bronze sculpture (right) was created by Santa Fe artist Buck McCain and was dedicated on April 23, 1988, exactly 282 years after the city's founding. Albuquerque's city flag (above), designed by Richard T. Vann, features the city's founding date, a Zia symbol, and a stylized thunderbird. Reversing the Spanish royal colors of the New Mexico state flag, its yellow images lie on a field of red.

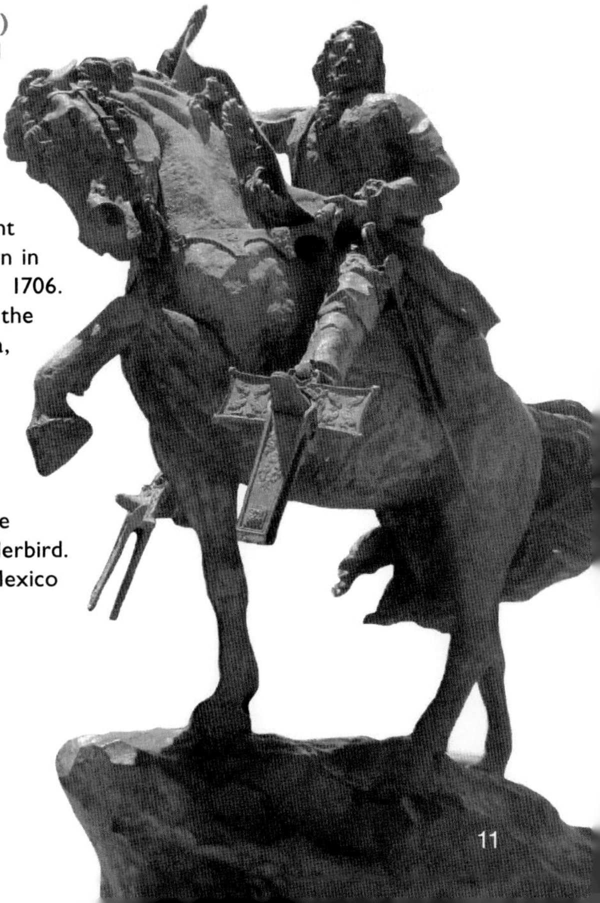

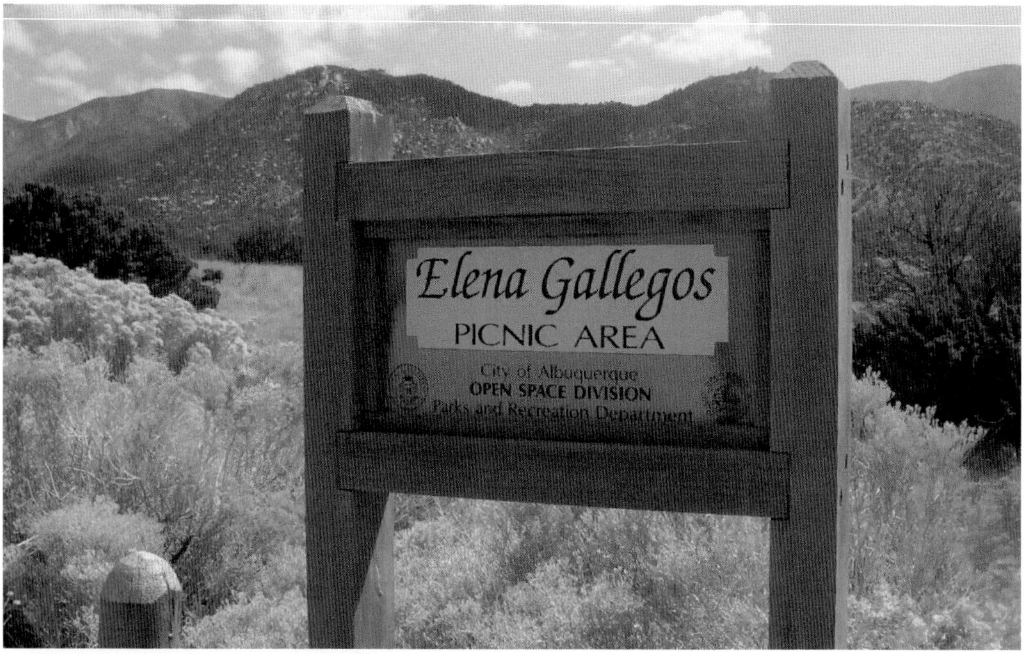

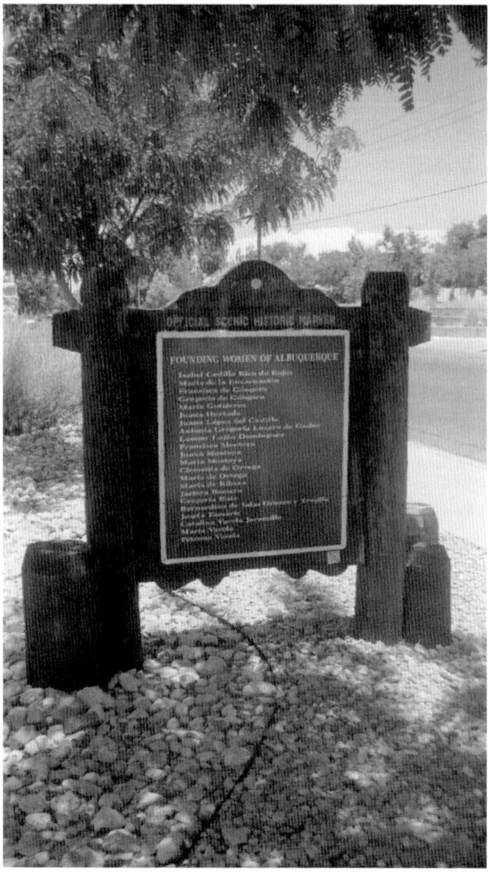

Elena Gallegos (c. 1680–1731) and the Founding Matriarchs

Elena Gallegos's family joined hundreds of Spanish refugees who fled New Mexico after the Pueblo Revolt of 1680. She returned to New Mexico with the Reconquest and married Jacques Grolet when she was 19. Left a widow 12 years later, she acquired a huge Spanish land grant from her neighbor, Diego Montoya. It was not uncommon for women, especially widows, to own land under Spanish law. By the 1930s, Albert G. Simms had acquired the grant and later donated much of it to the Albuquerque Academy. It is now part of the Elena Gallegos Picnic Area (above), created in 1984. Other women played important roles in the city's early history. A historical marker near the Albuquerque Museum in Old Town (below) lists 22 of Albuquerque's founding matriarchs.

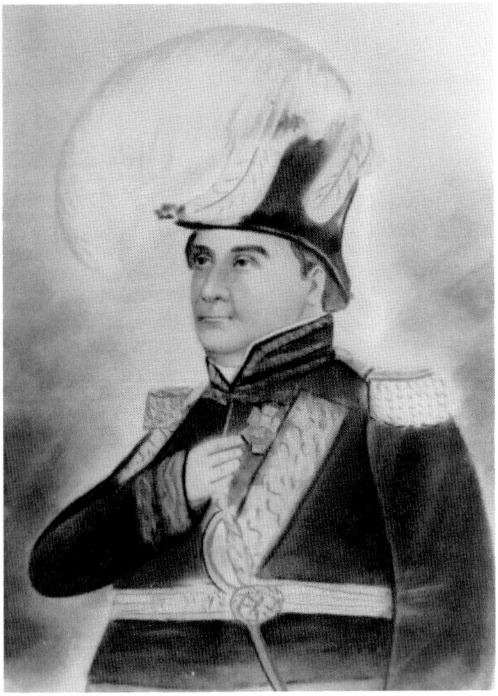

Manuel Armijo (1790–1853)
Born into an Albuquerque family of privilege and wealth in 1790, Manuel Armijo served as the governor of New Mexico three times during the Mexican period (1821–1848), for a total of eight years. His terms were filled with controversy involving land grants, the American invasion of New Mexico in 1846, and the influence of gambling-hall owner Gertrudis Barceló (Doña Tules). (Courtesy of the Museum of New Mexico, 50809.)

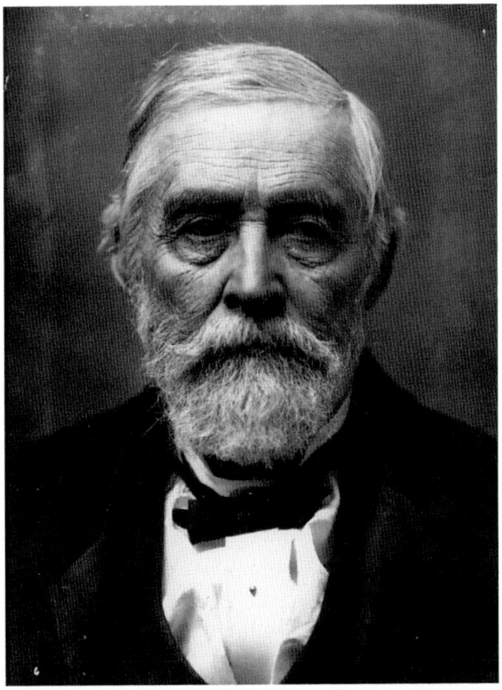

Edmund G. Ross (1826–1907)
Edmund Ross is most famous for casting the deciding vote in the impeachment trial of Pres. Andrew Johnson in 1868. Shunned in his home state of Kansas, Ross moved to Albuquerque, where Pres. Grover Cleveland appointed him New Mexico's 12th territorial governor. Ross worked hard to counter the powerful Santa Fe Ring. He also signed legislation that created New Mexico's first colleges, the University of New Mexico (UNM), the New Mexico School of Mines, and New Mexico A&M. (Portrait by William Cobb, courtesy of the Albuquerque Museum, PA1990-013-374.)

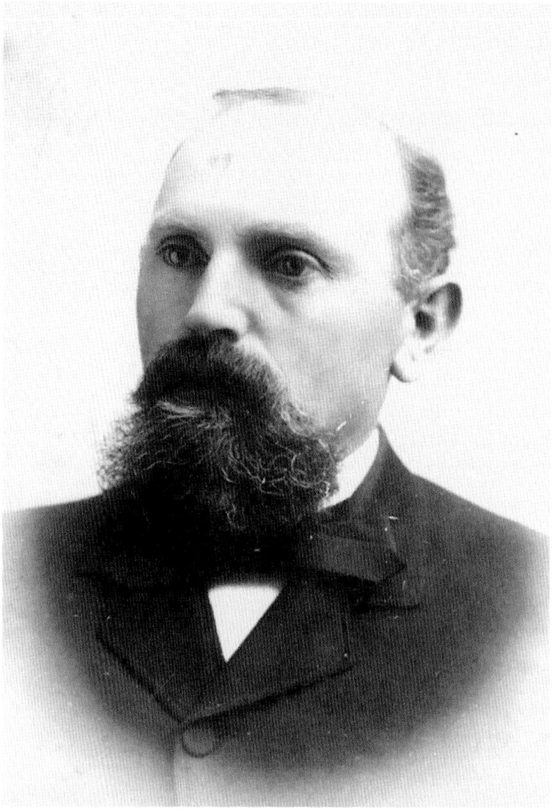

Henry N. Jaffa (1846–1901)
Jaffa was a member of the dynamic generation of leaders who helped Albuquerque grow in the decades following the arrival of the Santa Fe Railroad in 1880. When the city incorporated in 1885, Jaffa became Albuquerque's first democratically elected mayor, winning in a crowded field of eight candidates. Jaffa also served as the first president of Congregation Albert, Albuquerque's first Jewish congregation. (Courtesy of the Albuquerque Museum, PA1978-050-281.)

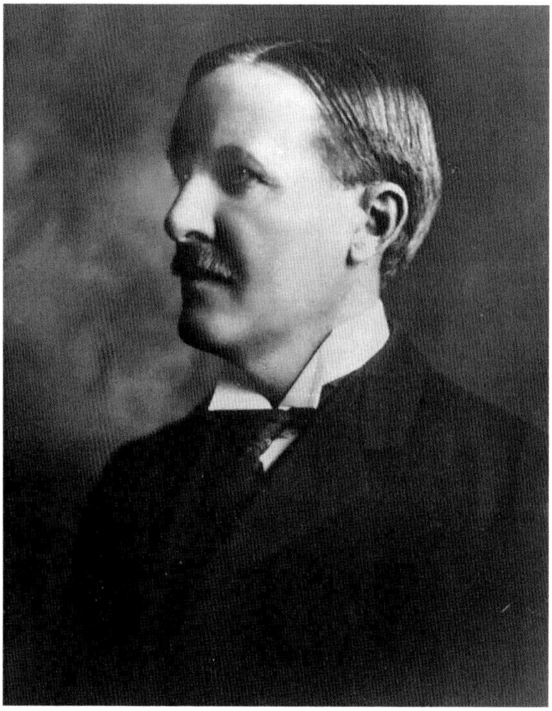

Bernard Rodey (1856–1927)
Republican Bernard Rodey arrived in Albuquerque in 1881, founding a law firm that remains one of the most influential in the state. He is known as the "Father of the University of New Mexico" because he helped draft legislation that led to the school's creation in 1889. Later, as New Mexico's congressional delegate in Washington, he was such a persistent advocate for statehood that some recommended "Statehood" should be his middle name. (Courtesy of the Albuquerque Museum, PA1978-050-410.)

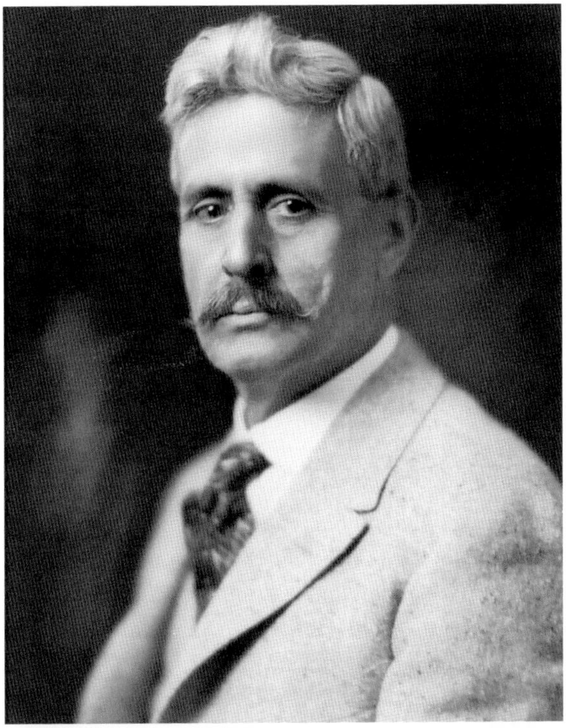

Octaviano Ambrosio Larrazolo Sr. (1859–1930)
Born in Mexico, Octaviano Larrazolo migrated to the United States in 1870. Known for his oratorical skills in both Spanish and in English, he served as the first and only Mexican-born governor of New Mexico (1919–1921). In 1928, he became the first Hispanic to serve in the US Senate. Sadly, one of the state's greatest orators could no longer speak after he suffered a stroke. He died in his Albuquerque home in 1930.

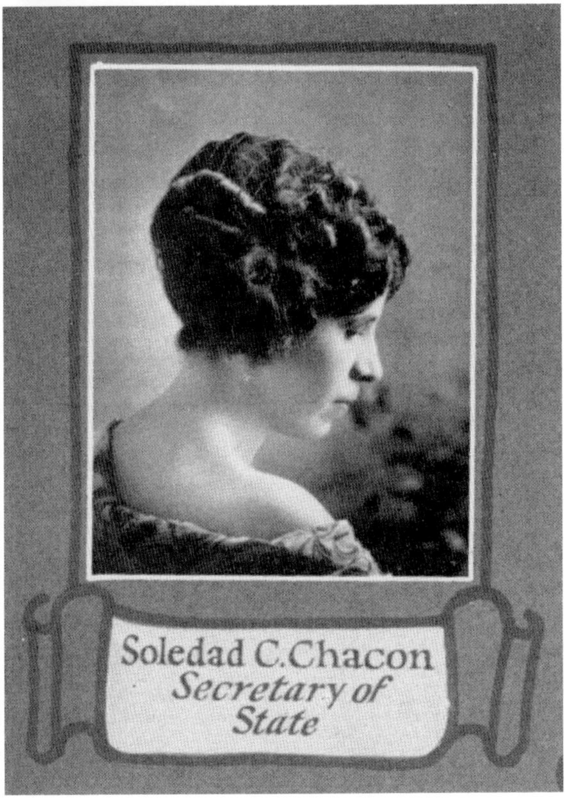

Soledad Chávez de Chacón (1892–1936)
Many believe that Susana Martinez was the first Hispanic female governor of New Mexico. Governor Martinez was the first *elected* female governor, but Secretary of State Soledad Chávez de Chacón, seen here in an image from the *New Mexico Blue Book, 1923–1924*, served as the temporary governor for 16 days while Gov. James Hinkle attended a national convention in 1924. Chacón's time as governor drew national attention, although reporters often focused on the color of her dresses rather than the value of her political ideas.

Clyde Tingley (1882–1960)

Clyde Tingley followed his fiancée, Carrie Wooster, from their native Ohio to Albuquerque when she was diagnosed with tuberculosis (TB). She recovered, and the couple wed in Albuquerque in 1911. Clyde entered Albuquerque city politics, becoming the dominant force on the city commission by the 1920s. A Democrat, in 1934, he was elected governor and served two terms in the midst of the Great Depression. Visiting Washington as many as 19 times, he was successful in securing many valuable New Deal projects for New Mexico, including construction or remodeling of the old Municipal Airport, the Albuquerque Little Theatre, the Monte Vista Fire Station, and almost every school in the city. Nearly every community in the state benefited from Works Progress Administration (WPA), Civilian Conservation Corps (CCC), and other New Deal programs. Thousands of families survived the Depression with wages earned while employed in these programs. Many of Albuquerque's public works were named in Tingley's honor, including Tingley Beach, Tingley Field, and Tingley Coliseum. He returned to Albuquerque following his two terms as governor, continuing to serve on the city council and influencing the city's development until 1954. Tingley enjoyed everything about being a politician, from power to publicity. He especially enjoyed meeting and having his photograph taken with celebrities, including Will Rogers, Douglas Fairbanks, Charles Lindbergh, and New York mayor Jimmy Walker. Never fond of proper grammar, he was famous for his declaration, "I ain't gonna quit saying 'ain't.'" Probably a political ploy, his poor grammar was meant to appeal to the common man and to secure his vote. (Courtesy of the Albuquerque Museum.)

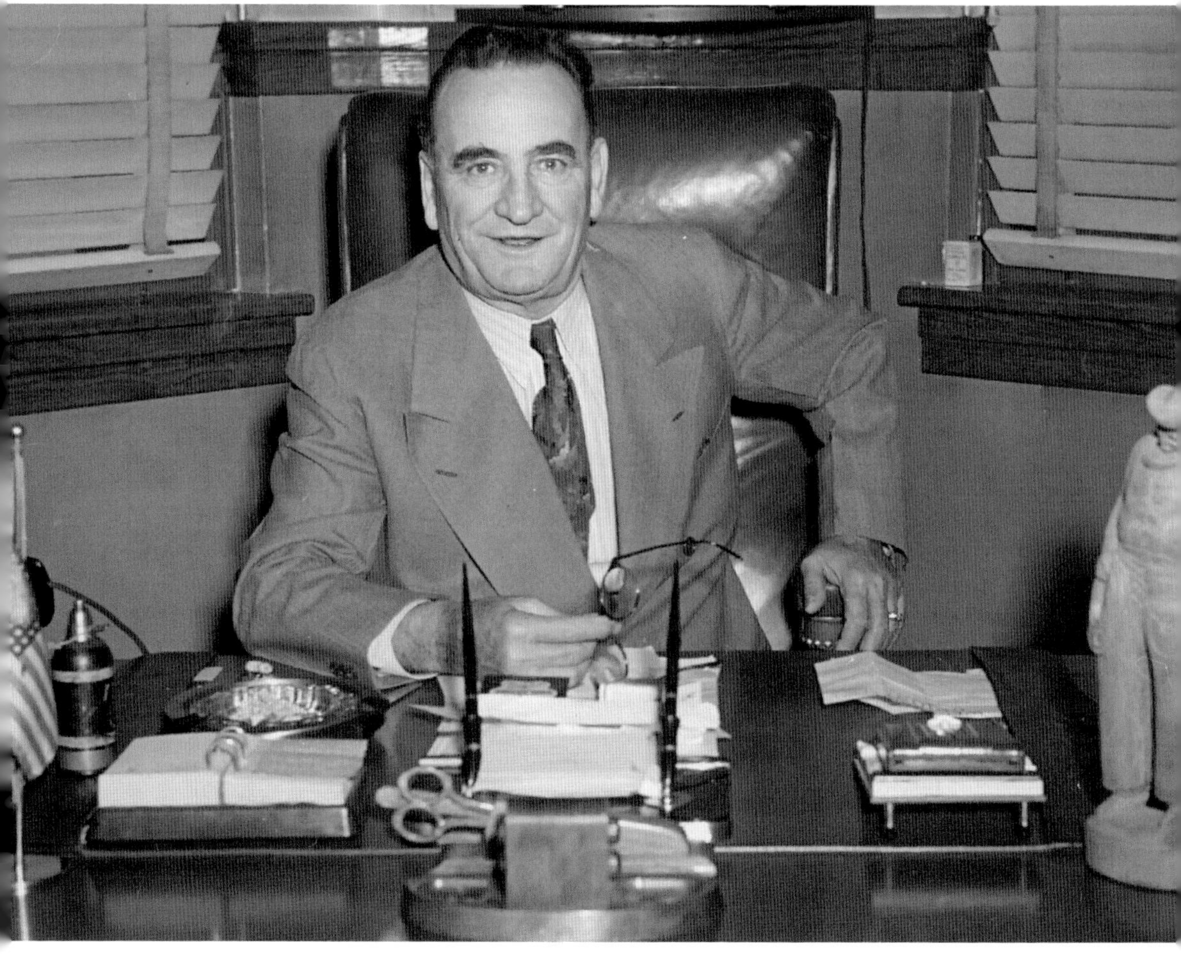

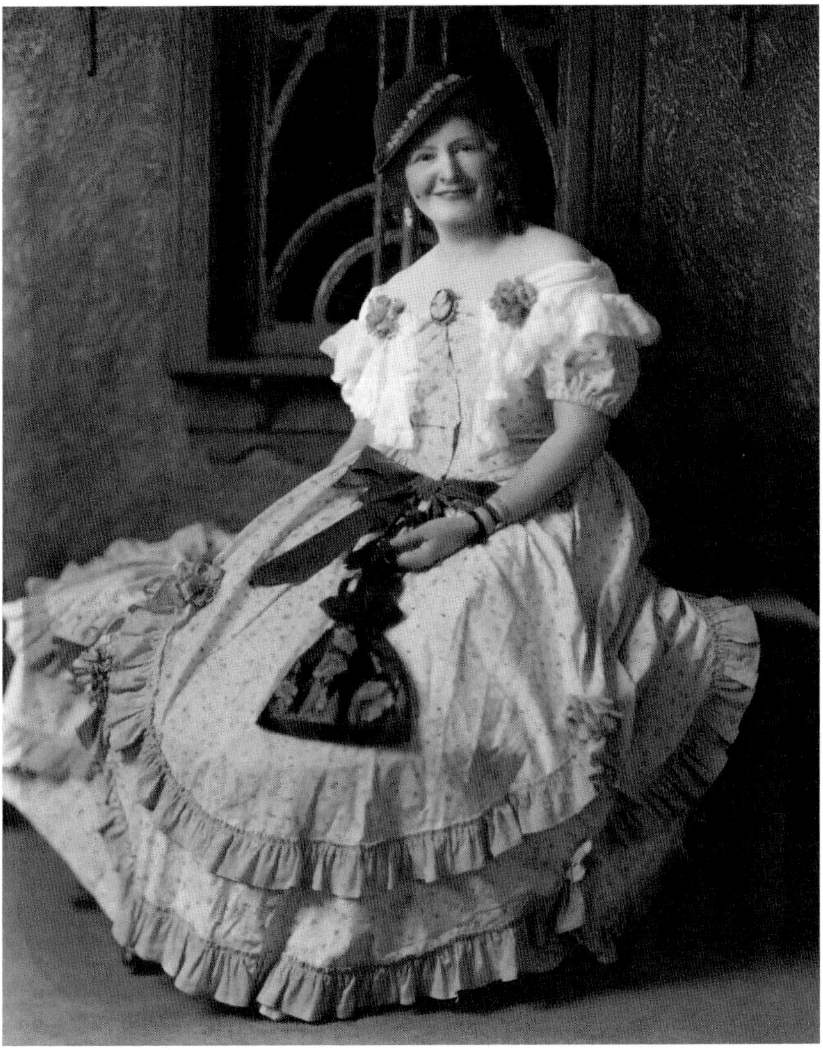

Carrie Tingley (1877–1961)
Born into a wealthy Ohio family, Carrie Wooster was 33 years old when she was diagnosed with tuberculosis. Like thousands of other victims of this dreaded disease, Carrie came to the Southwest in search of a cure. She recovered in Albuquerque and married her fiancé, Clyde Tingley, in 1911. Clyde rose in the political ranks to become Albuquerque's leading politician and, by the mid-1930s, the governor of New Mexico. While helping Clyde with his political career, Carrie Tingley did everything possible to help victims of TB, making visits, giving presents, and helping to create a public TB sanatorium near Socorro. Childless, she also cared for crippled children, especially those suffering from polio. A new health facility in Hot Springs (now Truth or Consequences) was named the Carrie Tingley Hospital for Crippled Children when it was built during Clyde's second term as governor. (The hospital is now located on the UNM campus in Albuquerque.) Carrie loved the color purple, elaborate hats, valuable antiques, and Hollywood movies; she had a permanently reserved seat at the Sunshine Theatre on Central Avenue. The Tingleys lived at 1523 Silver Avenue Southeast, where Carrie died in 1961, within a year of Clyde's death. Concerned about children to the end, she left $75,000 to St. Anthony's Home for Boys in Albuquerque. Carrie Tingley was, without a doubt, the most colorful first lady of New Mexico—and Albuquerque. (Courtesy of the Albuquerque Museum, PA1994-020-001.)

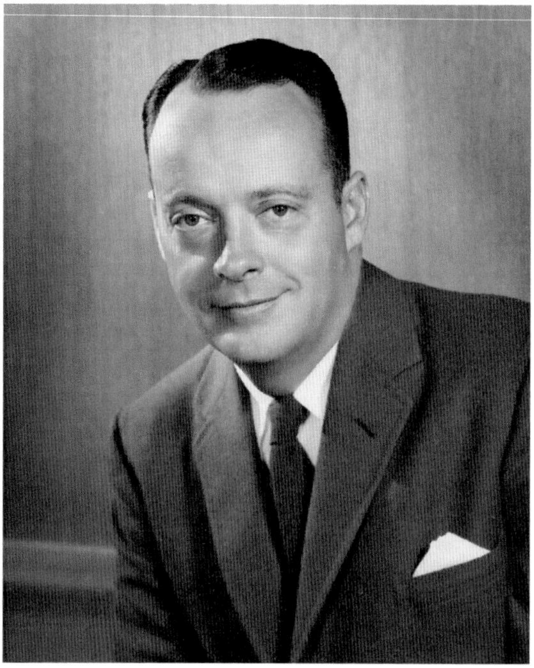

John Field Simms Jr. (1916–1975)
Democrat John Field Simms Jr. was the son of New Mexico Supreme Court justice John Field Simms Sr. and the nephew of US congressman Albert G. Simms. At age 38, Simms Jr. was elected the youngest state governor until that time in New Mexico history. Residing on a large estate on Rio Grande Boulevard, the Simms family built Albuquerque's 13-story Simms Building, the tallest structure in New Mexico when it was completed in 1952. (Courtesy of the Albuquerque Museum, PA1982-181-122.)

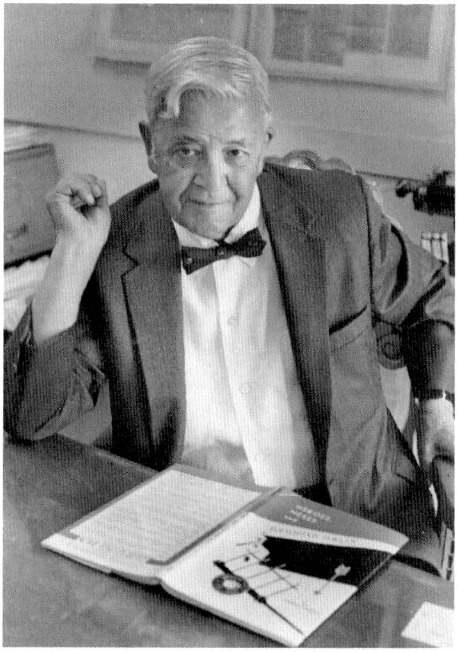

Antonio Gilberto Espinosa (1897–1983)
The descendant of an original Spanish family, Gilberto Espinosa graduated from Albuquerque High, served in World War I, and completed law school at Georgetown University. He practiced law in Albuquerque for the next 60 years. He also studied New Mexico history, translating Gaspar Perez de Villagra's *Historia de la Nueva Mexico, 1610* and helping to organize Coronado's Cuarto Centennial Celebration. His tie-breaking vote led to the annexation of Old Town to Albuquerque in 1949. (Courtesy of Margaret Espinosa McDonald.)

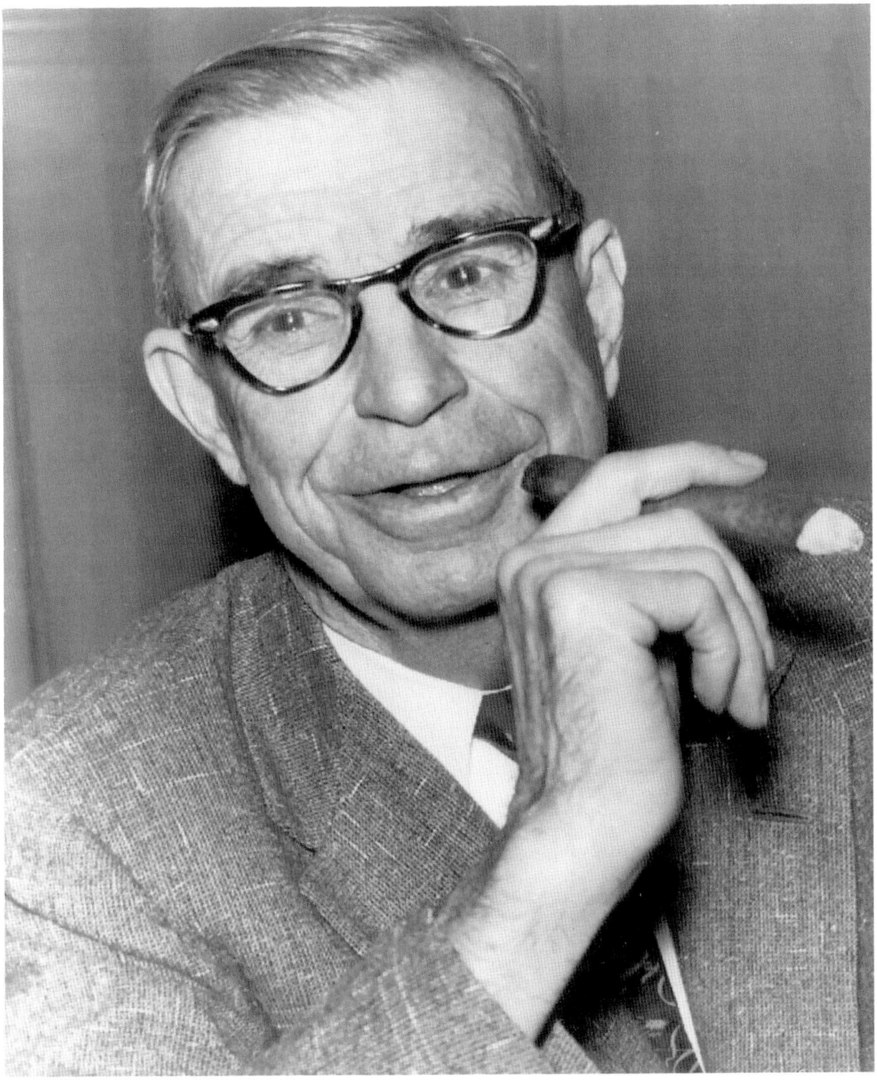

Dennis Chavez (1888–1962)
Chavez was born in Los Chavez, a small farming community in New Mexico's Valencia County. His family moved to Albuquerque, where Dennis had to quit school to help support his parents and their seven other children. Largely self-educated, he studied at nights and passed the bar in 1920. A dedicated Democrat, he quickly rose in political office, becoming a US congressman (the first American-born Hispanic in Congressional history) in 1930. In 1935, he lost a heavily contested race for the US Senate, but was appointed to that senate seat when his opponent, Bronson Cutting, died in a tragic plane crash in Missouri. Chavez never lost another election, serving 27 years as the most powerful Hispanic senator in American history. He was instrumental in bringing New Deal projects to the state in the 1930s and defense projects to New Mexico during the Cold War. His pioneering legislation led to the Civil Rights Act of 1964. Chavez's statue, by Felix de Weldon, represents New Mexico in Capitol Statuary Hall in Washington, DC. A less formal statue, by Cynthia Rowland, showing "El Senador" chatting with an elderly woman, is on display in Albuquerque's city plaza. A postage stamp was issued in his honor in 1991. A federal office building in downtown Albuquerque and an elementary school in the Northeast Heights were also named in Chavez's memory.

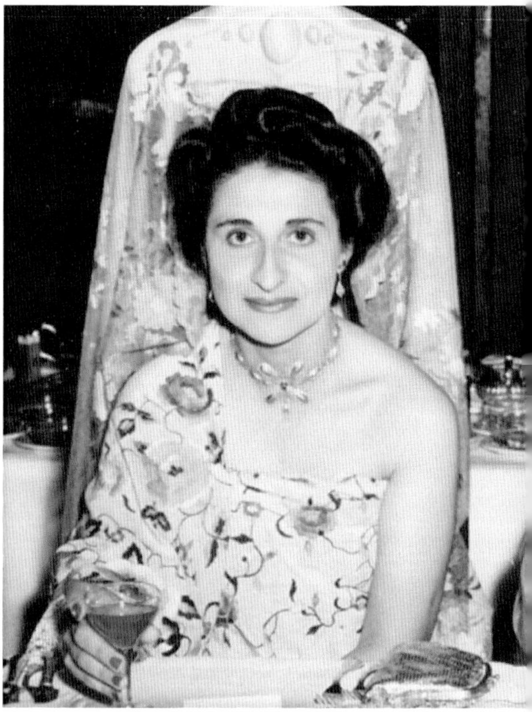

Concha Ortiz y Pino de Kleven (1910–2006)
Ortiz y Pino de Kleven's roots in New Mexico date to the 1690s. While serving three terms in the New Mexico House of Representatives, she became the nation's first female minority whip. She devoted her life to many social causes, including crippled children and prison inmates. Known as the "grande dame" of New Mexico, she was chosen as one of the "Ten Outstanding Women in New Mexico History Since 1850." (Courtesy of the Albuquerque Museum, PA1993-010-022.)

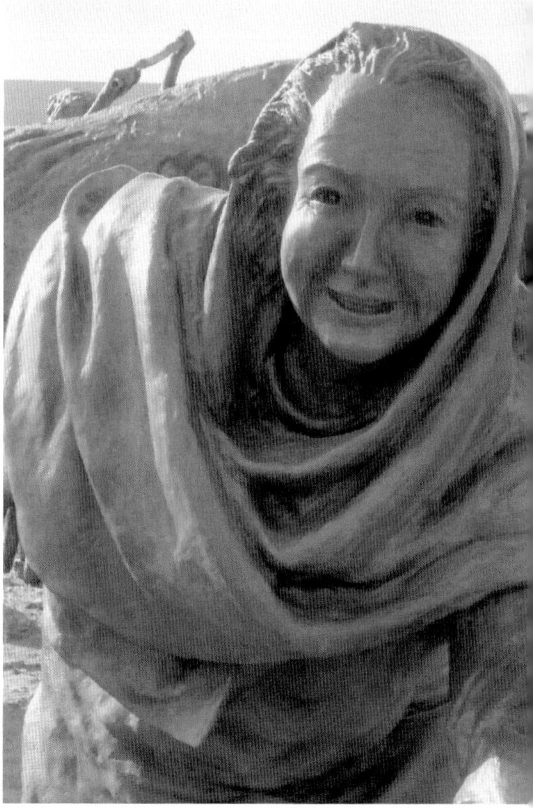

Millie Santillanes (1933–2007)
Born in Albuquerque's Old Town, businesswoman Millie Santillanes was passionately proud of her Hispanic heritage. She helped create the Albuquerque Museum and helped organize Albuquerque's annual Founders Day. In 1998, she supported the creation of a controversial statue of Don Juan de Oñate on the 400th anniversary of his conquest of New Mexico. Rather than honor Oñate alone, statues honoring all Spanish settlers were created. Fittingly, Santillanes's image (pictured) is among the bronze statues of the "Colonizers Memorial."

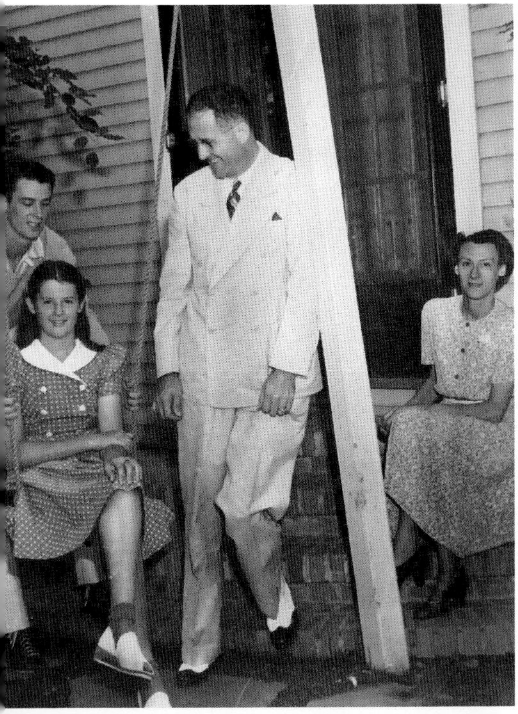

Clinton P. Anderson (1895–1975)
Democrat Clinton P. Anderson (shown here with his family) first came to New Mexico in search of a cure for his case of tuberculosis. Recovering, he administered several New Deal programs before winning election to Congress in 1941. He also served as the nation's secretary of agriculture before returning to New Mexico, where he was elected to the US Senate in 1948. He described his 24 years in the Senate in his 1970 memoir, *Outsider in the Senate*.

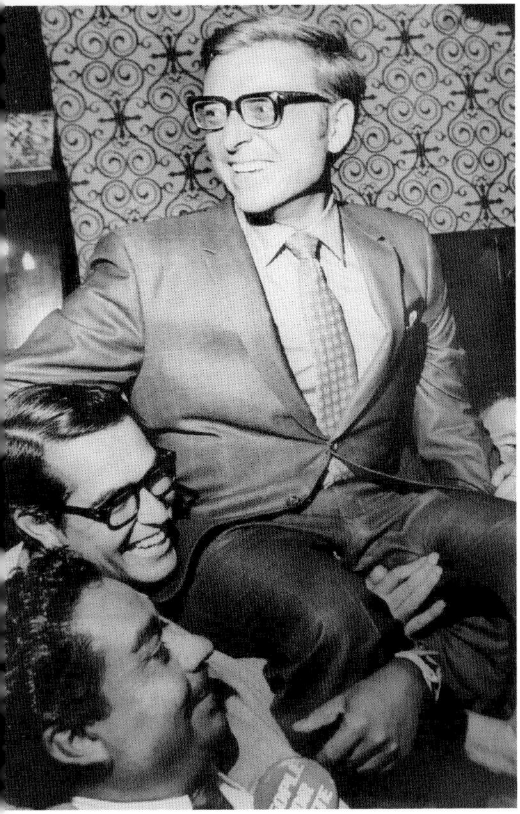

Pete V. Domenici (b. 1932)
The son of Italian immigrants, Pete Domenici graduated from UNM and, as a good athlete, pitched for the Albuquerque Dukes. A Republican, he was elected to the Albuquerque city council and, in 1972, ran successfully for the US Senate. Domenici served longer than any other senator in state history. "Saint Pete" brought many federal programs to the state and performed political miracles by saving several threatened ones.

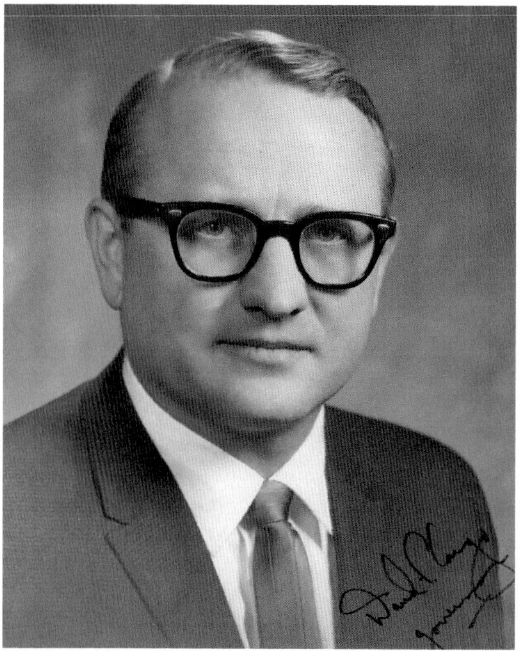

David Cargo (1929–2013)
Originally from Michigan, David Cargo came to Albuquerque to practice law. He soon entered politics, serving in New Mexico's House of Representatives. In 1967, he ran an unorthodox campaign for governor, driving through much of New Mexico in his old Chevrolet. A reporter soon dubbed him "Lonesome Dave." Based on his broad appeal and the popularity of his wife, Ida Jo Anaya, Cargo won the election at the age of 37 and became the state's youngest governor.

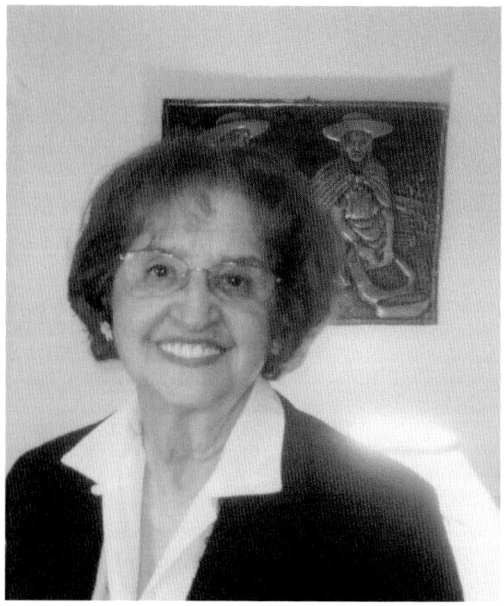

Mari-Luci Jaramillo (b. 1928)
Jaramillo grew up in a loving, working-class family in Las Vegas, New Mexico. Overcoming poverty and discrimination, she graduated from New Mexico Highlands University. She completed a doctoral degree at UNM in 1971. Jaramillo rose to become a UNM vice president and, at the request of Pres. Jimmy Carter, the American ambassador to Honduras (1977–1981). She succeeded by remaining faithful to her values and by never forgetting her humble roots.

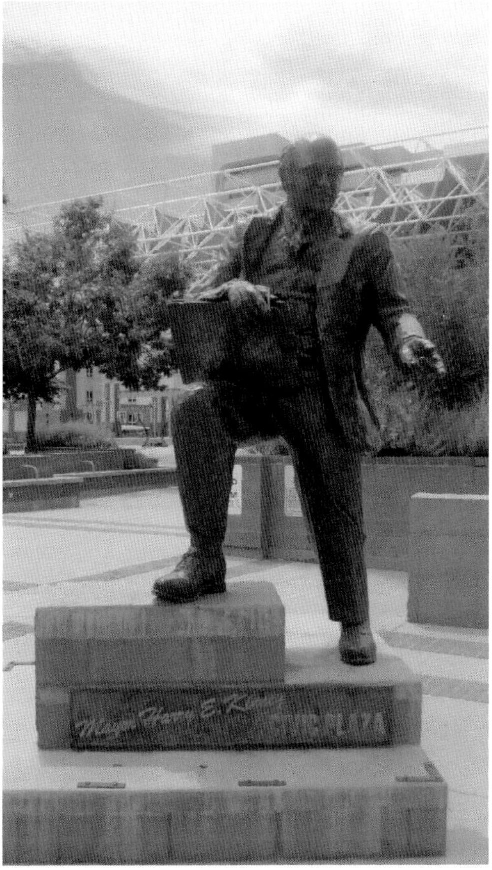

Harry Kinney (1924–2006)
Kinney was elected to both the Bernalillo County Commission and the Albuquerque City Commission, serving as the chairman (de facto mayor) of the latter. After almost 60 years of using a commission-manager form of city government, Albuquerque returned to a mayoral form of government in 1974. Kinney was elected mayor and served two terms in office (1974–1977, 1981–1985). His statue (pictured), by Sonny Rivera, was placed in Albuquerque's Civic Plaza, now named Kinney Plaza.

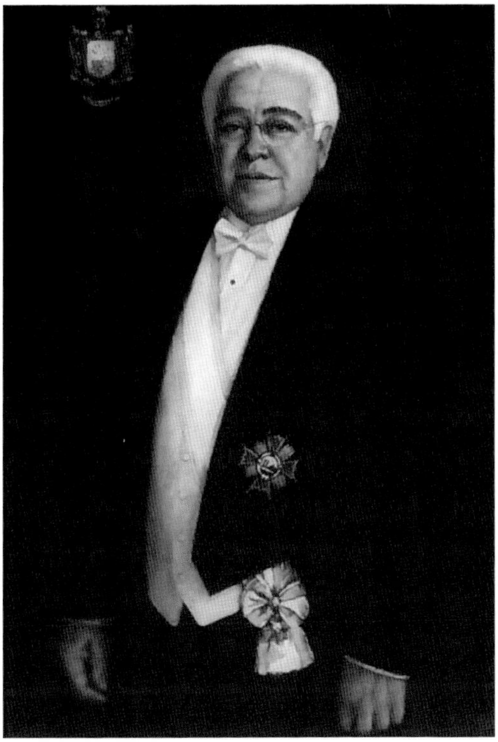

Edward Romero (b. 1934)
The descendant of a Spanish family dating to 1598, Ed Romero served in the Korean War before moving to Albuquerque and founding Advance Sciences, Inc. He enjoyed great business success before selling his company in 1998. He was a founder of Albuquerque's National Hispanic Cultural Center and a founding member of the Albuquerque Hispanic Chamber of Commerce. In 1998, Pres. Bill Clinton appointed Romero as the first Hispanic US ambassador to Spain.

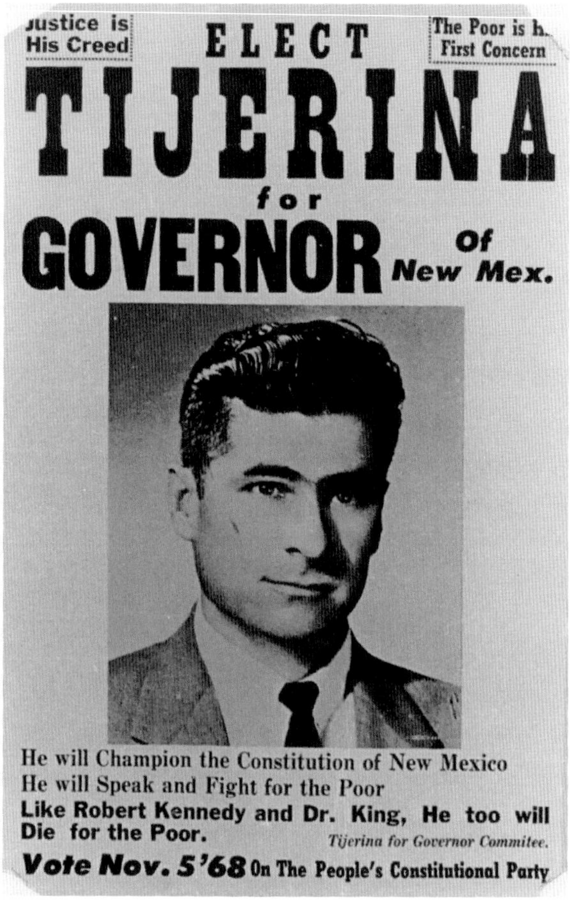

Reies López Tijerina (1926–2015)
López Tijerina was born in Texas and raised in a poor migrant laborer family. Although he worked as an itinerant Christian preacher in various parts of the Southwest, he recognized his true calling when he came to New Mexico and lamented the loss of most Spanish and Mexican land grants. Equating land grants with Hispanic culture and power, he worked hard to have the grants returned to their rightful heirs. Starting nonviolently, López Tijerina organized La Alianza Federal de Merced and led several peaceful marches and demonstrations in the early 1960s. Unfortunately, La Alianza turned to more aggressive forms of protest. In 1966, López Tijerina led a temporary "invasion" of the Carson National Forest, declaring it to be part of the old San Joaquín land grant. La Alianza's violence escalated with its infamous Tierra Amarilla courthouse raid of June 5, 1967. Armed forces, from the state police to the National Guard, searched for him in the wilderness of northern New Mexico until he was finally arrested in Bernalillo. Put on trial for his part in the courthouse raid, he defended himself, using most of his defense to pontificate on the injustices of land-grant losses. In a surprise verdict, the jury found him innocent of all charges. Known as "King Tiger," he became one of the most controversial civil rights leaders of the 1960s. He staged an unsuccessful campaign for governor of New Mexico in 1968. Living to his late eighties, he contributed his papers to UNM, wrote his memoir (*They Call Me "King Tiger"* [2000]), and continued to make public appearances, including at the Roundhouse in Santa Fe. He was unsuccessful in winning the return of a single land grant, but he succeeded in raising Hispanic awareness of the importance of defending what few land grants remain. (Courtesy of Karl Kernberger Pictorial Collection, 2000-008-0001, Center for Southwest Research, University Libraries, University of New Mexico.)

CHAPTER TWO

The Military

Albuquerqueans have faced many foreign enemies in their 300-plus-year history. In each case, they have risen to the occasion and fought bravely on their country's behalf, be it under Spain (1706–1821), Mexico (1821–1848), or the United States (since 1848). Each nation stationed small contingents of soldiers in Albuquerque. Under American rule, New Mexicans have volunteered to fight so readily that their numbers usually represent the highest participation per capita of any territory or state in the country. Tragically, their casualty rates have been equally high, meaning that they are willing to sacrifice their safety—and often their lives—to help defend the United States and its freedoms.

Albuquerqueans have sacrificed on the home front as well. During World War II, Albuquerque Army Air Base (renamed Kirtland Army Air Field in 1942) was built southeast of town, bringing thousands of newcomers to join local residents in building the facility, maintaining it, and using it to train air crews for combat. Although the atomic bomb was developed in Los Alamos in northern New Mexico, parts of the bomb were created from research conducted at the base.

Albuquerque's military role grew even larger during the Cold War. Kirtland Army Air Field (renamed Kirtland Air Force Base in 1947) and Sandia National Laboratories (as of 1949) were created in direct response to the threat of war against the Soviet Union and its communist allies. Albuquerque became a central part of the nation's defense system, especially when thousands of nuclear warheads were stored in a top-secret facility known as Site Able and, later, in the Kirtland Underground Munitions Storage Complex (KUMSC).

More than 75,000 New Mexicans served in the Korean and Vietnam conflicts. Almost 400 New Mexicans died in Vietnam; many were from Albuquerque and more than half were younger than 22 years old. Protests against the Vietnam War and nuclear energy served as reminders that military solutions are not always the preferred alternative in every crisis.

The city is now an essential part of America's counterterrorism infrastructure. Scientists at Sandia National Laboratories have developed important new antiterrorist devices. Air Force personnel at Kirtland train to combat foreign terrorists. And local residents continue to volunteer to serve in the military and make their country safe, just as they have always done in times of need.

Veterans are provided good healthcare in Albuquerque's Veterans Hospital, opened in southeast Albuquerque in 1932. About 300 local men and women were employed at the hospital in the 1940s. Over 2,100 dedicated people are employed today; about a third of the staff are veterans. All veterans are honored at Albuquerque's impressive 25-acre New Mexico Veterans Memorial Park at 1100 Louisiana Boulevard Southeast, where a monument for every foreign conflict has been erected.

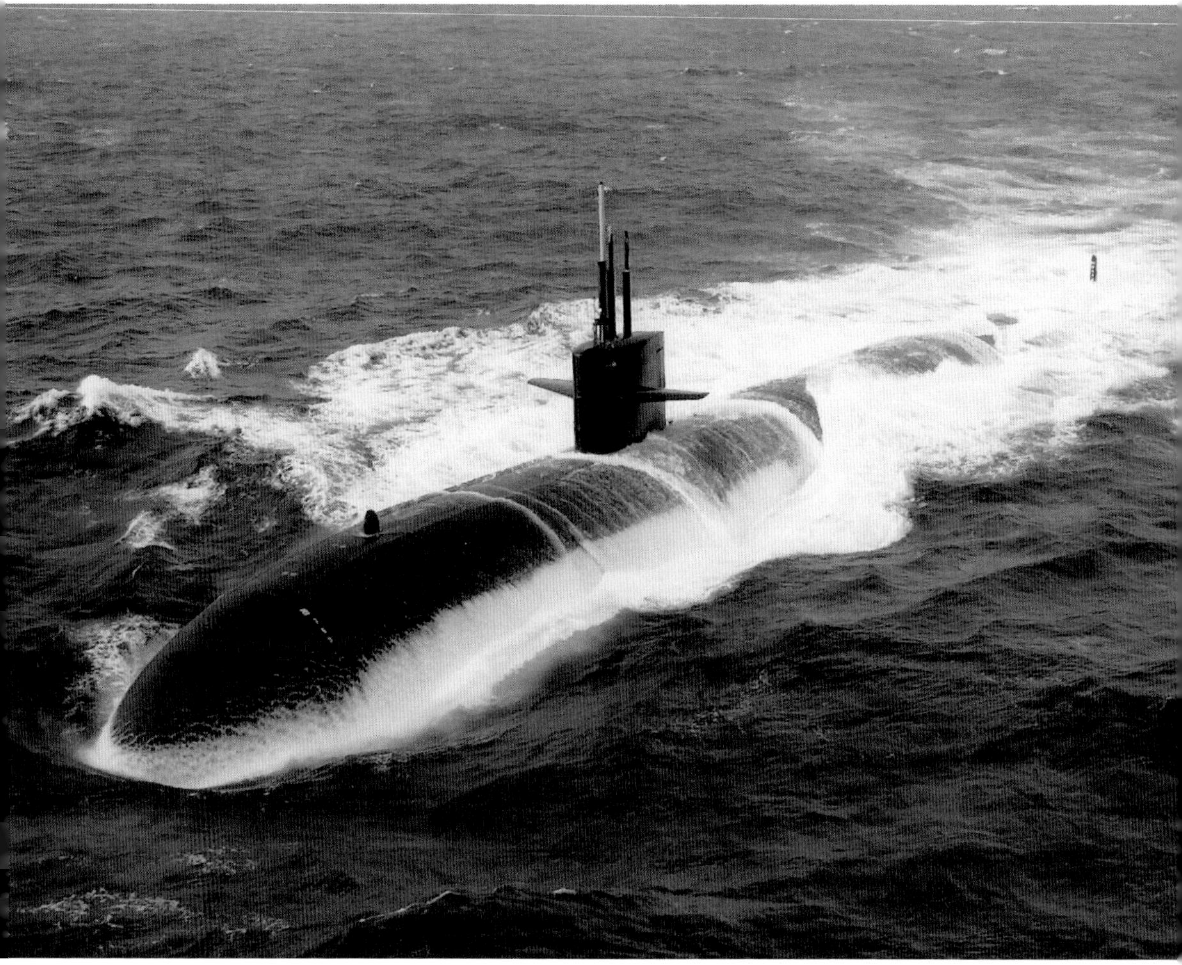

USS *Albuquerque*

There have been two naval ships named in honor of Albuquerque. The first USS *Albuquerque*, a frigate, was launched in 1943 and saw mostly escort and patrol duties in World War II. Curiously, in 1945 the ship was lent to the Soviet Union, an ally in World War II. It was returned to the United States in 1950 in time to see duty in the Korean conflict. In another twist of fate, the ship was lent to the Japan Maritime Self-Defense Force from 1961 to 1968. It was decommissioned in 1969. The second USS *Albuquerque* (pictured) is a nuclear submarine, launched on March 13, 1982, with a champagne bottle broken across its bow by Nancy L. Domenici, Sen. Pete V. Domenici's wife. Capt. Richard Hartman was its first commander; its crew included 12 officers and 98 men. The submarine has toured many parts of the world, with calls in countries like England, Scotland, Italy, and Spain. Engaged in the Kosovo conflict of 1999, its Tomahawk land-attack cruise missiles were so accurate that the submarine acquired the nickname "Sureshooter." Members of the crew have been honored guests in Albuquerque, while many residents of the city, including Mayor Richard Berry, have visited and helped support the submarine and its mission. The ship is scheduled to be decommissioned in 2015.

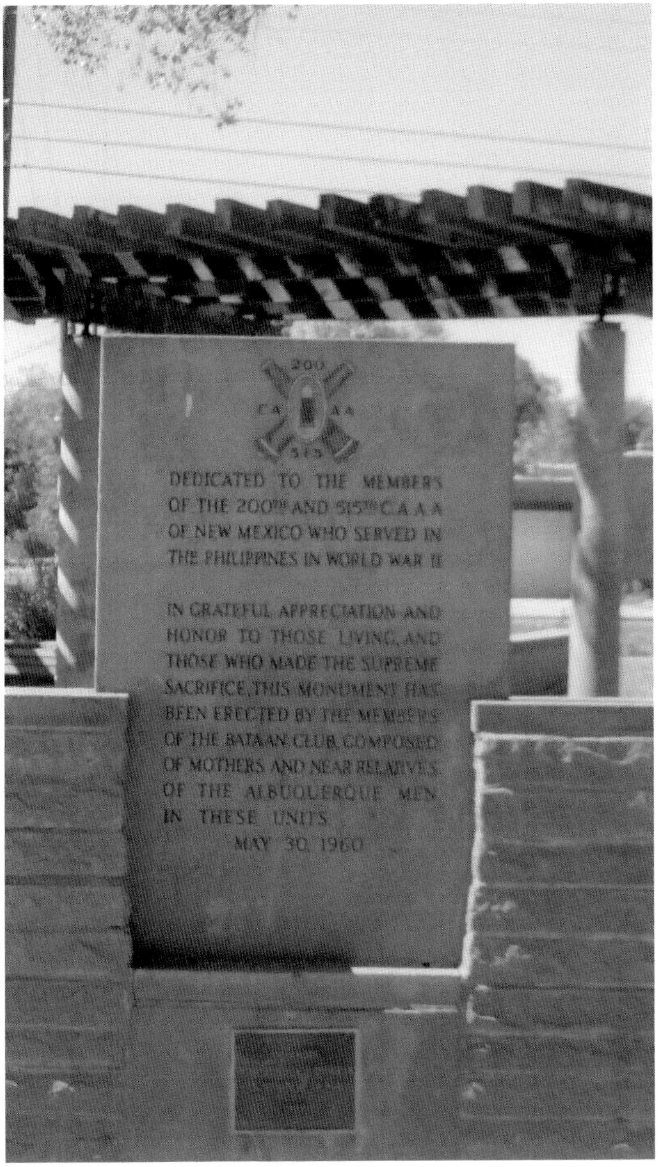

Bataan Death March Monument

In late 1941, just months before the Japanese invasion of the Philippines, 1,800 New Mexico National Guardsmen were deployed to the Philippines as the 200th Coast Guard Artillery Regiment. About a third, 542 men, were from Albuquerque. With no reinforcements and dwindling supplies, the New Mexicans, along with approximately 70,000 other US and Filipino soldiers, held out as long as they could before finally surrendering to the Japanese on April 9, 1942. Those who surrendered were forced on a terrible, 65-mile death march with little food, water, or medical supplies. Those who survived faced years of agony in Japanese prison camps. In all, 687 New Mexicans, including 253 Albuquerqueans, died during the Death March or in POW camps. They are honored in Albuquerque with the renaming of the local Methodist hospital (from 1952–1965), with a monument at the New Mexico Veterans Memorial Park on Louisiana Boulevard, and with a second monument (pictured), placed in Bataan Park at the corner of Carlisle and Lomas Boulevards, dedicated in 2002.

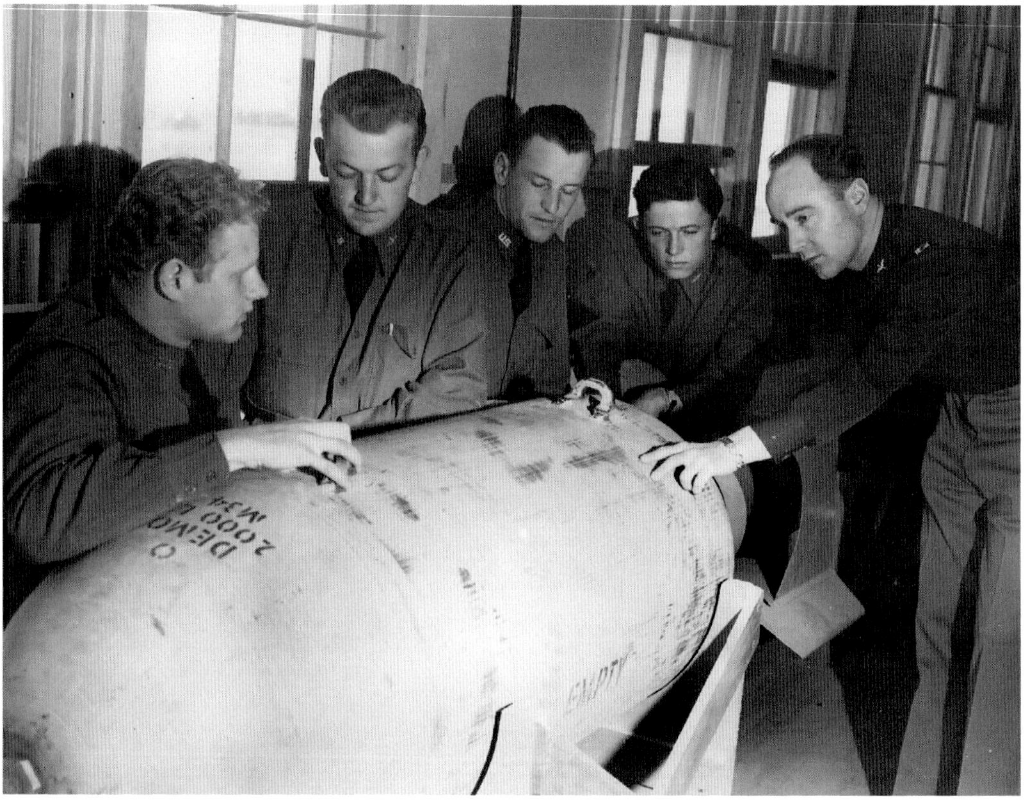

World War II Bombardier Cadets
Kirtland Army Air Field trained hundreds of pilots and bombardiers during World War II. Here, four bombardier cadets are seen with their instructor in an Army recruiting photograph. Cadets dropped bombs on targets (often identified with swastikas) in the surrounding countryside. Each cadet dropped as many as 160 bombs before graduating from the program. By 1945, instructors at Kirtland had trained 5,719 bombardiers and over 1,750 pilots for combat in the war.

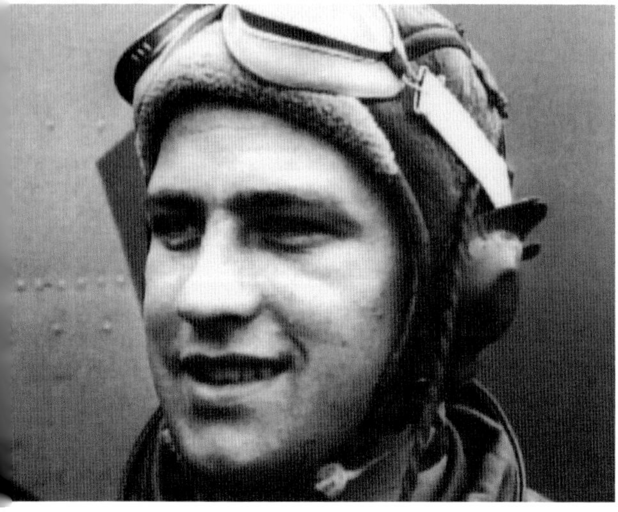

Sabine R. Ulibarri (1919–2003)
Educated at UNM and UCLA, Sabine Ulibarri wrote many books about Hispanic culture. But the turning point of his life came in World War II, when he served as a bombardier. As he wrote, the war caused great sorrow, but it "was the greatest thing that ever happened to the Hispanic population of New Mexico. . . . We saw vistas and horizons we didn't even think existed. . . . Now we wanted something more."

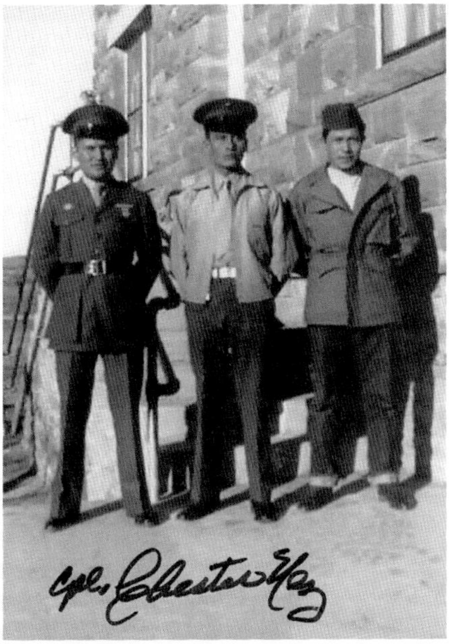

Chester Nez (1921–2014)

Nez (pictured on the left in the image at left) was born into a family of nine children on the Navajo Reservation near Gallup. Early in World War II, he was recruited to become one of the original 29 Navajo Code Talkers. These young Marines helped develop a secret code that proved essential in sending messages during nearly every Marine invasion in the Pacific theater. Returning home, Nez worked at the VA hospital in Albuquerque for 23 years before retiring and writing his memoir, *Code Talker* (2012), with Judith Avila. He was the last surviving member of the original 29 when he died at 93 in mid-2014.

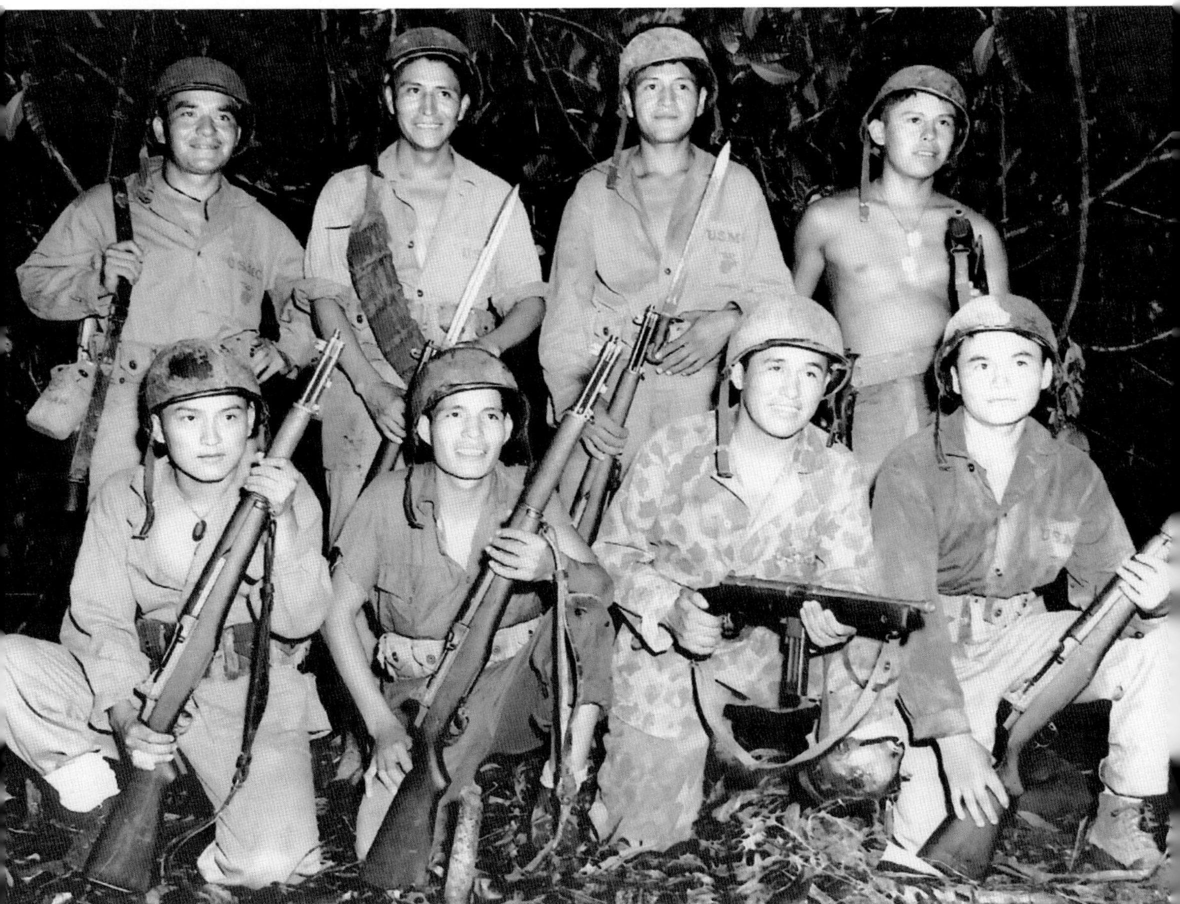

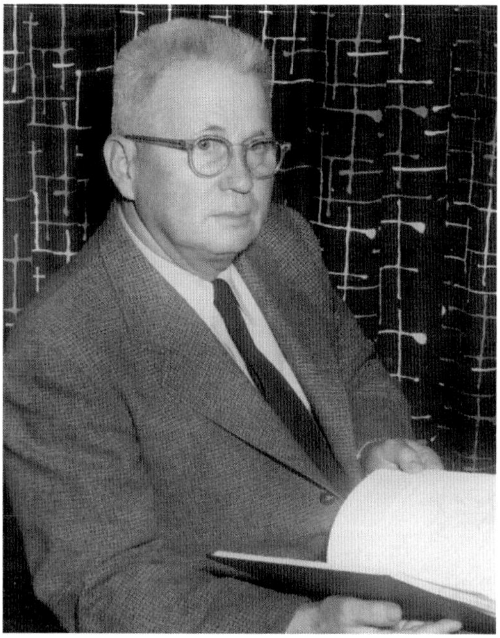

E.J. Workman (1899–1982)

Jack Workman joined UNM's small physics department in 1933, specializing in atmospheric physics and opening the school's new Research and Development Division. With the outbreak of World War II, Workman and his Albuquerque division engaged in several important phases of the top-secret Manhattan Project in Los Alamos. At war's end, Workman and his research division moved to Socorro, where he served as New Mexico Tech's president until 1964. (Courtesy of New Mexico Tech Archives.)

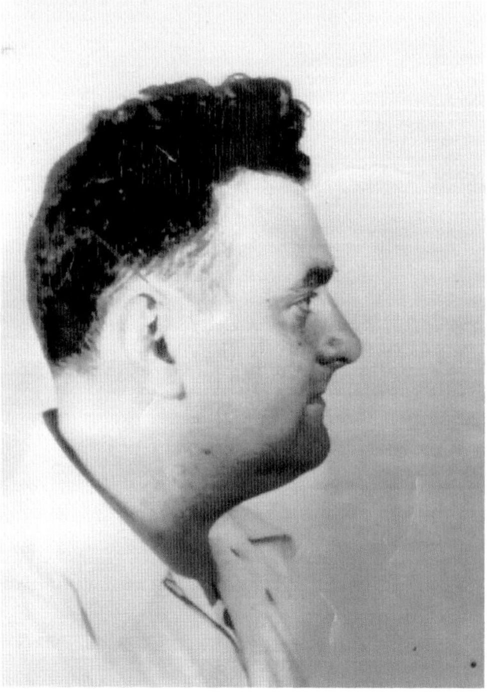

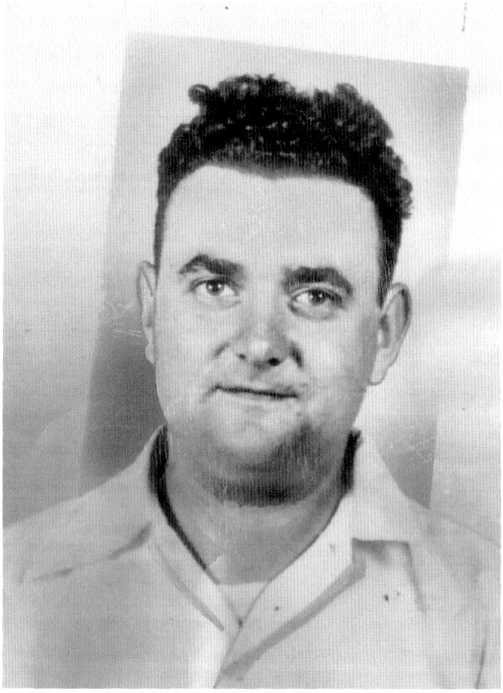

David Greenglass (1922–2014)

A communist, Army sergeant David Greenglass worked on the top-secret project to develop an atomic bomb in Los Alamos during World War II. Learning of the bomb, Greenglass alerted his relatives, Julius and Ethel Rosenberg, who arranged for Greenglass (code name "Bumblebee") to share what he knew with Soviet agent Harry Gold in mid-1945. Gold picked up the information at Greenglass's Albuquerque apartment at 209 North High Street, now a bed-and-breakfast known as the "spy house."

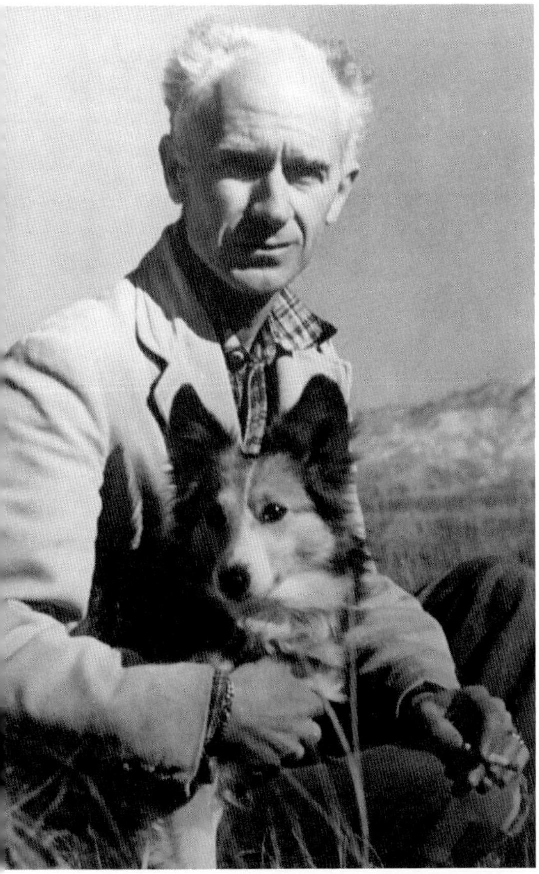

Ernie Pyle (1900–1945)
Pyle was the most famous American war correspondent during World War II. He and his wife, Jerry, traveled through every state in the country in the 1930s, when he worked as a reporter. Seeking a place to periodically rest, the Pyles chose Albuquerque for its scenery, mild weather, diverse cultures, and kind residents. Pyle wrote about their choice in a famous *New Mexico Magazine* article, "Why Albuquerque?" The Pyles enjoyed their neighbors, their small house at 900 Girard Avenue Southeast, and their toy collie, Cheetah (pictured above with Pyle), but they also experienced horror when Jerry suffered mental breakdowns, drank too much, and twice attempted suicide. After years as a Pulitzer Prize–winning reporter in war-torn Europe, Pyle was reassigned to the Pacific, where he was killed by a sniper on Ie Shima on April 18, 1945. Jerry died several months later. Without heirs, their house became the first branch library (below) in the Albuquerque Public Library system in 1948. A middle school, a beach, and a movie theater were also named in his honor. By 1950, so many places were being named after Ernie Pyle that one woman wrote to a local newspaper and facetiously suggested that the city should simply change its name to Ernie Pyle, New Mexico. (Courtesy of the Albuquerque Museum, PA1975-063-888.)

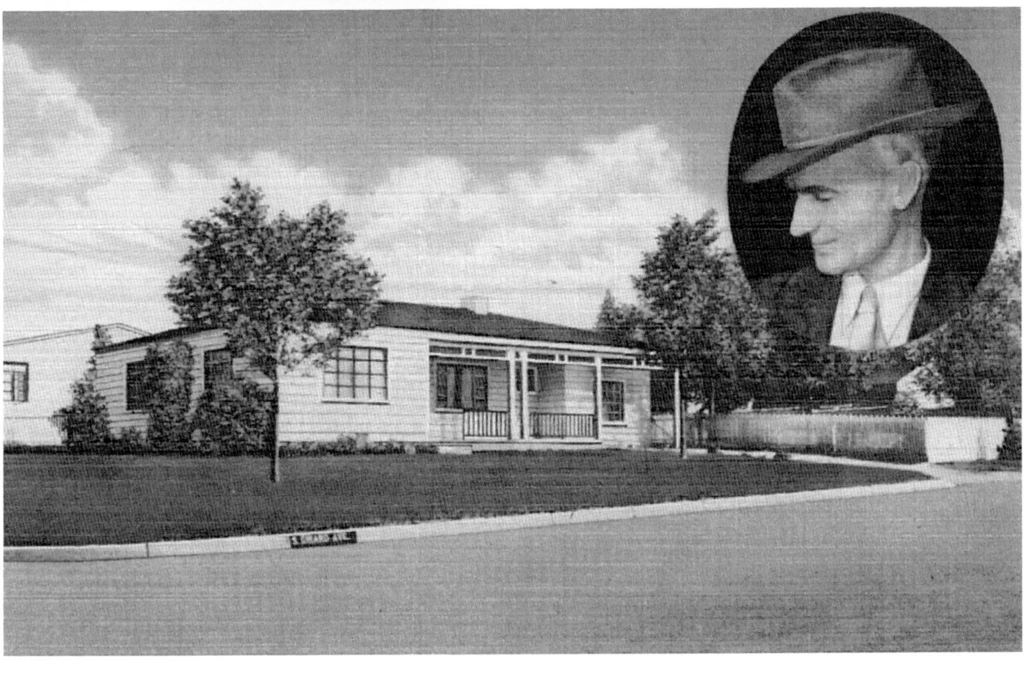

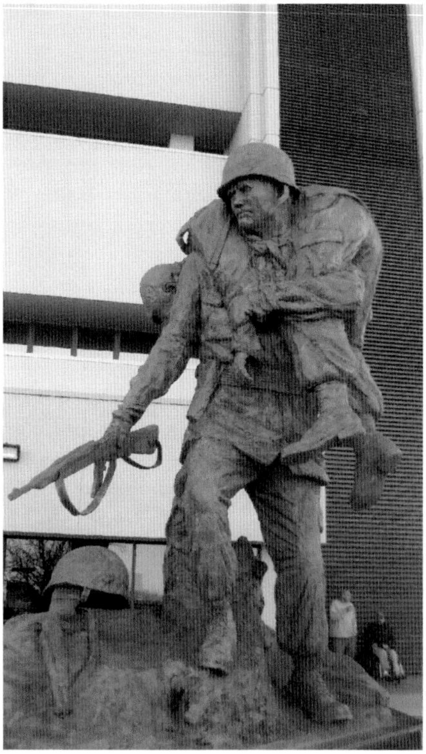

Raymond G. Murphy (1930–2007)
Lt. Raymond Murphy won the Medal of Honor for his bravery in attempting to rescue the bodies of members of an American machine-gun crew killed in the Korean conflict. Leaving the Marines in 1959, he continued to "rescue" his fellow Marines, first for 24 years as an employee of the Veterans Administration hospital in Albuquerque, and then as a volunteer. Albuquerque's VA hospital was named in his honor in 2008. This statue stands at the medical center's main entrance.

Luis Richard Rocco (1938–2002)
Rocco was born in Albuquerque's Barelas neighborhood. Crossing the law as a teenager, he was given the option of serving in the Army or facing prison time. Accepting the military option, Rocco served as a medic on a helicopter evacuation crew in Vietnam. Despite his own wounds, Rocco rescued his fellow crew members when their helicopter crashed on May 24, 1970. He received the Medal of Honor and spent the rest of his life working for veterans' causes.

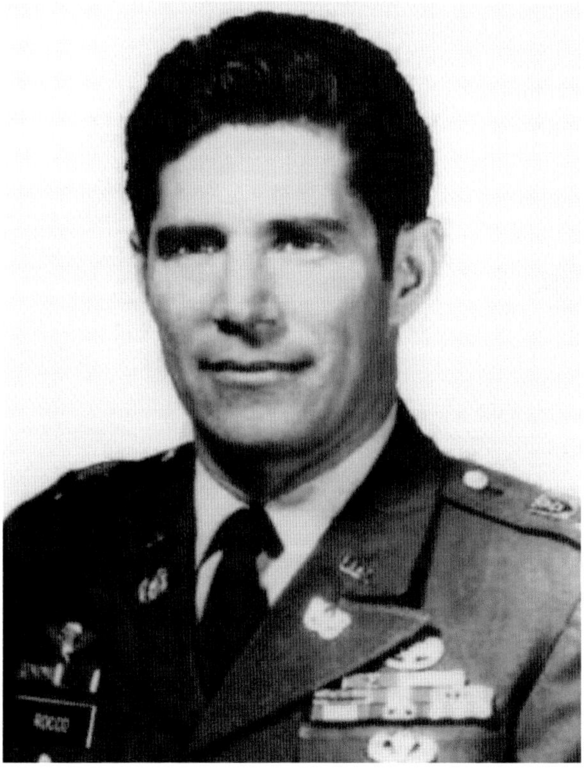

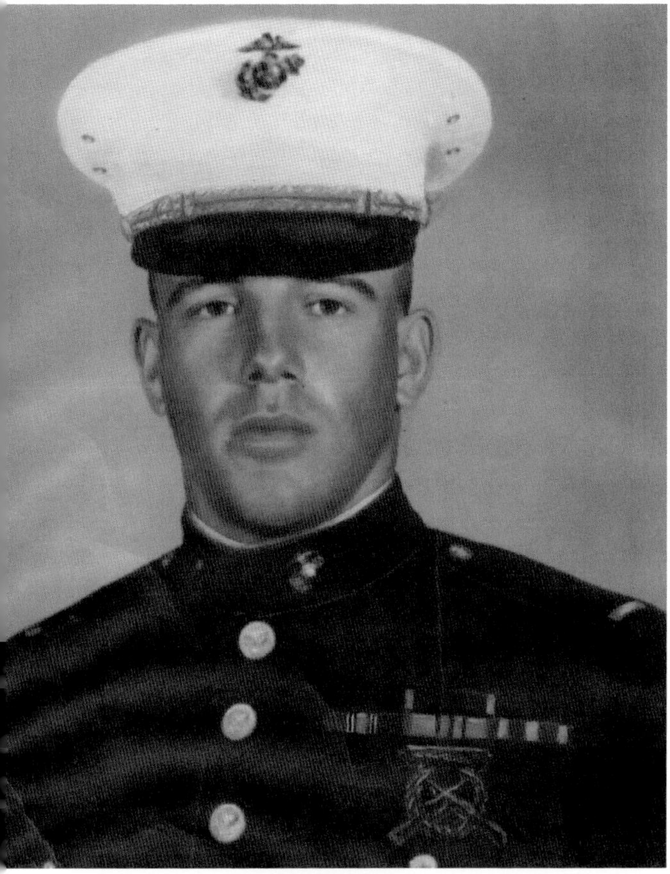

Victor David Westphall III (1940–1968)
Raised in Albuquerque, David Westphall graduated from Highland High School. He was a US Marine first lieutenant on patrol near Con Thien, Vietnam, when he and 16 of his fellow Marines were killed by enemy fire on May 22, 1968. Crushed by the loss of his son and other American youths in Vietnam, David's father, Victor Westphall, used money from David's life insurance and land that the Westphall family owned near Angel Fire, New Mexico, to construct the Vietnam Veterans National Memorial, the first Vietnam memorial in the United States. It was completed in 1971, on the third anniversary of David's death. Thousands of visitors have come to the memorial and its chapel (below), where Dr. Westphall greeted people from around the world until the day before his death in 2003. The Vietnam memorial is now a New Mexico state park. (Courtesy of the Vietnam Veterans National Museum.)

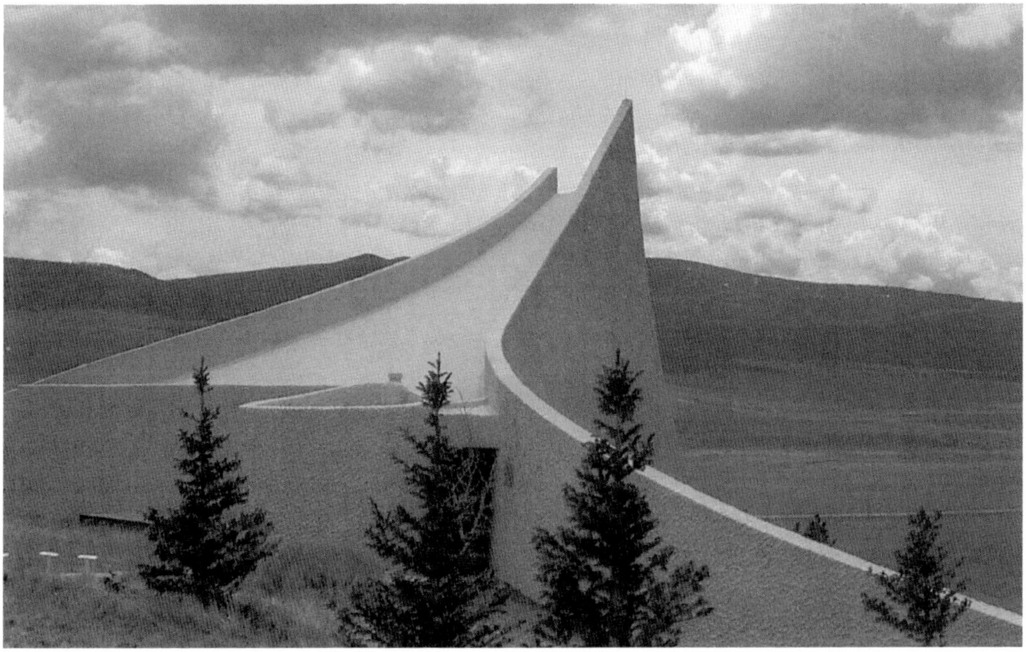

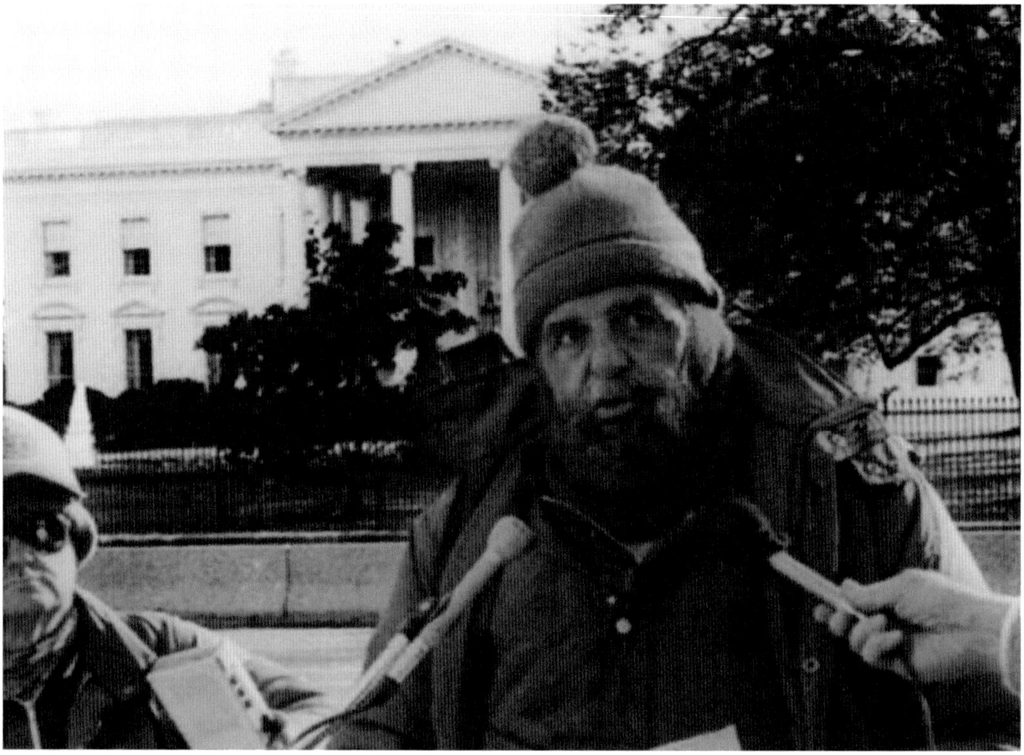

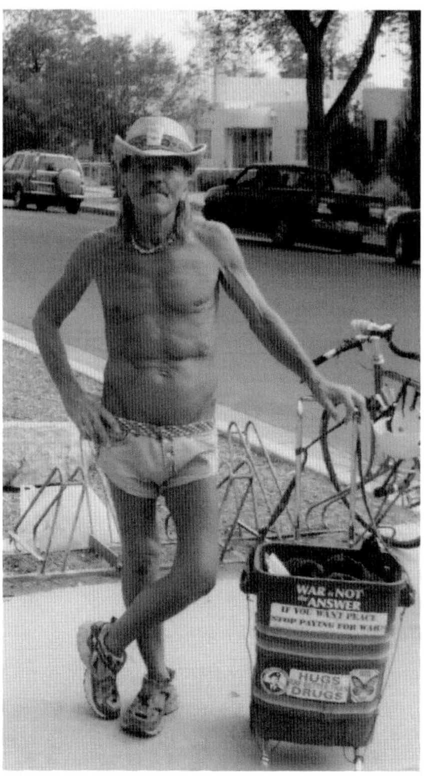

Charles Hyder (1930–2004)
Hyder was born in Albuquerque, graduated from Albuquerque High, and earned two degrees in science at UNM before deciding to devote his life to opposing nuclear war and nuclear waste storage. To draw attention to his causes, Hyder engaged in a famous 217-day hunger strike at Lafayette Park in Washington, DC. He later held an 85-day hunger strike to protest the opening of the Waste Isolation Pilot Project outside Carlsbad.

Don Schrader (b. 1945)
Don Schrader first came to Albuquerque as a conscientious objector during the Vietnam War. He has become the most recognized protester in Albuquerque history. According to Schrader, he protested against war and other issues at the gates to Kirtland Air Force Base and Sandia National Labs 300 times from 1989 to the 1990s and daily on Central Avenue by the University of New Mexico for a total of 641 days from 1998 to 2001.

CHAPTER THREE

Law and Order

Albuquerque was a rather tranquil town for much of its history, at least from its founding in 1706 to the coming of the Santa Fe Railroad in 1880. Even in the late 19th century, Albuquerque could be considered an Old West town, not a Wild West one. The city had its share of saloons (like the Bucket of Blood), ladies of the night (Lizzie McGrath), and hangings, including of its own town marshal in 1883! But, unlike Wild West towns like Tombstone, Arizona, Albuquerque had no infamous shoot-outs, major bank robberies, or resident outlaw gangs.

The main reason for this relative calm was that Albuquerque was a railroad town rather than a railhead or mining town populated by single young cowhands or miners with few roots to the community and limited interest in law and order. Given these fortunate circumstances, Albuquerque's police force grew and matured under the strong, steady leadership of police chief Patrick O'Grady. The city's firemen were also admired as among the strongest, most reliable men of their community.

Like many Western cities of the post–World War II era, conditions began to change in Albuquerque with rapid expansion, the influx of newcomers, and the accompanying problems of modern society. A few examples reflect the unfortunate trend. By the late 1960s, anti-Vietnam protests sometimes erupted into tragic violence. Albuquerque was shaken to its core by the abduction, rape, and murder of young Linda Lee Daniels in 1986. In 1996, three employees and two of their relatives were killed in the Hollywood Video store murders. In 2009, police uncovered the bodies of 11 women, aged 15 to 34, buried on the West Mesa. Arrests for driving while intoxicated remain alarmingly high. In an example of art imitating life, the television series *Breaking Bad*, filmed in Albuquerque, depicted the violence and crime that have accompanied the city's drug trade. Even the police have been accused of using excessive force in recent years.

But daily life is still largely tranquil in most parts of Albuquerque, thanks to the good work of most policemen, including a dozen lawmen who have been killed in the line of duty since Alexander Knapp lost his life as Albuquerque's first slain officer, in early 1912. Despite its strains, Albuquerque's justice system usually serves the best interests of most local citizens.

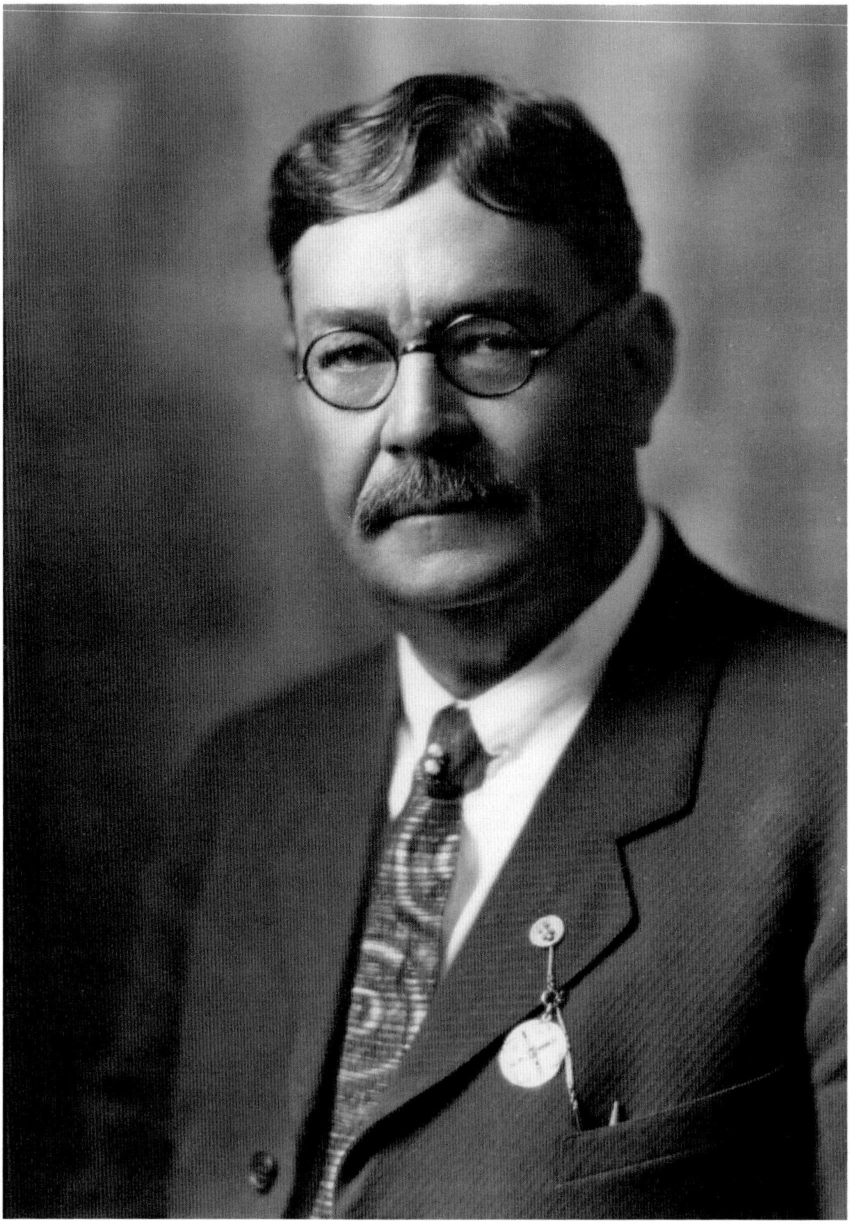

Elfego Baca (1866–1945)
Baca is most famous for his 33-hour shootout with 80 Texas gunmen in Reserve, New Mexico, in 1884. As a result of that and other incidents that proved his bravery, Baca became one of the most feared lawmen in the West. In 1910, he moved to Albuquerque, changed careers, and became a lawyer/private investigator. According to historian Marc Simmons, Baca walked through downtown Albuquerque "dressed in a flowing cape and trailed by a bodyguard." Baca handed out business cards that read, on one side, "Elfego Baca, Attorney-at-Law, Fees Moderate," and, on the other side, "Private Detective, Divorce Investigations Our Specialty, Discreet Shadowing Done." At the end of an exciting life, Baca died "with his boots off" in his Albuquerque home while listening to the radio. (Courtesy of the Albuquerque Museum, PA1978-153-869.)

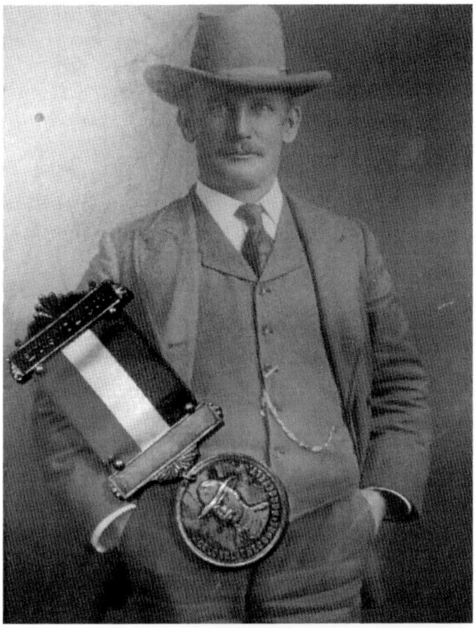

Fred Fornoff (1859–1935)
Fornoff served as one of Albuquerque's first town marshals (1894–1896 and 1897–1898) before fighting as a Rough Rider in the Spanish-American War. He also served as a captain of the New Mexico Mounted Police. Fornoff was called on to deal with many controversial events, including the famous boxing match between black boxer Jack Johnson and white fighter Jim Flynn in 1912. Fornoff broke up the fight in the ninth round. (Courtesy of Chuck Hornung.)

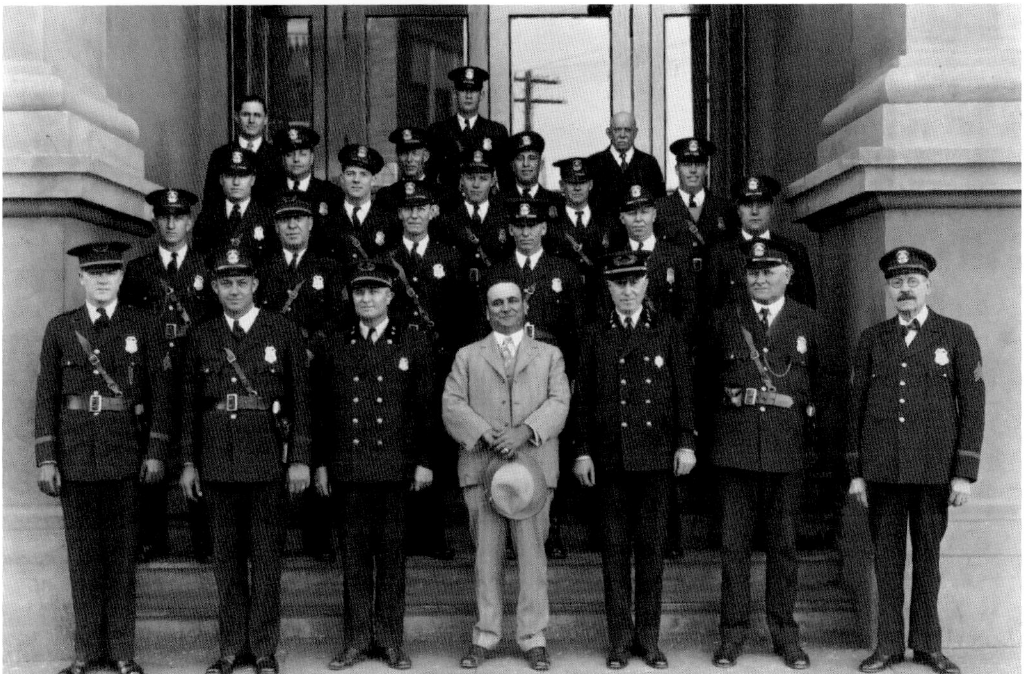

Patrick O'Grady (1875–1945)
Patrick O'Grady migrated from Ireland and joined Albuquerque's fledgling police force in 1908. He reportedly worked the night shift for 17 years without a day off. Rewarded for his persistence, he became the city's police chief in 1925. Over the next 20 years, he increased the size of the force, replaced horses with motor vehicles, began a fingerprinting department, refused to carry a weapon, and scrupulously avoided all scandal. Here, O'Grady (first row, third from right) poses with Clyde Tingley (first row, center) and the city's police force. (Courtesy of the Albuquerque Museum, PA1978-152-091.)

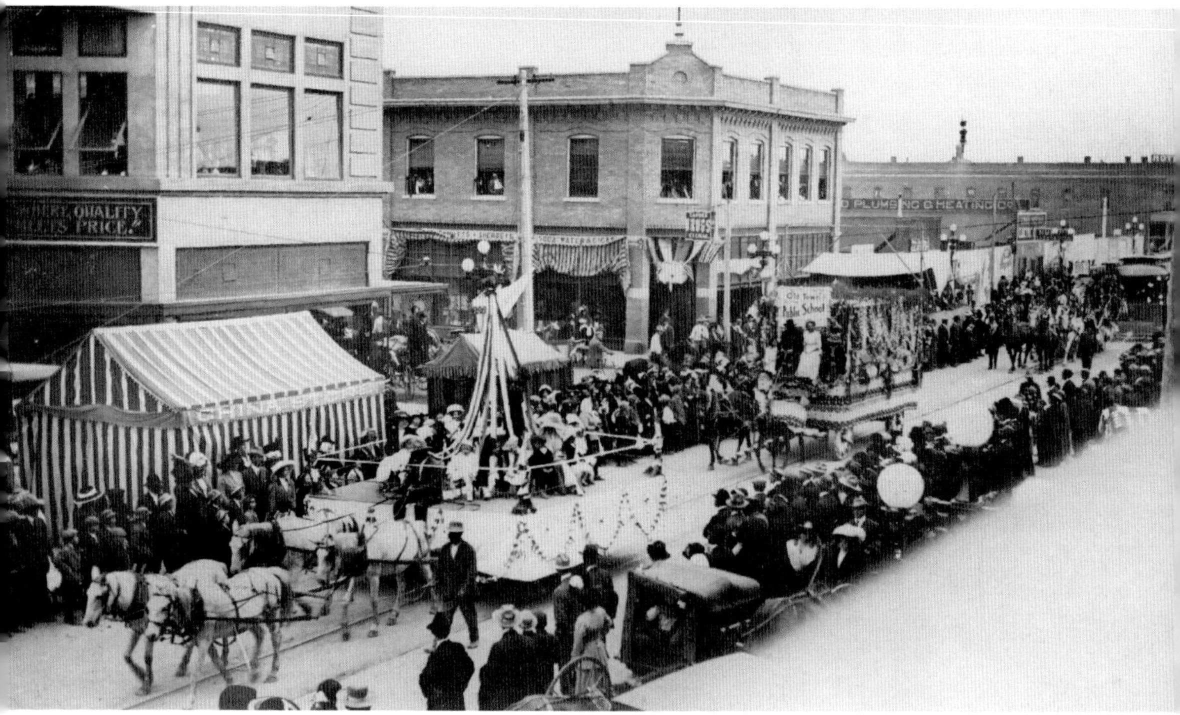

John Braden (c. 1822–1896)

Little is known of John Braden before October 19, 1896, when he drove a horse-drawn wagon filled with fireworks in a parade on the final night of that year's territorial fair. As the parade headed east on Railroad (now Central) Avenue, there was an explosion on Braden's wagon. His horses ran out of control as fireworks exploded and his wagon burst into flames. Only Braden's courage and skill prevented his wagon from colliding with a float carrying the fair queen and her attendants. In the words of a poem written in the aftermath of the accident, "Now the danger safely past, / The hero, overcome at last, / Falls burned and helpless from his seat, / While Death's cold hands stretch out to greet / His glorious deed, and soon in peace, / He from his sufferings finds release."

Braden's funeral was said to be the largest ever held in the city. A small monument recognizing his heroism was erected at Robinson Park, not far from the disaster. Despite his fame, Braden was buried in an unmarked grave at Fairview Cemetery and is all but forgotten today. (Courtesy of the Albuquerque Museum.)

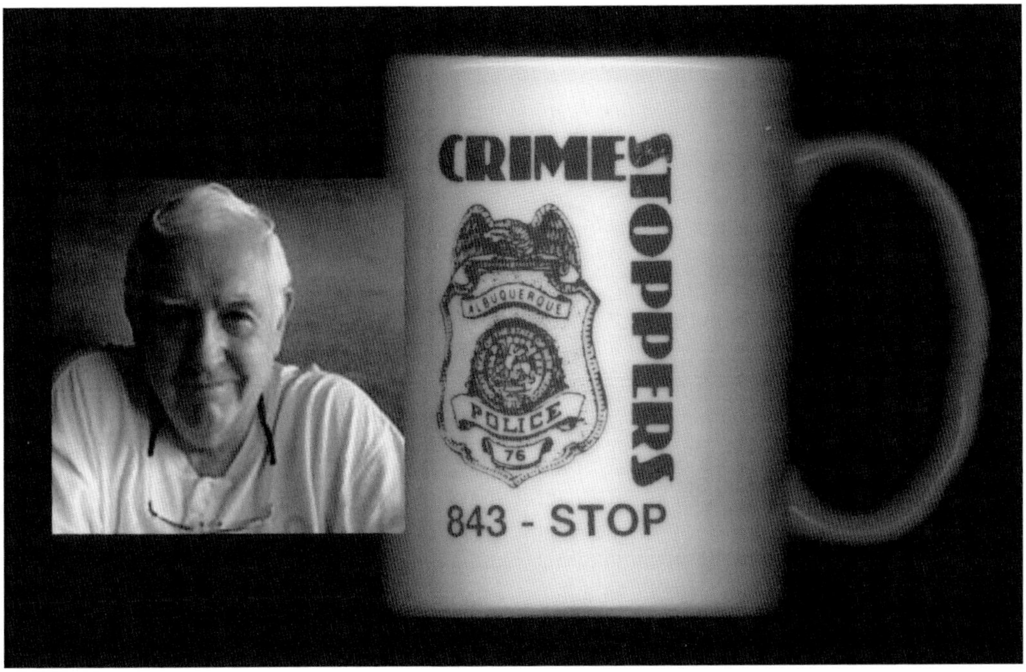

Greg MacAleese (b. 1948)
MacAleese was an Albuquerque detective assigned to a case involving the murder of a young gas-station employee in 1976. MacAleese worked with KOAT-TV to reenact the crime and offer monetary rewards to anonymous tipsters. The crime was solved, and the Crime Stoppers program was born. MacAleese was deservedly chosen as the National Police Officer of the Year. Copied in cities around the world, Crime Stoppers has helped solve over one million major crimes.

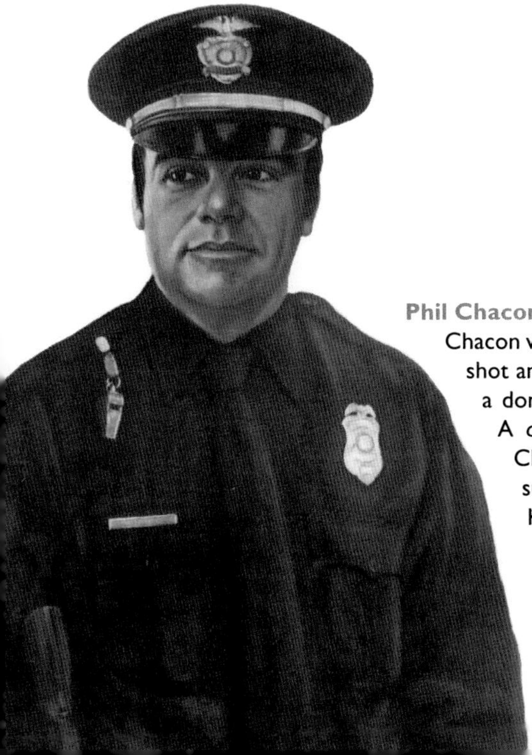

Phil Chacon (1944–1980)
Chacon was an off-duty Albuquerque police officer when he was shot and killed while attempting to stop an armed robbery of a donut shop on Central Avenue on September 10, 1980. A *descanso* (roadside memorial) marks the spot where Chacon perished. An Albuquerque park and police substation are named in his honor. This portrait, by L. Henry, hangs in the substation's lobby.

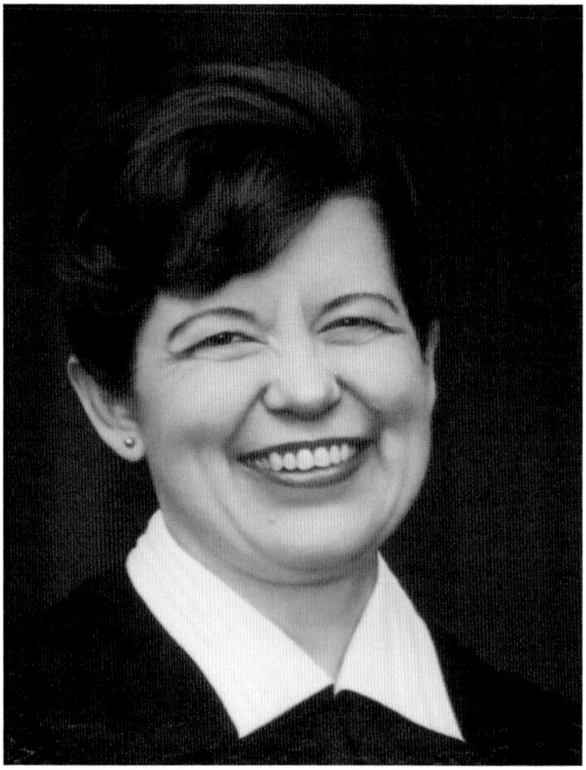

Pamela Minzer (1944–2007)
Minzer taught at UNM School of Law prior to her appointment to the state court of appeals. In 1994, Gov. Bruce King appointed her to serve on the New Mexico Supreme Court. Five years later, she became the first woman to serve as the high court's chief justice. A historical marker on the UNM Law School's campus honors her work. This portrait, by Davids, hangs in the law school's lobby. The court of appeals building is named for her as well.

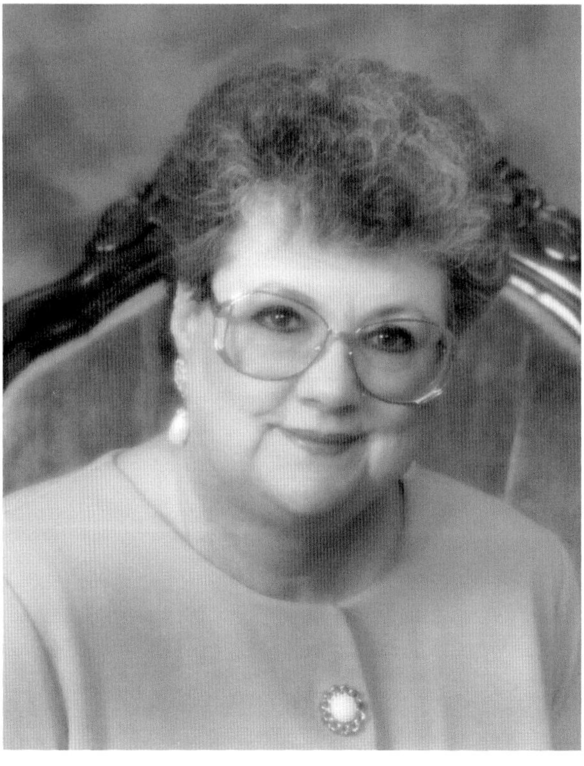

Nadine Milford (b. 1938)
Melanie Cravens and her three young daughters were killed in a terrible car crash involving a drunk driver on Christmas Eve, 1992. Lobbying lawmakers and serving as the president of the Albuquerque chapter of Mothers Against Drunk Driving (MADD), Melanie's mother, Nadine Milford (pictured), has worked tirelessly to toughen DWI laws in New Mexico. Although great strides have been made, DWI remains a major problem in Albuquerque and throughout New Mexico. (Courtesy of Nadine Milford.)

CHAPTER FOUR

Religion and Education

Most Americans would find it strange to read a history of an American city that includes religion and education in a single chapter. A majority of Americans cherish the concept of separation of church and state, especially in regards to education. But Albuquerque, and much of New Mexico, was different for a large part of its history. The Catholic Church dominated nearly every aspect of life, including education, dating back to Spanish colonial times. Even when public school bills were proposed after the American conquest of 1846, they were regularly defeated, largely for fear that Catholic children would lose their religion—and culture—in Anglo-dominated schools.

Religion left its mark on local schools long after a territory-wide public school bill was finally passed in 1891. Many Catholic families continued to send their children to parochial schools like St. Mary's (founded in 1892), St. Pius X High School (founded in 1956), and St. Joseph's College, later the University of Albuquerque (founded in 1950). Other families, including converted Hispanics, sent their children to Protestant schools, such as Albuquerque's Menaul School (opened by the Presbyterian Church) and the Harwood School (opened by the Methodist Church). With a shortage of qualified secular teachers, public schools often hired priests and nuns to teach classes. The famous Dixon court case (*Zellers v. Huff*) ended this practice in 1951.

A strong public-school system finally emerged in Albuquerque under the able leadership of John Milne, one of the longest-serving superintendents in American history. By 2014, the city had 89 public elementary schools, 27 public middle schools, 19 charter schools, and 13 public high schools. Prestigious private schools, like the Albuquerque Academy, Sandia Prep, and Bosque School, have provided additional educational opportunities for many students. The Albuquerque Indian School (1881–1981) and Southwestern Indian Polytechnic Institute (founded in 1971) taught Native American students for many years. Central New Mexico Community College (formerly the Albuquerque Technical-Vocational Institute) has offered training in valuable job skills for half a century. And the University of New Mexico, with its highly respected law and medical schools, is the largest, most diverse postsecondary institution in the state.

Meanwhile, the Catholic Church has continued to be the dominant religion. Starting with the San Felipe de Neri Church on Old Town Plaza in 1706, there are now 31 Catholic parishes in Albuquerque. Many Protestant churches, the Church of Jesus Christ of Latter-day Saints, and a few Jewish congregations have also been organized by faithful followers.

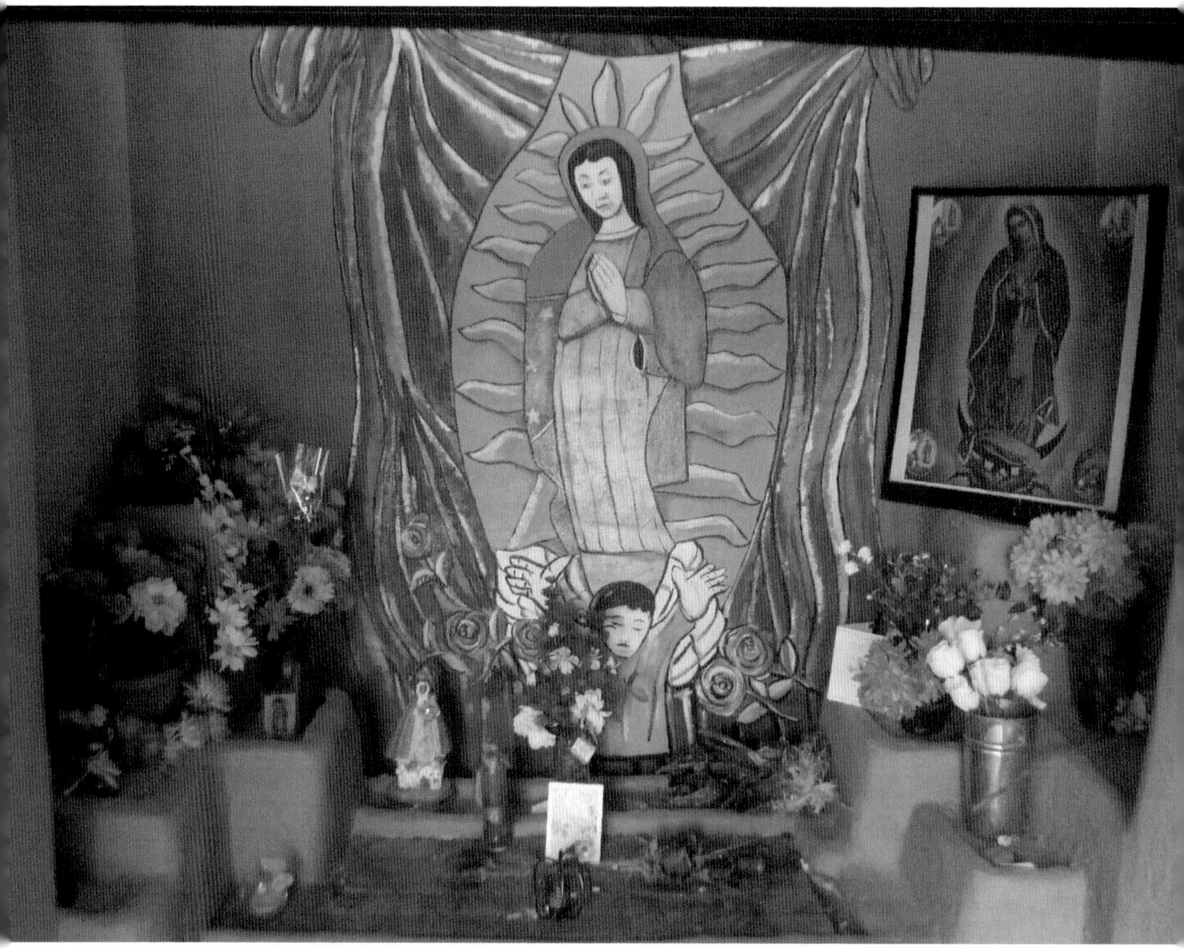

Virgin of Guadalupe

In 1531, the Virgin of Guadalupe appeared to a humble Indian named Juan Diego on the outskirts of Mexico City. The Virgin instructed Diego to meet with the archbishop of New Spain and have a shrine built in her honor at that location. Although intimidated, Diego convinced the archbishop, Fray Juan de Zumarraga, to build the shrine after Diego impressed the prelate by revealing a likeness of the Virgin in his *tilma* (cloak). Franciscan missionaries in New Mexico were able to use this miracle to help convert pueblo Indians, who were moved that the Virgin would appear to a fellow Native American. The Virgin's image appears throughout Mexico and its former territories, including in New Mexico. It is depicted on everything from paintings and sculptures to car windows and tattoos. This shrine stands in Old Town. Truly revered, her brassica in Mexico City is the most-visited shrine to the Virgin Mary in the world. Juan Diego was canonized as a saint in 2002.

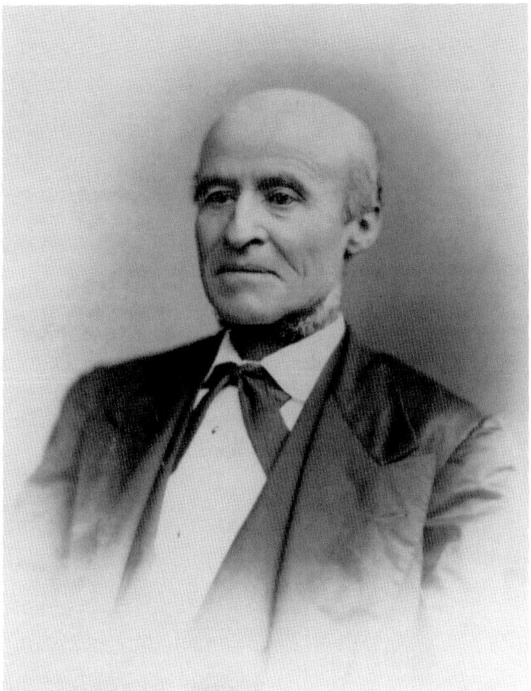

José Manuel Gallegos (1815–1875)
Gallegos was born in Abiquiu, educated in Taos, and prepared for the priesthood at a seminary in Durango, Mexico. Assigned to the San Felipe de Neri Church (below), Gallegos became a popular parish priest despite his interest in gambling, drinking, dancing, and commerce. His parishioners may have tolerated such behavior, but Bishop Jean Baptiste Lamy did not. Newly arrived in New Mexico in 1851, the French bishop accused Gallegos of "trying to do all the mischief he can." The prelate first suspended Gallegos and then replaced him as part of Lamy's campaign against traditional Hispanic priests. Turning to a career in politics, Gallegos served as New Mexico's congressional delegate, was speaker of the territorial House of Representatives, and held several other important offices. (Courtesy of the Museum of New Mexico, 009882.)

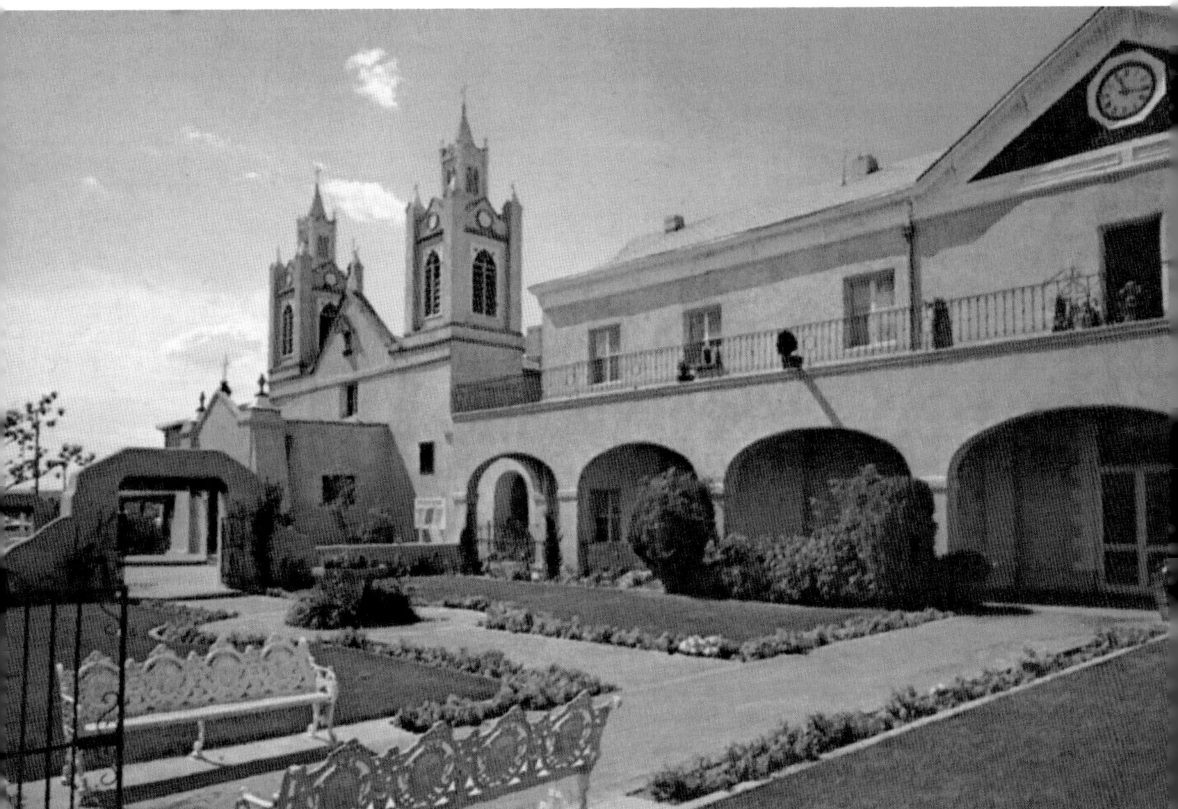

Fr. Donato Maria Gasparri (1834–1882)
Father Gasparri was one of five Spanish-speaking Italian Jesuit priests invited to New Mexico by Bishop Jean Baptiste Lamy. Arriving in 1868, Father Gasparri became the pastor at the San Felipe de Neri Church on Old Town Plaza. He established a new cemetery (Mount Calvary), opened a parish school, published *La Revista Catolica*, and helped found the Immaculate Conception parish in New Town. Father Gasparri's positive motto was, "God will provide. Let us begin!"

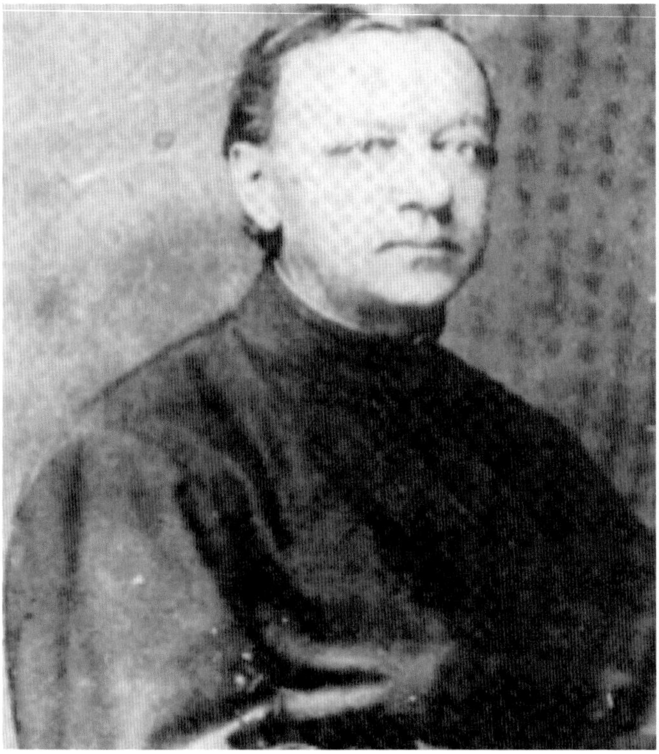

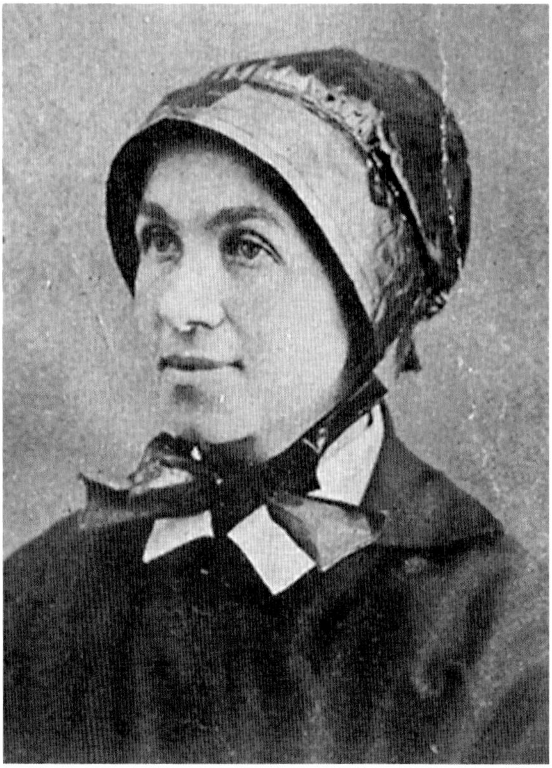

Sister Blandina Segale (1850–1941)
A member of the Sisters of Charity, Sister Blandina Segale arrived in Albuquerque in 1881 to help establish a new convent and school, Our Lady of Angels, in the San Felipe de Neri parish. She also helped establish Albuquerque's first hospital, St. Joseph, opened in 1902. Her memoir includes a story about how she befriended Billy the Kid. She is the first person in New Mexico history to be nominated for Catholic sainthood. (Courtesy of the Albuquerque Museum, PA1978-050-841.)

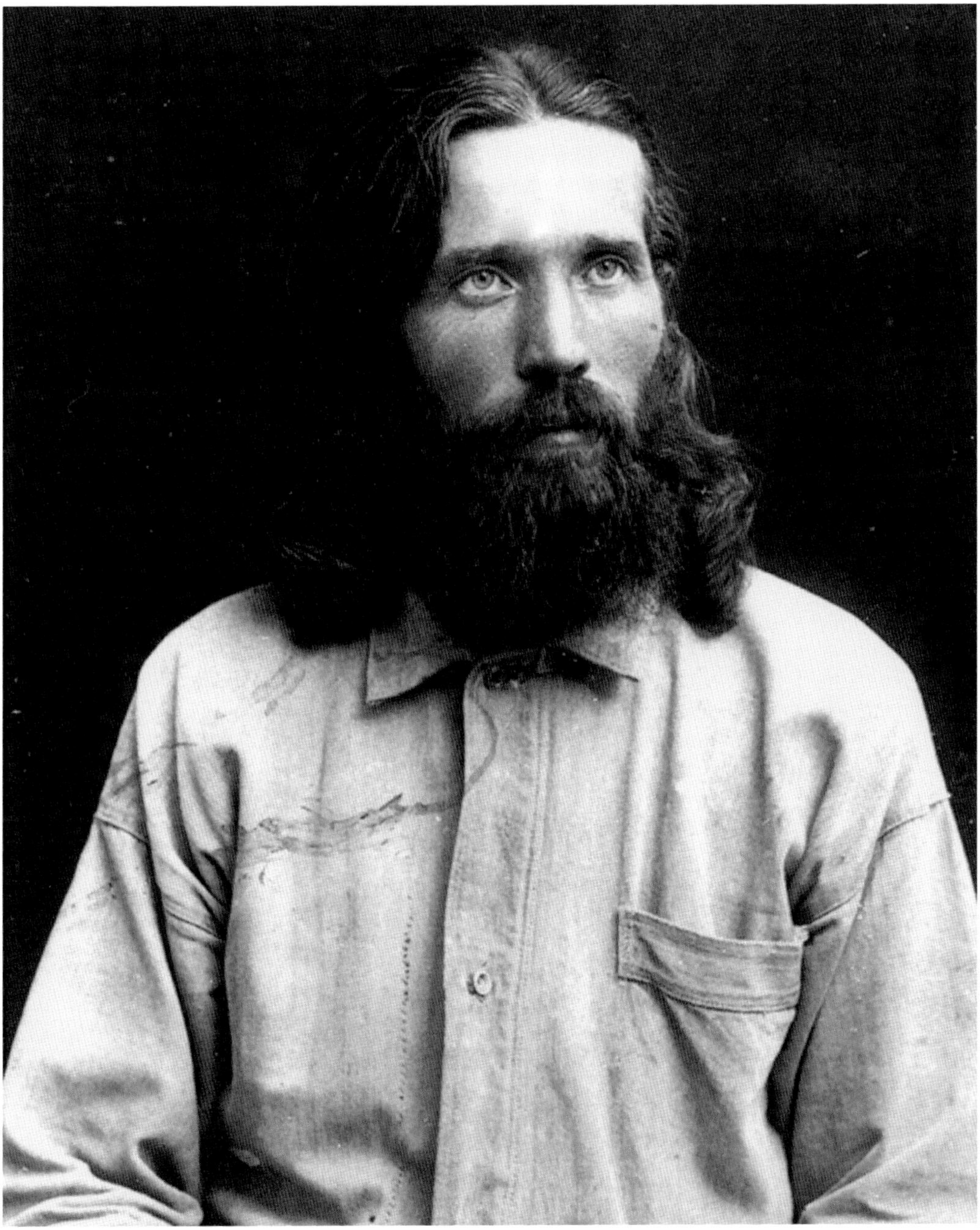

Francis Schlatter (1856–?)
Better known as "The Healer," Francis Schlatter was a European immigrant who came to Denver, Colorado, in 1892. He became known for his deeply spiritual life and remarkable healing powers. He visited many states in the West, including New Mexico in 1895. While staying in Albuquerque, he drew large crowds and reportedly healed several blind and crippled residents. Unlike other healers, Schlatter lived in poverty and refused to take money for his work. Many believed that he died in Mexico, where a body was found beside the large copper rod he carried everywhere in his travels. (Courtesy of the Albuquerque Museum, PA1978-050-226.)

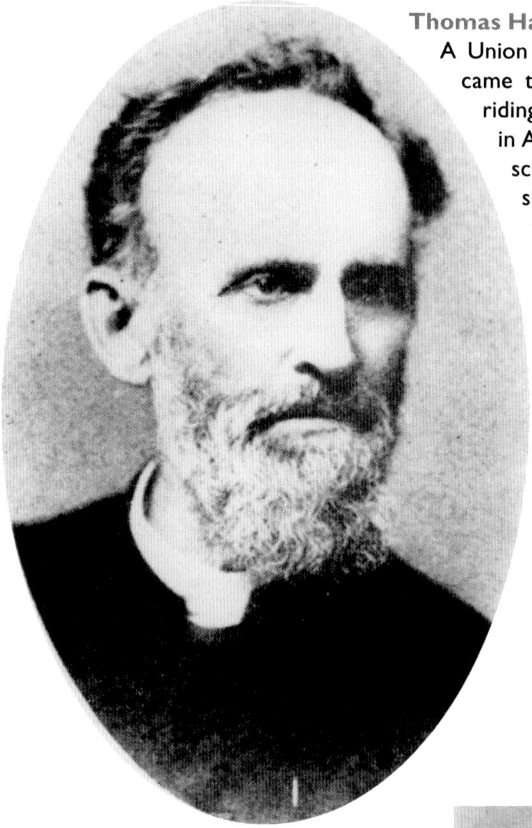

Thomas Harwood (1831–1917)
A Union army chaplain during the Civil War, Harwood came to New Mexico in 1869 to serve as a circuit-riding missionary for the Methodist Church. Settling in Albuquerque, he opened a "Biblical and Industrial" school for boys, while his wife, Emily, opened a similar school for girls to help counterbalance the great influence of the Catholic Church in local education. The Harwood School taught thousands of local students before its closing in 1976. (Courtesy of the Museum of New Mexico, 50137.)

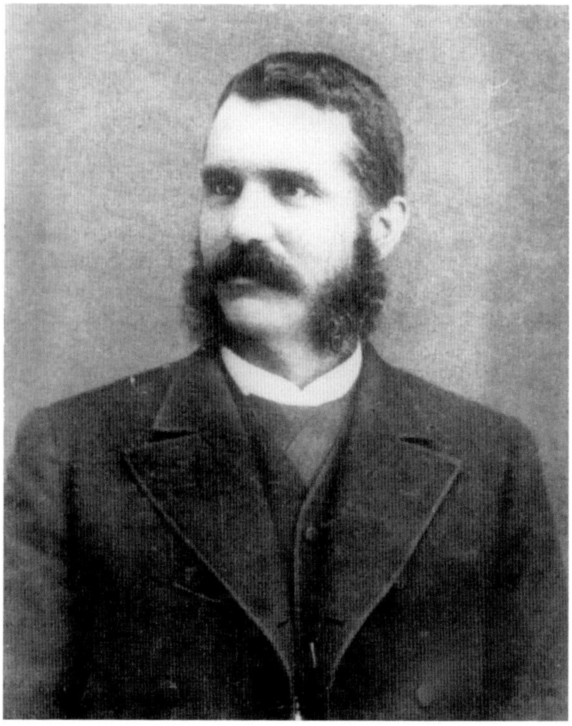

James A. Menaul (1842–1897)
Menaul arrived in New Mexico to serve as a missionary for the Presbyterian Church. After 16 years in the field, Menaul organized Albuquerque's First Presbyterian Church and served as its first minister. In 1896, he organized a boarding school for Hispanic boys who had converted to the Presbyterian faith. The school and the main road on which it is located were both named in Menaul's honor. (Courtesy of the Menaul Historical Library of the Southwest.)

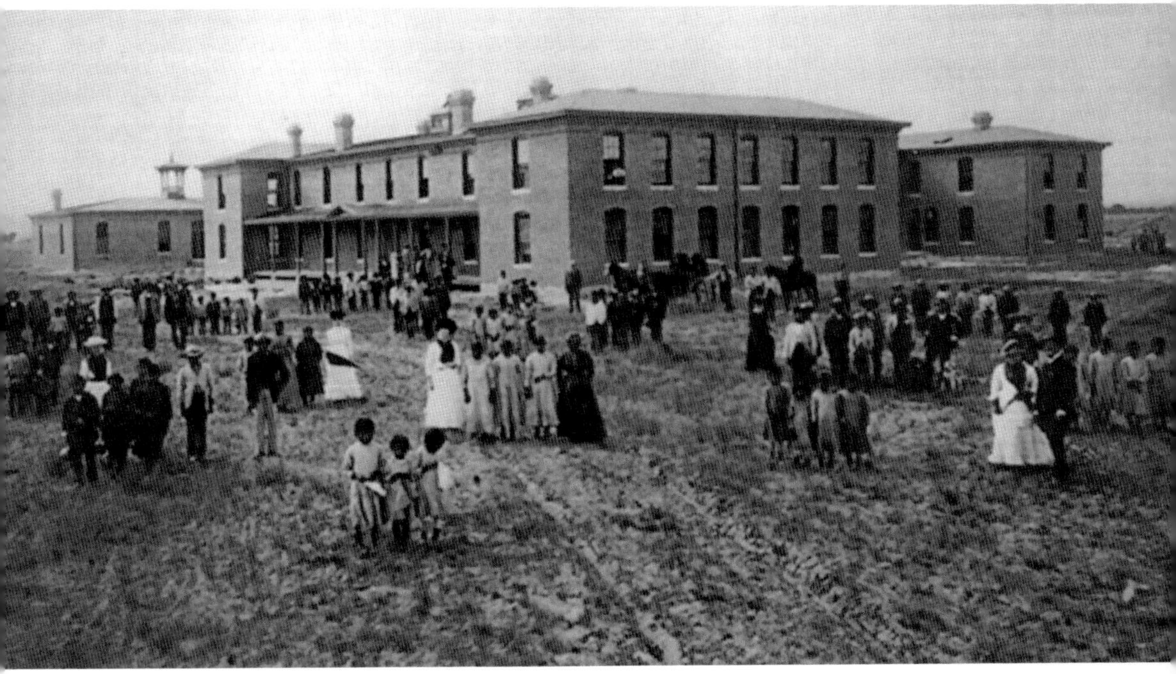

Albuquerque Indian Schoolchildren
Indian boarding schools of the 19th century believed that Native American culture had to be sacrificed to instill Anglo values in Indian children. Following this policy, the Albuquerque Indian School (AIS) was created by the Presbyterian Church in 1881. Pablo Abeita of Isleta was the first student to enroll. The federal government took control in 1886. The school eventually changed its philosophy to respect tribal cultures, not eliminate them. AIS closed in 1981.

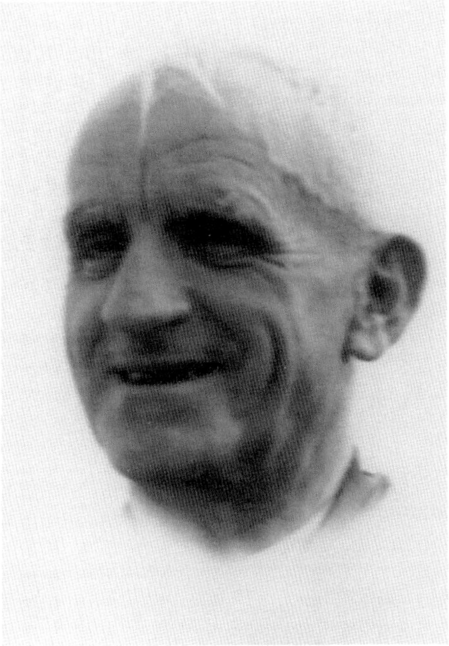

Brother Mathias Barrett (1900–1990)
In 1951, Irish-born Mathias Barrett established the Little Brothers of the Good Shepherd and opened a refuge for transient men in Albuquerque's downtown area. Using donated beds and supplies, he was able to help countless "Knights of the Road," as he called the men who turned to him for help. A fundraising St. Patrick's Day dinner (featuring corned beef and cabbage) is still held in Albuquerque each year. (Courtesy of the Little Brothers of the Good Shepherd.)

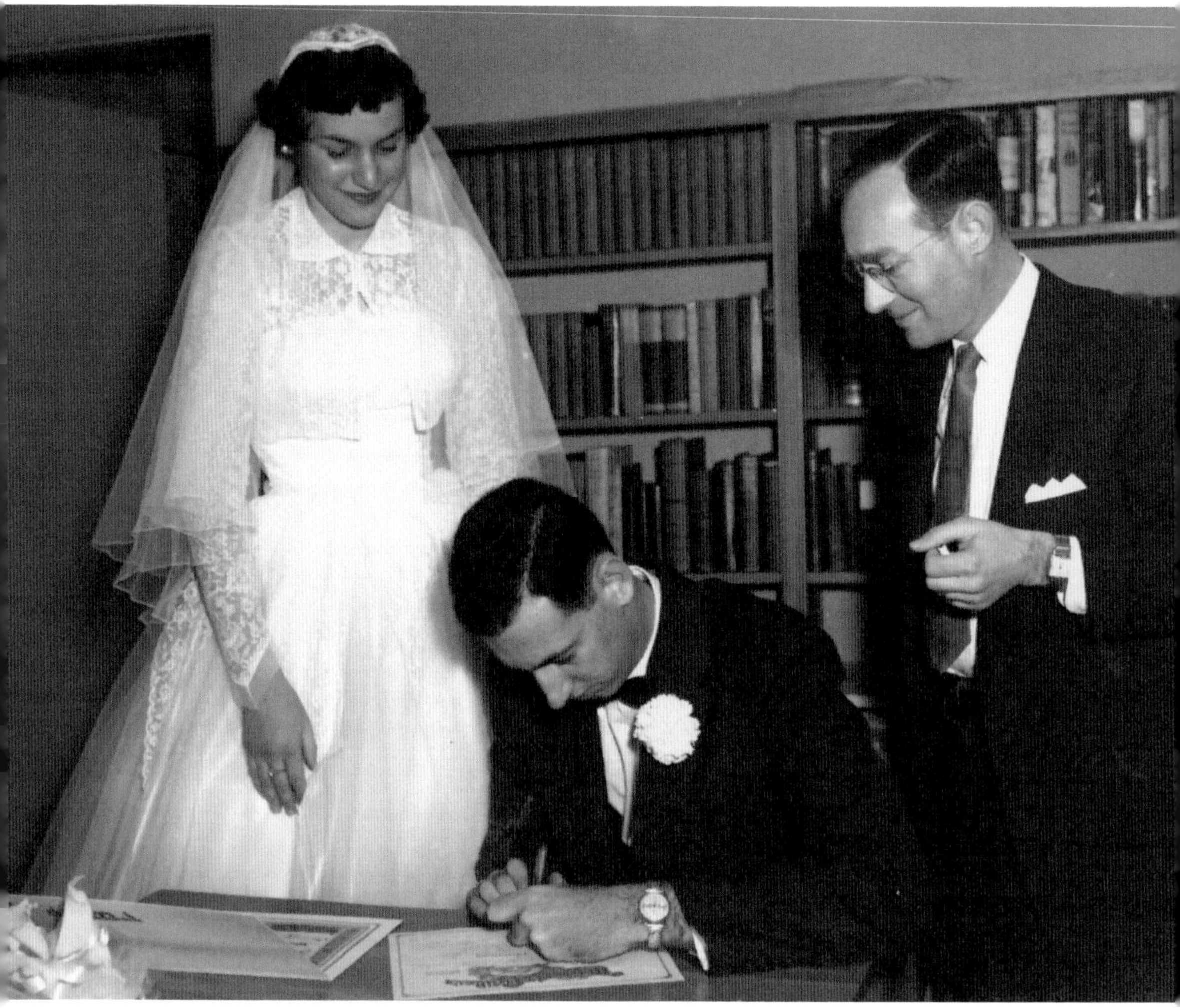

Rabbi David D. Shor (1913–1998)

After graduating from Hebrew Union College and serving as a chaplain in Europe during World War II, Rabbi Shor arrived in Albuquerque in 1948. He served as Congregation Albert's rabbi for the next 30 years. He was so respected and admired that Congregation Albert voted to change its bylaws and award him a lifetime contract. As the rabbi of the second congregation in New Mexico (the first was in Las Vegas), he worked hard to increase Congregation Albert's membership (which doubled in his first 10 years as rabbi), while also fostering strong ties and understanding between all faiths in the city. Here, the rabbi (right) officiates at the marriage of Arthur and Ailene Cohn on January 30, 1955. Jews have played important political and economic roles in New Mexico, including as Albuquerque's first mayor (Henry N. Jaffa), as a US congressman (Steven Schiff), and even as the governor of nearby Acoma Pueblo (Solomon Bibo). According to Sam Sokolove, executive director of the Jewish Federation of New Mexico, Jews have enjoyed a tradition of inclusion in New Mexico and have experienced relatively little anti-Semitism. There are now 15 synagogues in New Mexico, serving as many as 24,000 Jews, including about 13,200 in Albuquerque. Many Hispanic families have identified themselves as crypto-Jews whose ancestors escaped the Spanish Inquisition by fleeing to the New Mexico frontier. (Photograph by C.E. Redman, courtesy of the Israel C. Carmel Archives, Congregation Albert.)

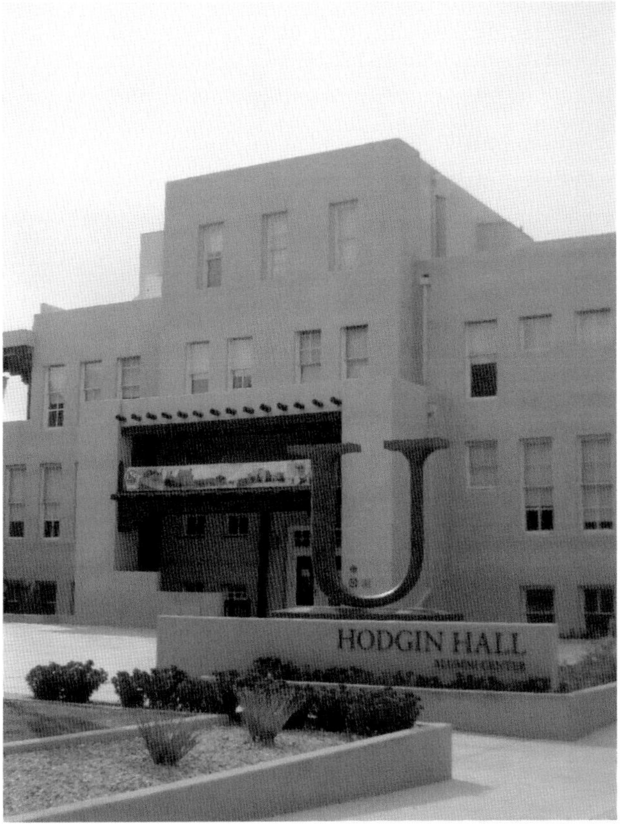

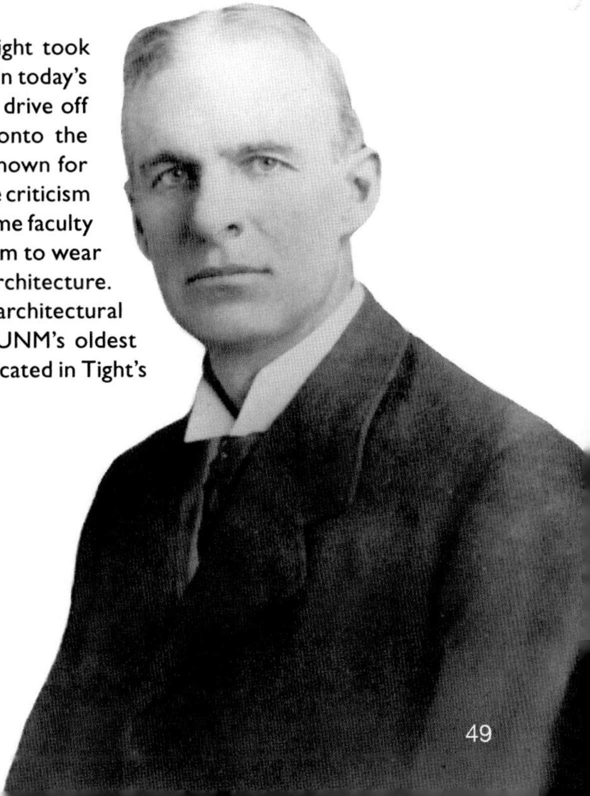

William G. Tight (1865–1910)

The University of New Mexico's third president, Tight took office in 1901 for an annual salary of $2,000 ($55,000 in today's money). He was known to ride his horse at night to drive off any cattle and coyotes that might have wandered onto the school's campus from the nearby mesa. He is best known for introducing Pueblo-style architecture to UNM, despite criticism from many on the faculty and the board of regents. Some faculty facetiously claimed that Tight would soon require them to wear Indian blankets to match the school's Indian-style architecture. According to historian Marc Simmons, this "architectural indiscretion" largely cost him his job. Hodgin Hall, UNM's oldest building and now its alumni hall (above), has been dedicated in Tight's memory. (Courtesy of the Albuquerque Museum.)

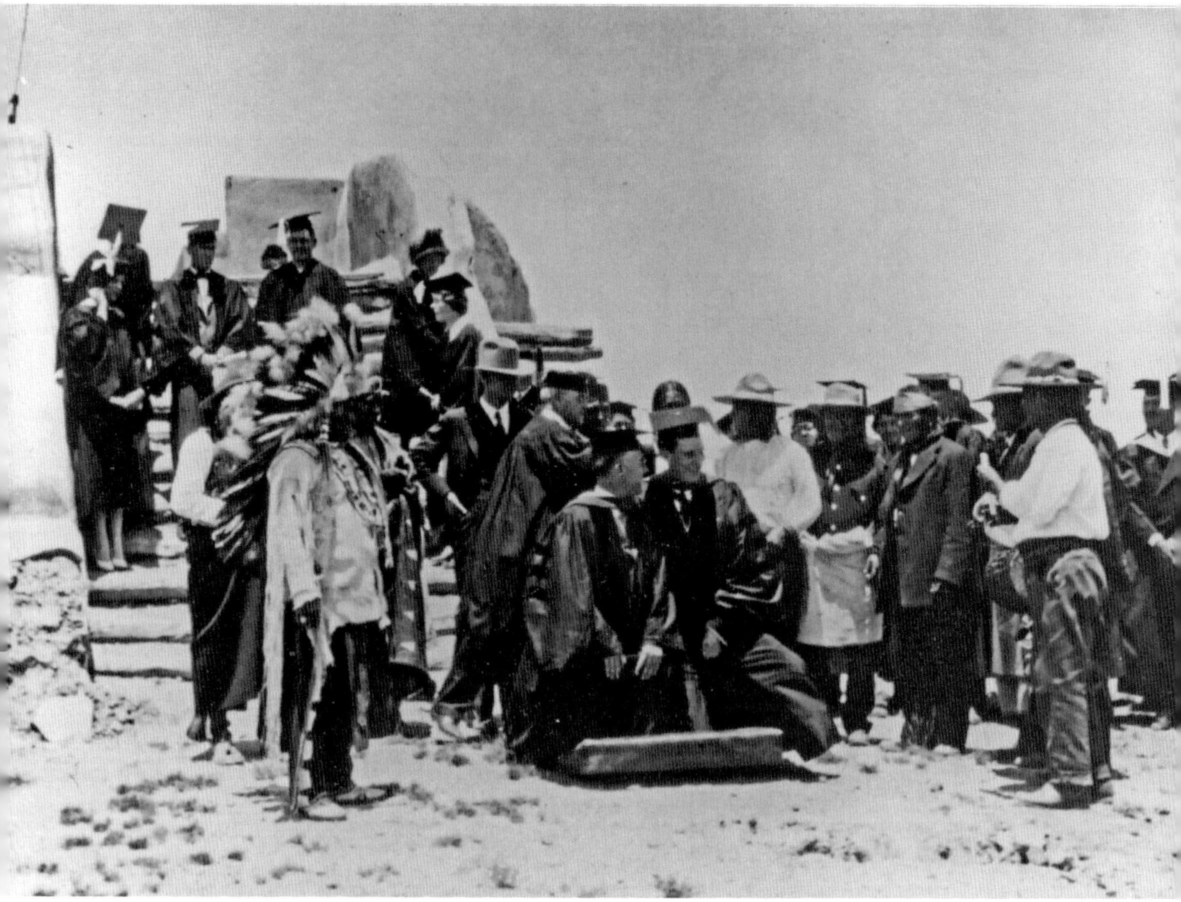

James F. Zimmerman (1887–1944)
Zimmerman came to the University of New Mexico to teach history, which he did for a year and a half, and he stayed to serve as UNM's president for 17 years (1927–1944). He is probably best known for adopting Pueblo Revival as UNM's standard architectural style by the 1930s. UNM's most distinctive structures, including Scholes Hall, the Student Union Building (now the anthropology building), and the main library (named in his honor), were products of this change in style. Even his inauguration (pictured) was conducted near a kiva-shaped structure. Symbolically, UNM's Pueblo architecture represents Zimmerman and the university's strong commitment to New Mexico and Latin American history and culture. Historian Bud Davis wrote that Zimmerman was known to be "gracious without being ingratiating, proud, but with a true humility, and aggressive but not arrogant." (Courtesy of UNM Department of Facility Planning Records, Box 46, Center for Southwest Research, University Libraries, University of New Mexico.)

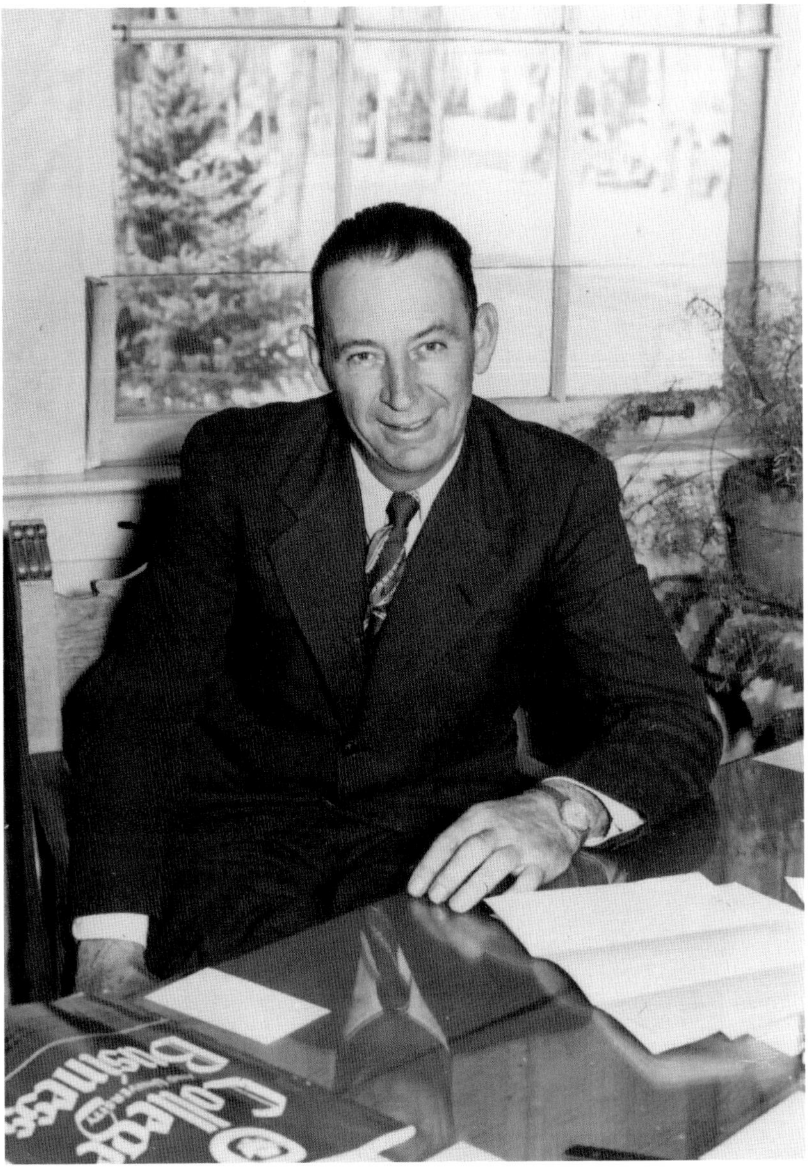

Thomas Lafayette Popejoy (1902–1975)
Tom Popejoy attended UNM, taught on the faculty, was named comptroller, and, in 1948, was inaugurated as the school's ninth president. He was the first native New Mexican to serve as president, a position he held with distinction for 20 years. The school experienced great changes during his tenure, from increased enrollment and the construction of many new buildings, to new academic programs and considerable athletic prowess. A lover of golf, Popejoy built the University Golf Course on what is now UNM's North Campus. Bud Davis, a later UNM president, wrote that Popejoy "was the stuff legends are made of, and there never was or will be a lack of tall tales about [him]." According to UNM's longtime university architect, Van Dorn Hooker, "No person ever contributed more to UNM than Tom Popejoy and I doubt if anyone ever will." UNM's performance center was named in Popejoy's honor upon his retirement in 1968. (Courtesy of UNM Student Publications Board Records, Box 5, Center for Southwest Research, University Libraries, University of New Mexico.)

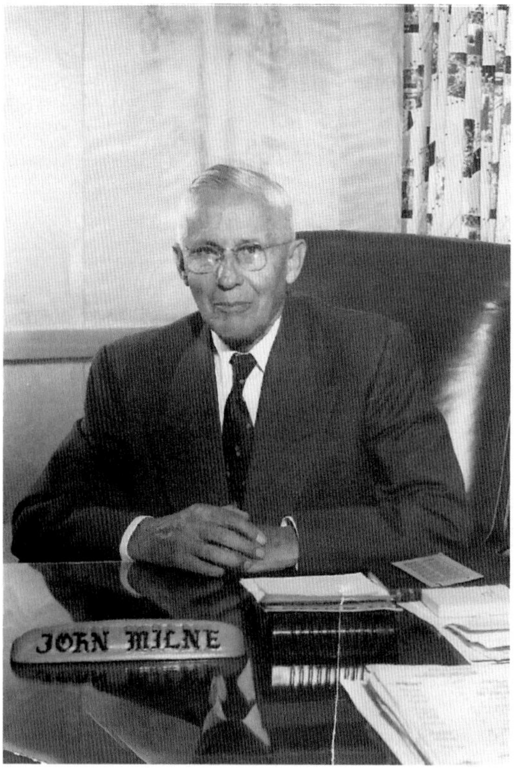

John Milne (1880–1957)
At the age of 25, John Milne arrived in Albuquerque to take a job as a high school math teacher in 1906. By 1908, he was the high school's principal, and in 1911, he was appointed the city's superintendent of schools, a job he held for the next 45 years. Milne prudently purchased land for the building of new facilities as the city expanded and enrollment in city schools jumped from an estimated 1,500 to almost 40,000 students. New facilities included Albuquerque High School (below), which opened in 1914, and Milne football stadium, built in 1939. (Courtesy of the Albuquerque Public Schools.)

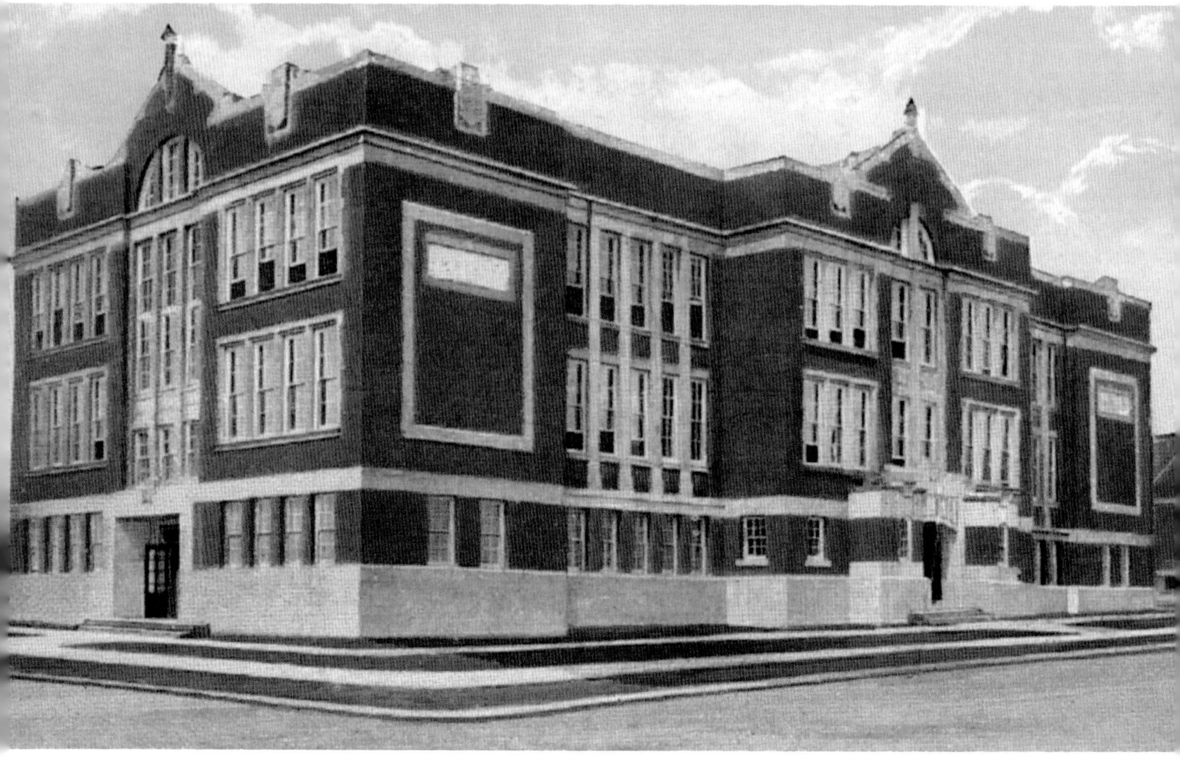

CHAPTER ONE

Authors, Artists, and Architects

When people think of artists and authors in New Mexico history, they usually think first of Taos and Santa Fe. It is only natural to remember these famous art colonies and their legendary residents of the first half of the 20th century. But a strong case can be made that the creative epicenter of New Mexico had shifted to Albuquerque in the second half of the 20th century. While Albuquerque has never boasted an art colony per se, its lineup of artists, photographers, architects, novelists, and poets is unsurpassed in the Southwest. Academic scholars at the University of New Mexico have added to the city's reputation as a magnet for creative minds.

Albuquerque's creative works are often very public. Authors regularly read from their works in public venues, like Bookworks and other local bookstores. Poets often read their newest poems at public slams. Architects design unique structures throughout the city. Public art, especially sculptures, are abundant. Most works evoked praise, as with Cynthia Rowland's sculpture of Sen. Dennis Chavez on Civic Plaza, but also controversy, as with Barbara Grygutis's so-called "Chevy-on-a-Stick" at Gibson and San Mateo Boulevards.

But that is the risk of true creativity. To their credit, Albuquerque's authors, artists, photographers, and architects have been willing to take risks to keep their work—and their community—fresh, vibrant, and never dull.

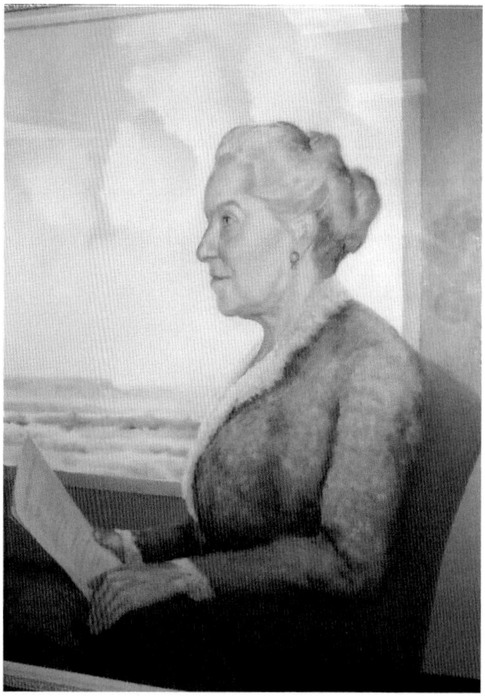

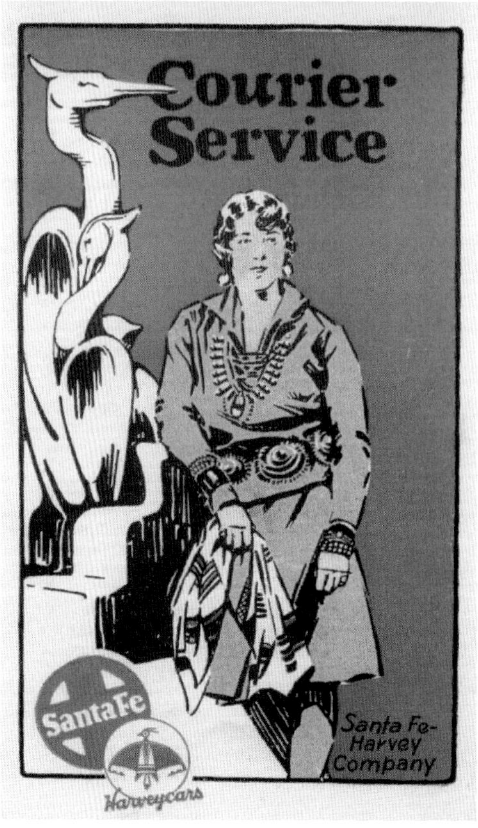

Erna Fergusson (1888–1964)
Albuquerque native Erna Fergusson was the daughter of politician Harvey B. Fergusson and the granddaughter of businessman Franz Huning. Graduating from UNM in 1912, she honed her writing skills as a reporter for the *Albuquerque Herald*. She later helped train dozens of talented young women (known as couriers) who led extensive tours of the Indian country. The Southwestern Indian Detours remained open from 1926 to the 1940s. She wrote many books about New Mexico, including *Dancing Gods* (1932), *Albuquerque* (1947), and *Murder and Mystery in New Mexico* (1948). She was known as the "Grand Dame of New Mexico Letters." A branch library of the Albuquerque Public Library is named in her honor.

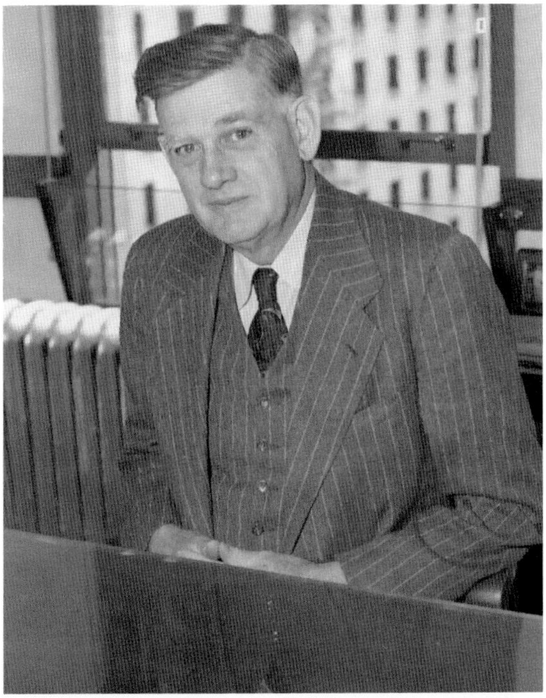

Will Keleher (1870–1970)
Starting as an Albuquerque newspaper reporter, Will Keleher began to practice law in 1915. By the 1930s, he also began writing history. He knew and wrote about many of the greatest figures in state history, from Elfego Baca to Albert B. Fall. As his son, Michael L. Keleher, has written, "It became his single-minded purpose to record his observations of persons and circumstances so they would . . . avoid the 'iniquity of oblivion.'" (Photograph by C.E. Redman, courtesy of the Keleher family.)

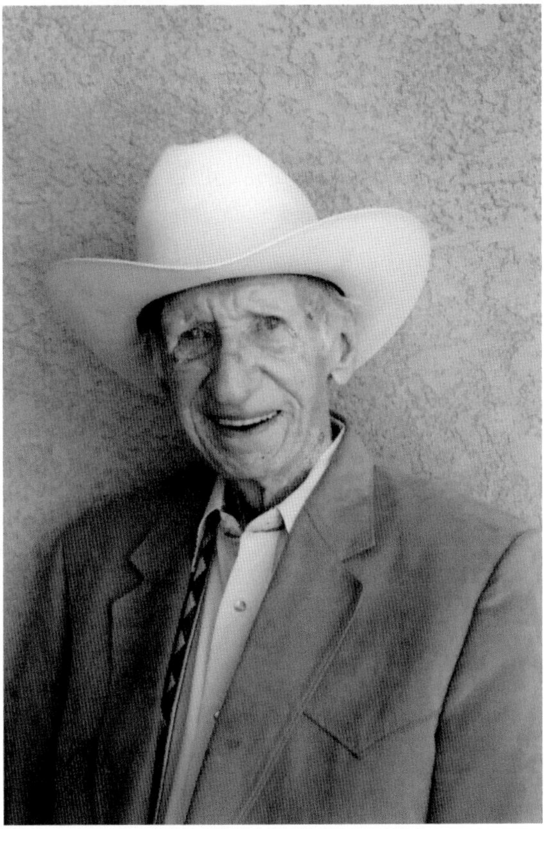

Howard Bryan (1920–2011)
A young World War II veteran, Howard Bryan arrived in Albuquerque to work for the *Albuquerque Tribune*. In 1953, he began to write "Off the Beaten Path," an immensely popular column about New Mexico's past. Bryan combed old newspapers and interviewed many of the people he wrote about. According to Tony Hillerman, Bryan was "the fellow hardest to beat at the game of swapping anecdotes" about history. (Courtesy of Rio Grande Books.)

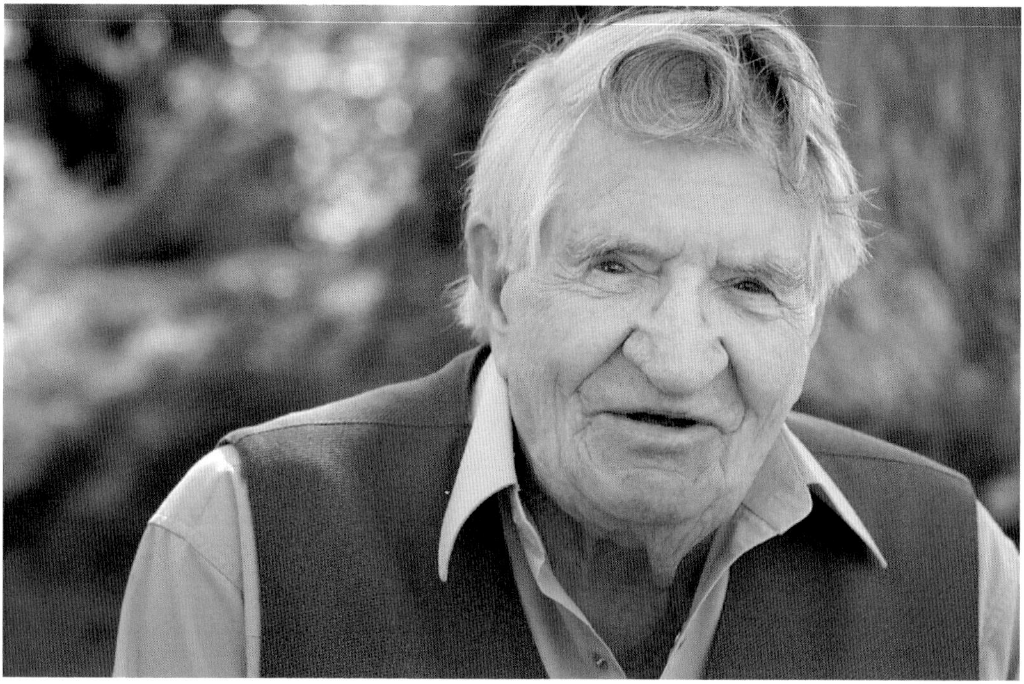

Max Evans (b. 1924)
Evans was a cowboy, a soldier, an artist, and a miner before he became an author. He wrote his first novel, *The Rounders*, in 1960. Evans wrote 24 additional books, mostly from his home in Albuquerque's Nob Hill neighborhood. He says that his beautiful view of the Sandia Mountains "rests my eyes and my soul," enabling him to become one of the most honored and admired authors in the West. (Courtesy of Rio Grande Books.)

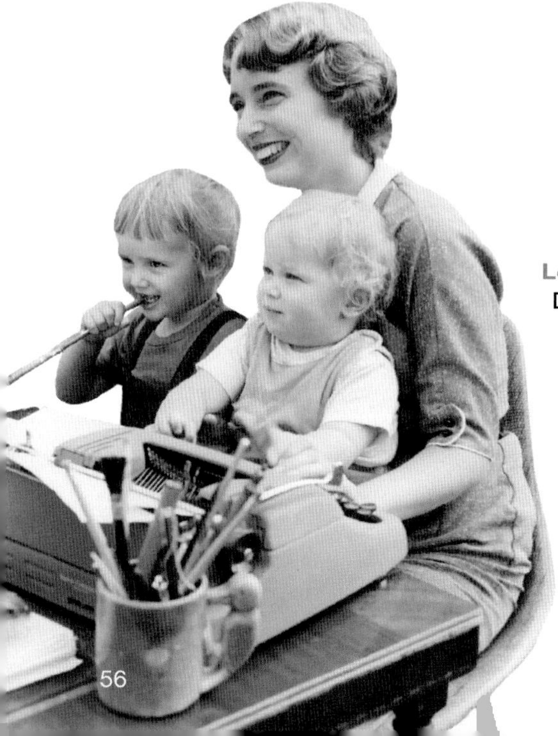

Lois Duncan (b. 1934)
Duncan (seen here with two of her children) is the author of 48 award-winning novels for young adults. She moved to Albuquerque to teach writing in 1962. In 1989, her 18-year-old daughter, Kaitlyn, was shot to death on Lomas Boulevard. The police ruled the shooting a random act, but Duncan believes that it was deliberate. She wrote a book on the subject called *Who Killed My Daughter?* and has appeared on many cold-case television shows in her endless search to solve the crime.

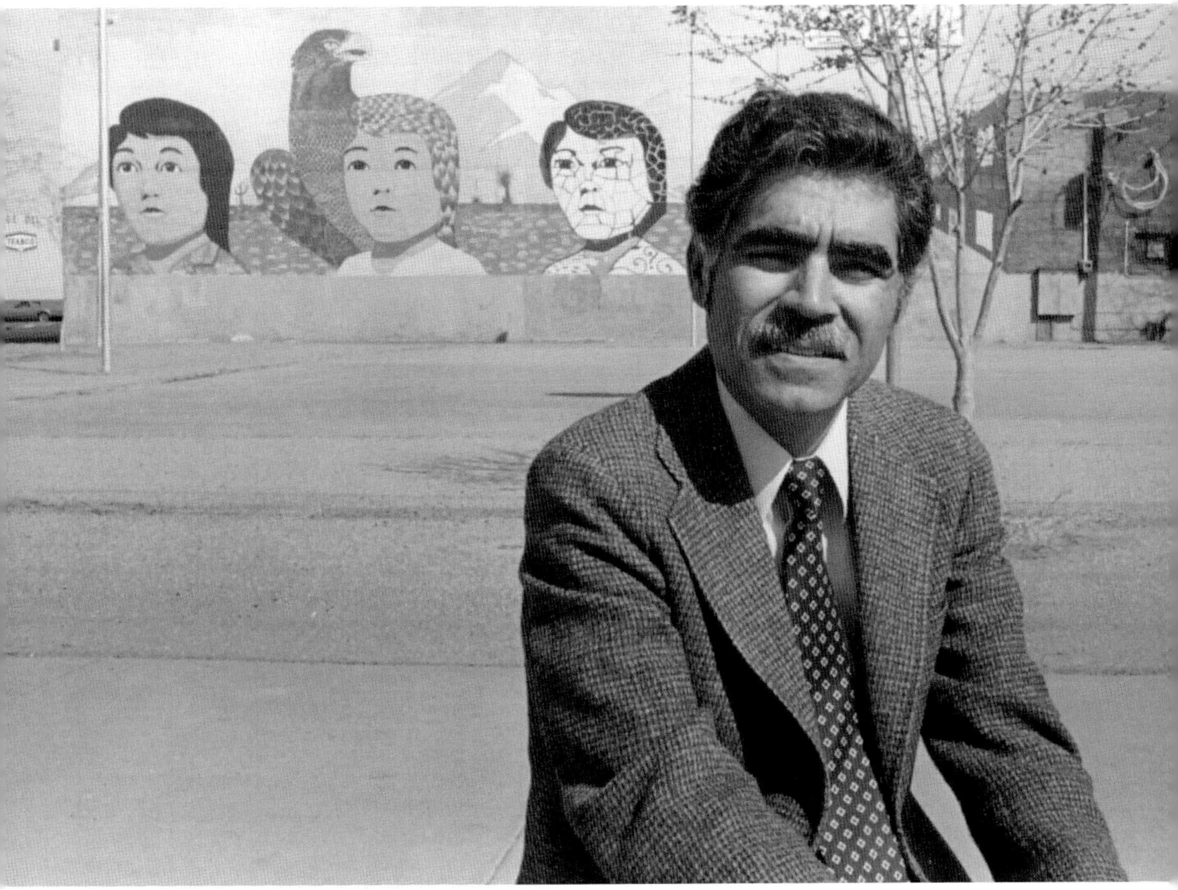

Rudolfo Anaya (b. 1937)

Hispanic novelist Rudolfo Anaya was born and raised in rural Guadalupe County. His first and most famous novel, *Bless Me, Ultima,* was largely based on the culture and values he learned as a young boy. The highly acclaimed book has been translated into several languages and was made into a popular motion picture in 2013. Its description of *brujas*, or witchcraft, made it so controversial that it has been banned in several communities, sparking debates regarding censorship of literature. Anaya has continued to write award-winning novels, poetry, plays, and children's literature. His later works include *Alburquerque* (1992), *Rio Grande Fall* (1996), *La Llorona* (2011), and *How Chile Came to New Mexico* (2014). Living on Albuquerque's west side, Anaya led the creative writing program at UNM for many years. (Courtesy of the Center for Southwest Research, 980-008-0002, University Libraries, University of New Mexico.)

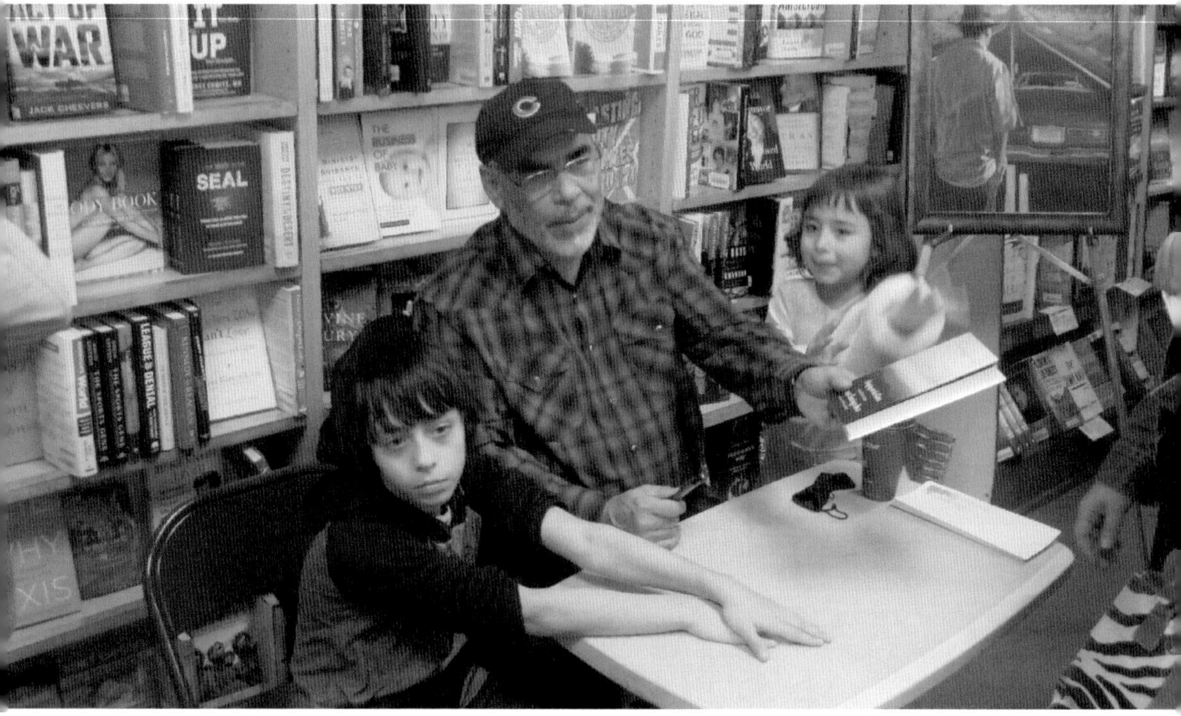

Jimmy Santiago Baca (b. 1952)
Baca grew up in a truly dysfunctional family filled with violence, abandonment, and betrayal. By the time he was 20, he had been convicted of drug possession and was sentenced to five years in the Arizona State Prison. Learning how to read and write in prison, he began writing powerful poems, some of which were published in *Mother Jones* magazine even before his release. He has since used his writings to become a powerful voice for men and women who face similarly troubled lives. His works include *Martín and Meditations of the South Valley* (1987) and *Spring Poems along the Rio Grande* (2007). His compelling memoir is titled *A Place to Stand* (2002). Baca, seen here with two of his children, has won many awards for his writing and has taught and encouraged countless other writers, from young children to incarcerated adults. His work is filled with love and passion.

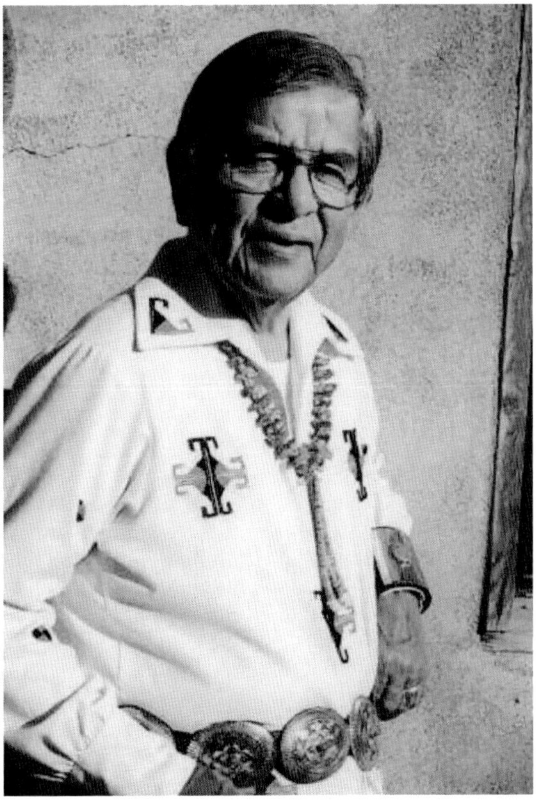

Joe S. Sando (1923–2011)
A native of Jemez Pueblo, Joe Sando graduated from the Santa Fe Indian School and Eastern New Mexico University. Teaching Pueblo Indian history at UNM, he realized that few books had been written about pueblo history and culture. He filled this void with exceptional works, including *Pueblo Profiles* (1998), becoming the state's acknowledged expert in Pueblo history. A true cultural broker, he thrived in both Pueblo and Anglo cultures.

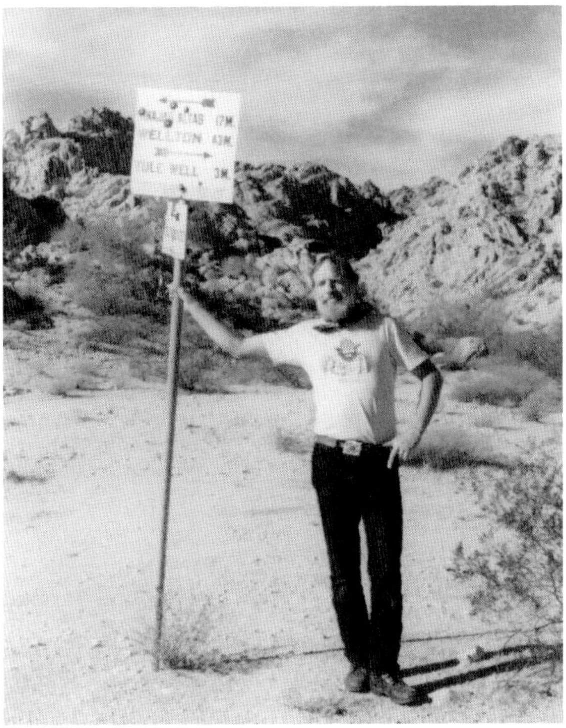

Edward Abbey (1927–1989)
Abbey attended UNM in the 1950s, using his GI Bill benefits to earn BA and MA degrees. His master's thesis focused on anarchism; at least one of his writings in a student newspaper was censored by university officials. Remaining in the Southwest, Abbey became a dedicated advocate for environmental issues and the author of such critically acclaimed novels as *The Lone Cowboy* (1956) and *The Monkey Wrench Gang* (1975). (Courtesy of Jack Loeffler.)

Tony Hillerman (1925–2008)

Arriving in Albuquerque after decorated service in World War II, Hillerman, like thousands of other newcomers, was impressed with the city's lights, sky, clean air, and friendly people. He worked for the *Santa Fe New Mexican* before taking a job as a special assistant to UNM president Tom Popejoy. By the late 1960s, he began writing enormously popular mystery novels, featuring Navajo police officers Joe Leaphorn, Jim Cree, and Bernadette Manuelito. His 18 novels include *The Blessing Way* (1970), *A Thief of Time* (1988), *Sacred Clowns* (1993), and *Skeleton Man* (2004). Receiving every imaginable award for his books about the people and culture of the Navajo Reservation, he asserted that "there's not much action from Albuquerque that goes into my books, but it is a wonderful place to write." His memoir, *Seldom Disappointed* (2001), reflected his philosophy that if a person does not have unrealistic expectations in life, he is seldom disappointed and often pleasantly surprised. An elementary school in northwest Albuquerque is named in his honor. Following his death in 2008, his talented daughter, Anne Hillerman, has helped preserve her father's legacy by continuing to write novels about many of the same characters, places, and beauties of the country's largest "res." Her first novel, *Spider Woman's Daughter*, was published in 2013. (Courtesy of Tony Hillerman Photograph Collection, 000-501-0002, Center for Southwest Research, University Libraries, University of New Mexico.)

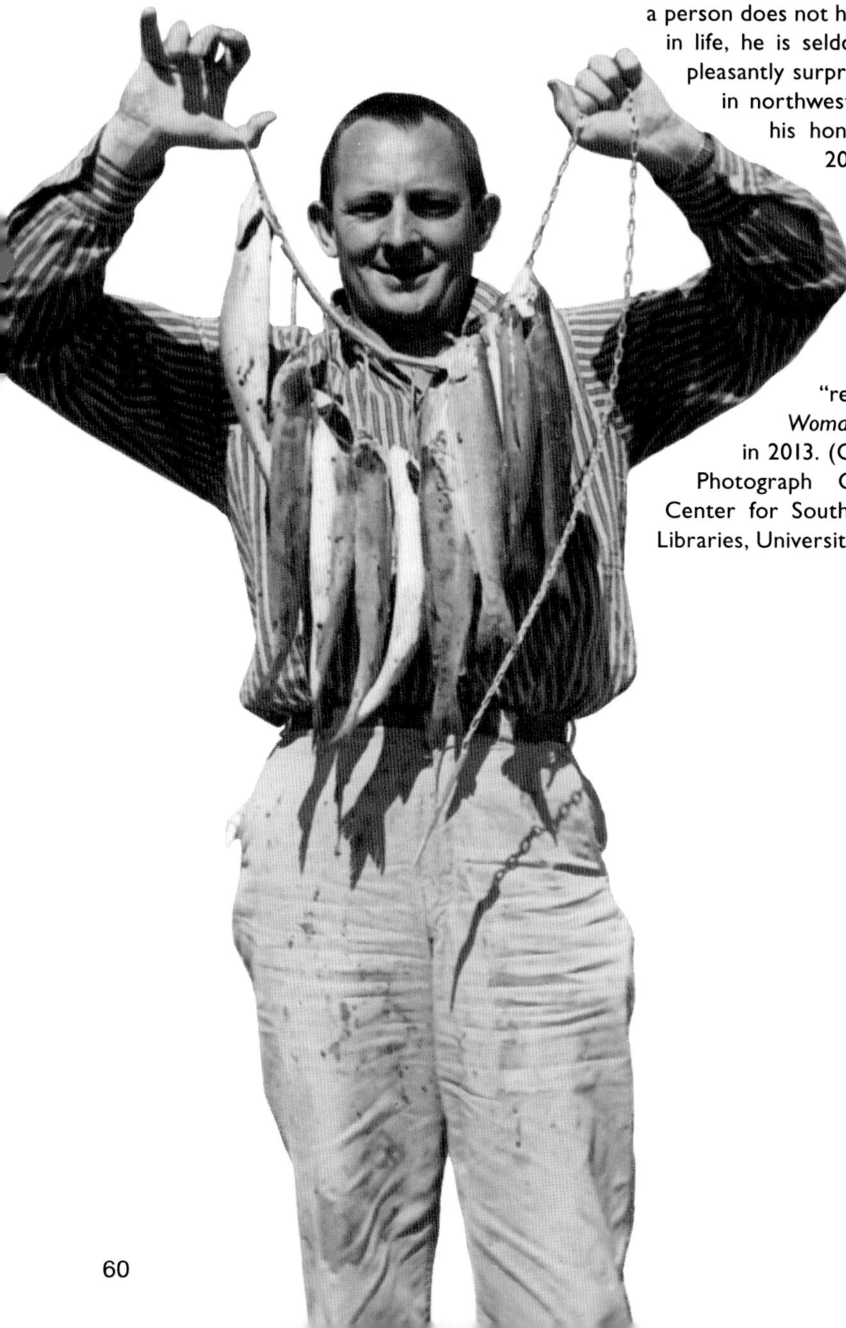

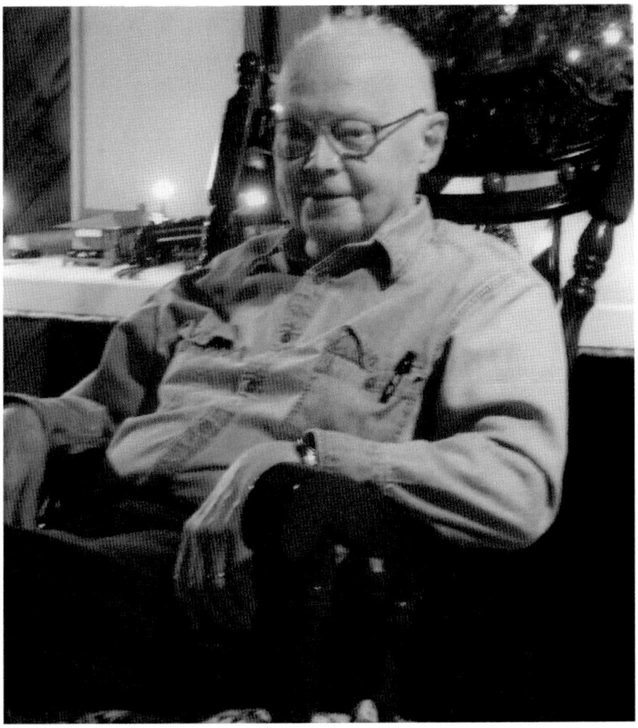

Fred Saberhagen (1930–2007)
A highly successful author of horror novels and science fiction, Saberhagen wrote 60 novels and hundreds of short stories, mostly at his home in Albuquerque over the last 20 years of his life. When a young fan told him that the day she met him was the most exciting day of her life, he replied, "Fortunately, you are young and have many days ahead of you."

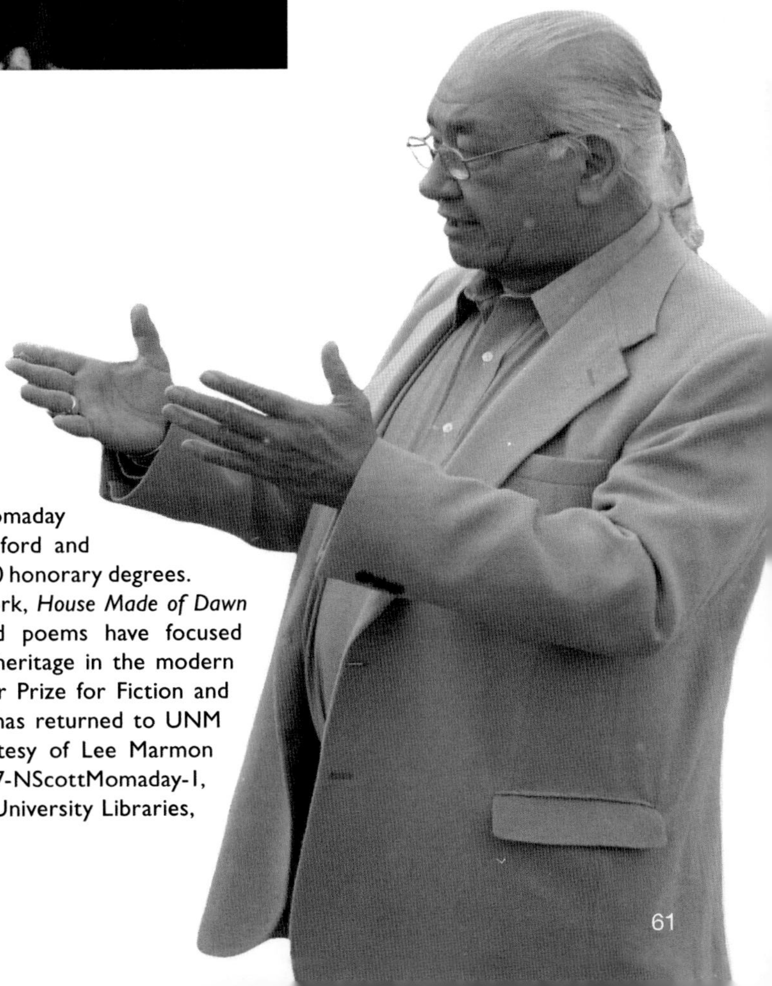

N. Scott Momaday (b. 1934)
After graduating from UNM, Momaday earned graduate degrees at Stanford and has been awarded no fewer than 20 honorary degrees. Starting with his most famous work, *House Made of Dawn* (1968), his memoir, novels, and poems have focused on the fate of Native American heritage in the modern age. He was awarded the Pulitzer Prize for Fiction and the National Medal of Arts. He has returned to UNM to teach creative writing. (Courtesy of Lee Marmon Pictorial Collection, 2000-017-NScottMomaday-1, Center for Southwest Research, University Libraries, University of New Mexico.)

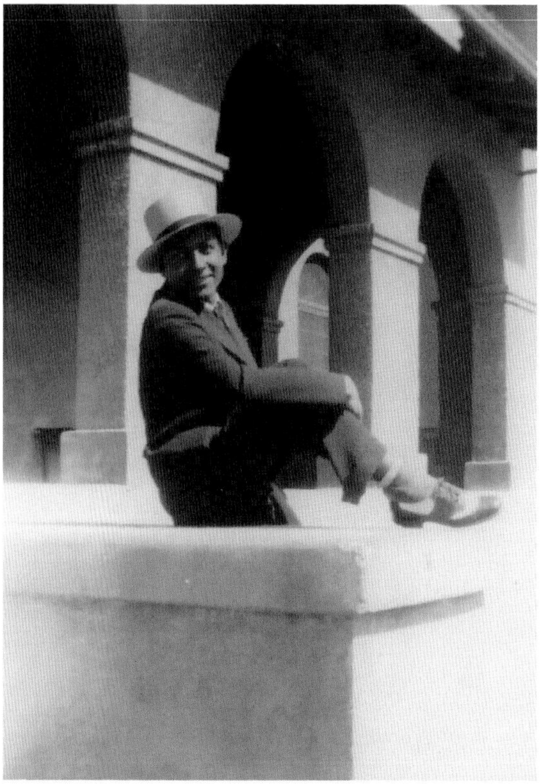

Rubén Cobos (1911–2010)
Rubén Cobos was a natural linguist. Even as a boy attending Albuquerque's Menaul School (pictured), he enjoyed listening to his classmates speak a kind of Spanish that was different from the Spanish of his native Mexico. During World War II, he used his language skills in military intelligence. Cobos taught at UNM from 1945 to 1976. He wrote many books, including his most famous, *A Dictionary of New Mexico and Southern Colorado Spanish* (1983). (Courtesy of Evelia Cobos and Rio Grande Books.)

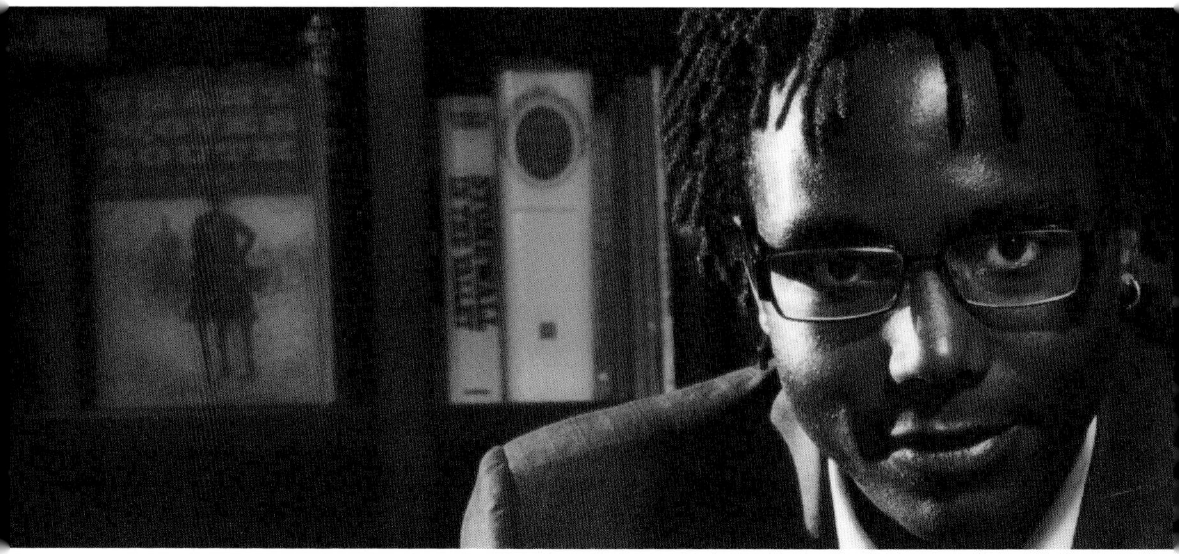

Hakim Bellamy (b. 1979)
Bellamy was named Albuquerque's first poet laureate in 2012. A national poetry-slam champion, he says that his "duty is to try to make poetry matter to populations it often doesn't matter to," including at-risk youths and prison inmates. Bellamy believes that to cultivate creativity, "I need to hear music, see a [play], watch documentaries, play with my son in the park, take in an art exhibit. Creativity begets creativity."

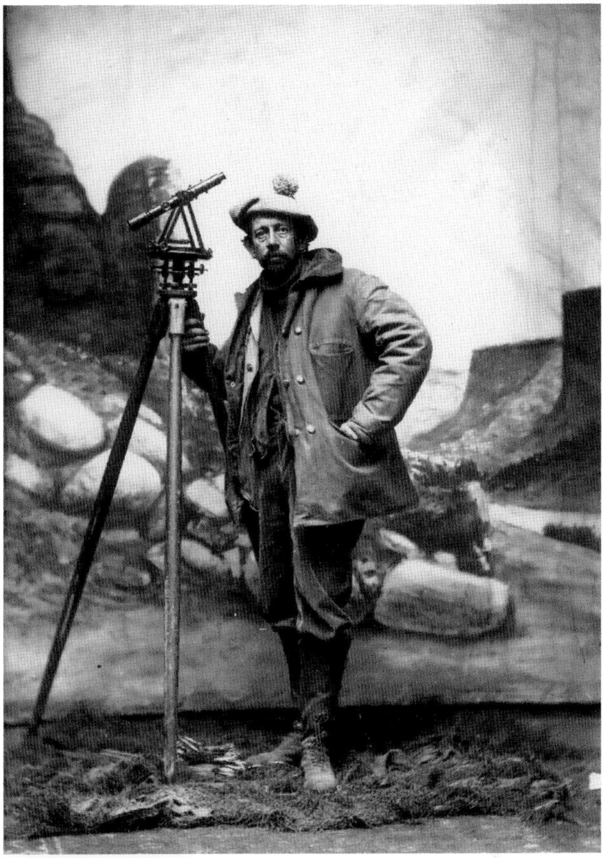

William Cobb (1860–1909)
A Harvard graduate, William Cobb came to Albuquerque to seek a cure for his tuberculosis. Once here, he opened a photography studio and, in 1891, married Edmundie "Eddie" Ross, the daughter of former governor Edmund Ross. The couple worked side-by-side for the next 18 years. According to historian Richard Ruddy, they came to dominate photography in the city in the late territorial period. Their collected works are archived in the Albuquerque Museum. (Courtesy of the Albuquerque Museum, PA1990-013-390.)

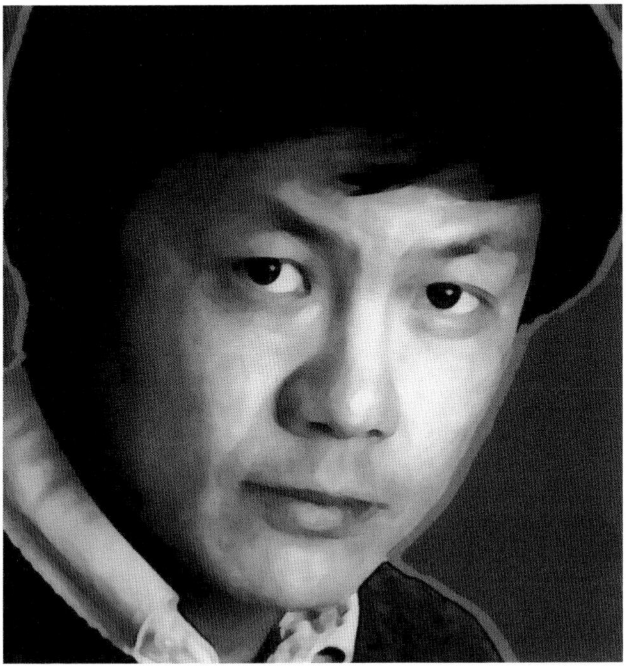

Kim Jew (b. 1952)
Kim Jew got his first camera when he was a student at Highland High School. He opened his first portrait studio in the Nob Hill neighborhood in 1976. Now the most esteemed portrait photographer in Albuquerque, his subjects have included many famous Americans, including four US presidents. Jew believes that "people's self-image comes from the last picture taken of them. It really does have an influence on the psyche and translates into self-esteem." (Courtesy of Kim Jew.)

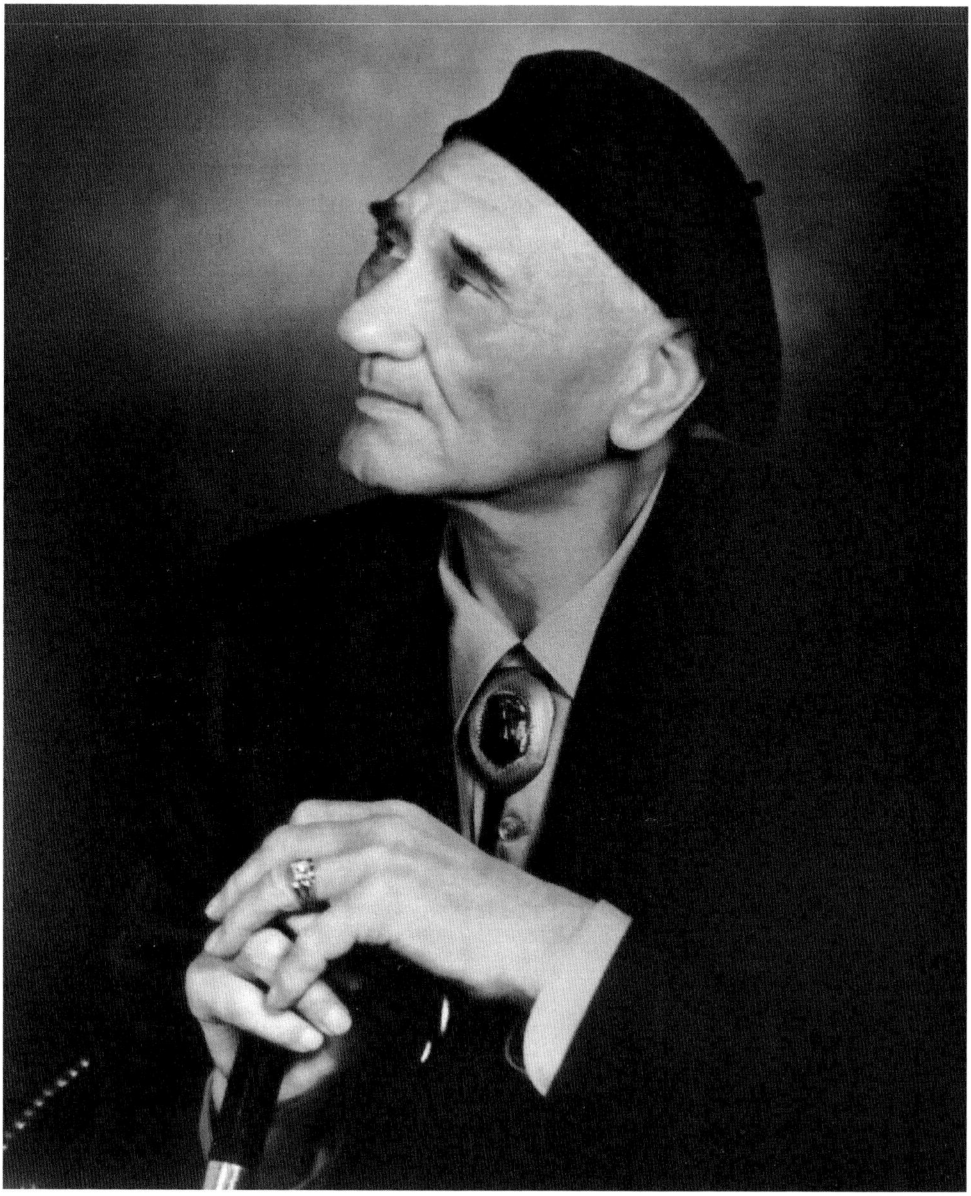

Carl Von Hassler (1887–1969)
At the age of 26, Carl Von Hassler migrated to the United States from his native Germany in 1912. A maverick, he became a member of the controversial Greenwich Village Ash Can school of modern artists. After serving in the US Army during World War I, he moved to Albuquerque in 1922, living in various parts of town, including Old Town, the Alvarado Hotel, and, for a while, upstairs at the KiMo Theatre. Recognized as the "dean" of Albuquerque artists, he is probably best known for his impressive murals, including those at the KiMo, the Franciscan Hotel, the old airport, and the Mineshaft Tavern in Madrid, New Mexico. Several talented artists, including Betty Sabo, studied under him. According to Von Hassler, "If an artist can come close to nature, he's doing damn well. Don't let anyone tell you that he is doing better than nature or improving on it." (Courtesy of Esther E. Berrenberg Estate; do not copy.)

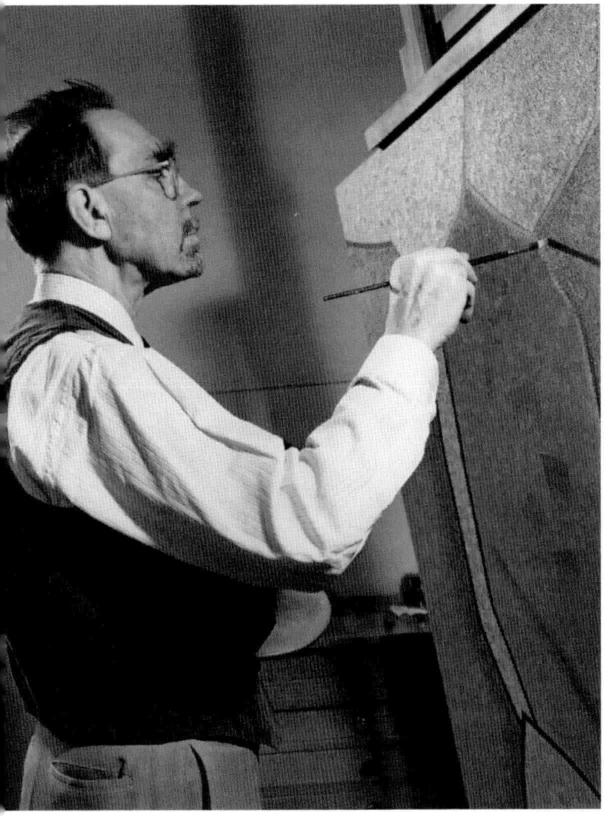

Raymond Jonson (1891–1982)
One of the most famous abstract artists in New Mexico history, Raymond Jonson began teaching at UNM in 1934 and became an artist-in-residence in 1950. His house on campus, designed by John Gaw Meem, served as his home, his studio, and an art gallery. It remains the Jonson Gallery today. It could be said that he is still in residence, because his ashes are stored in a vault on the premises, per his wishes. (Courtesy of Albuquerque Museum, PA1980-187-131.)

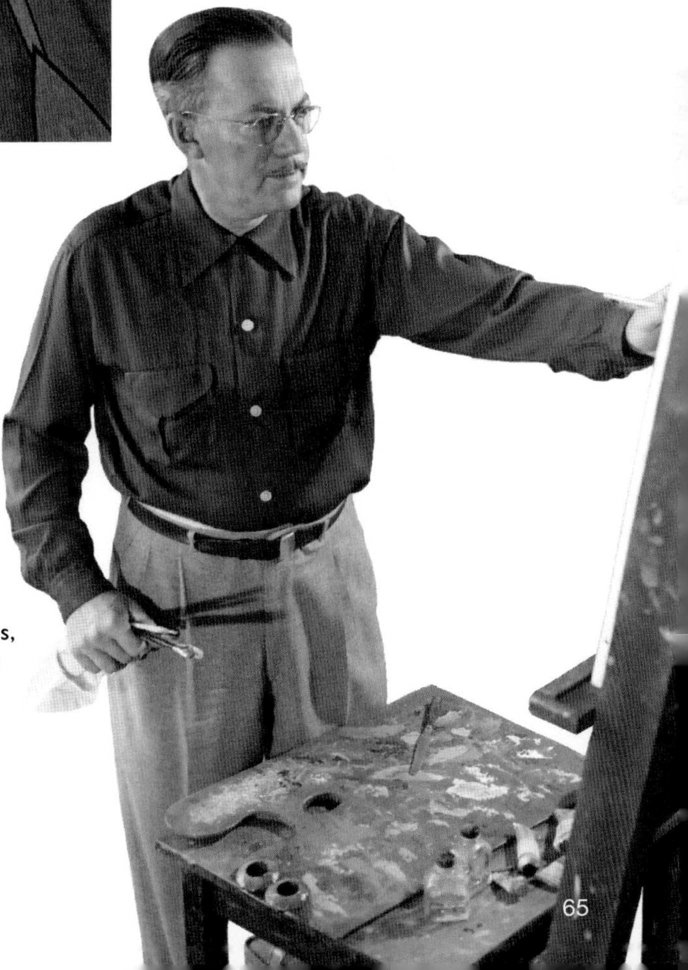

Kenneth Adams (1897–1966)
An accomplished painter by the 1920s, Kenneth Adams became the last member of the Taos Society of Artists before that prestigious organization disbanded in 1927. His impressive murals graced the interiors of several New Deal buildings of the 1930s. He served as an artist-in-residence at UNM from 1938 to 1963. While at UNM, he painted his most famous, most controversial mural, a four-panel work at the university's Zimmerman Library. (Courtesy of Albuquerque Museum, PA1980-187-114.)

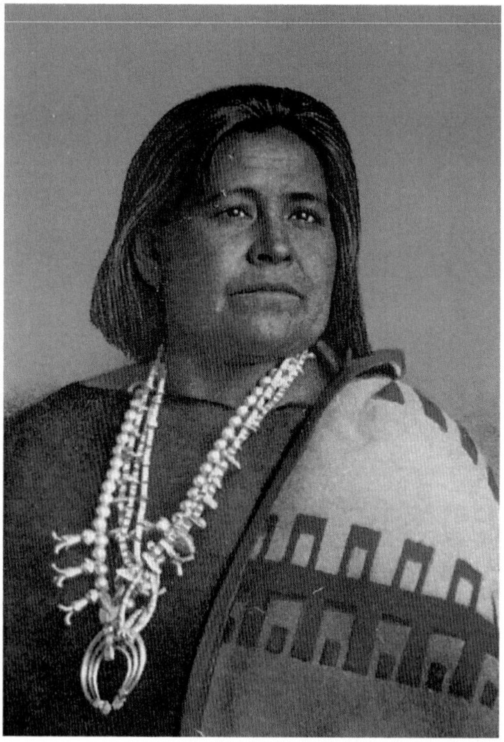

Asdzaa Lichii' (Red Woman), a.k.a. "Elle of Ganado" (c. 1853–1924)
Elle of Ganado was an expert Navajo weaver who demonstrated her craft at Fred Harvey's Indian Room in the Alvarado Hotel from 1903 to 1923. She wove rugs that were then given as gifts to presidents Teddy Roosevelt and William Howard Taft during their famous visits to Albuquerque. Unlike many Indians, she allowed her photograph to be taken and used on Fred Harvey postcards, magazine covers, and even playing cards.

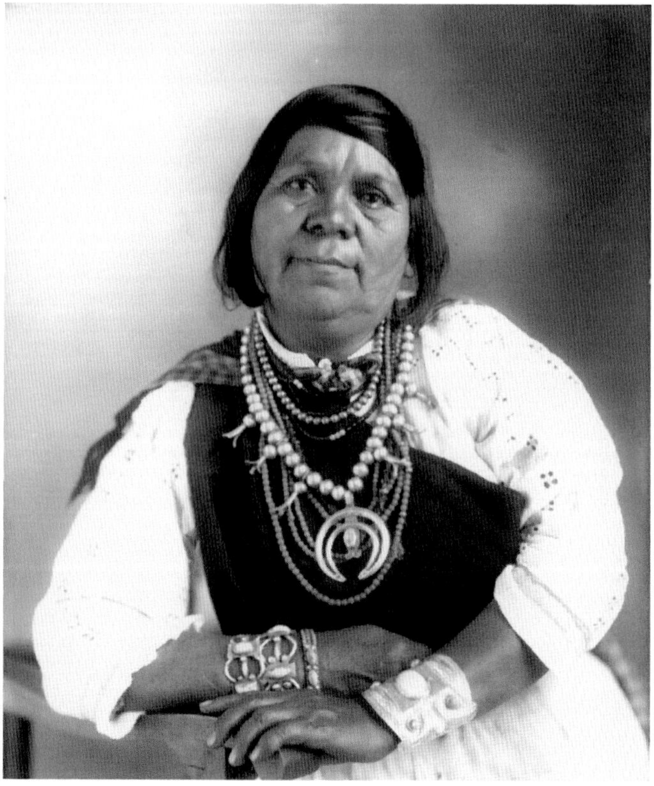

Maria Chiwiwi
Isleta Pueblo native Maria Chiwiwi attended the infamous Carlisle Indian School in Pennsylvania, where young men and women were forced to surrender their native cultures and adopt mainstream American values and behavior. Despite this traumatic experience, Chiwiwi returned to Isleta and learned the traditional art of pottery making. Becoming a highly accomplished artist, she sold her beautiful pottery to admiring tourists at the Albuquerque train depot and from her shop in Isleta. (Courtesy of Albuquerque Museum, PA1990-013-274.)

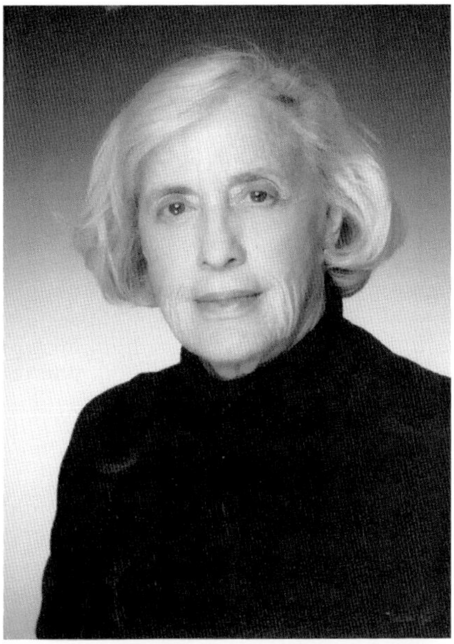

Betty Sabo (b. 1928)

Artist Betty Sabo graduated from Albuquerque High School and UNM before studying with Carl Von Hassler, the dean of Albuquerque painters. Her vivid paintings were said to be so popular that they were "snatched up before they could dry." Her equally popular bronze sculptures at the Albuquerque Museum and on the UNM campus depicted Albuquerqueans engaged in everyday life. Gov. Susana Martinez declared February 10, 2012, "Betty Sabo Day." (Courtesy of Mary Sabo.)

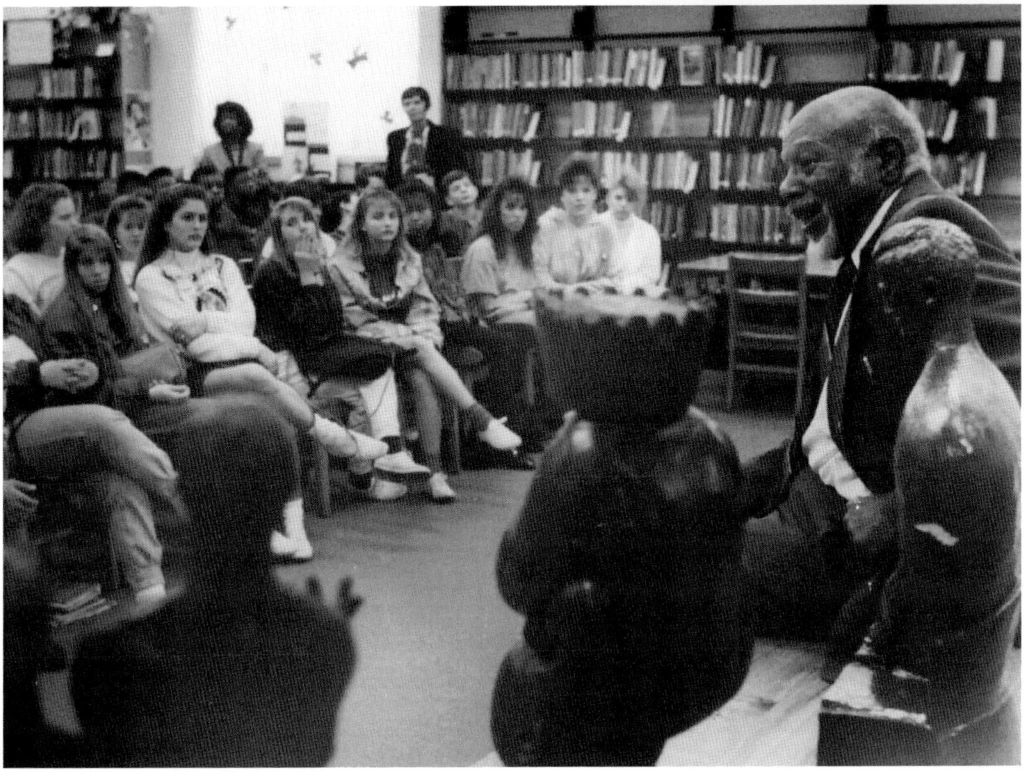

C. Oliver LaGrone (1906–1995)

LaGrone was a student at Howard University when his sister was diagnosed with tuberculosis and his family moved to Albuquerque to seek a cure for her disease. LaGrone became a WPA artist and one of UNM's first African American graduates. His 1935 sculpture *Mercy*, showing his mother comforting him when he had malaria, stood in the lobby of the Carrie Tingly Hospital for Crippled Children for years.

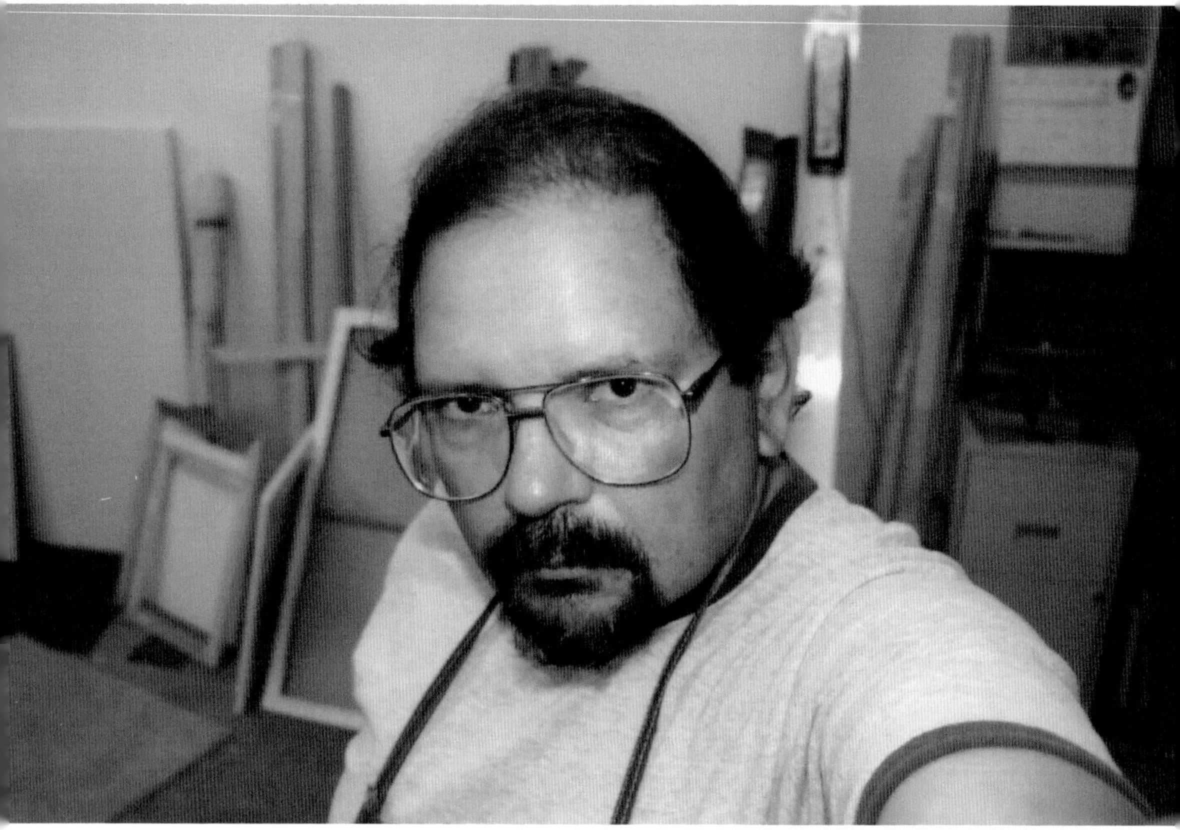

Edward Gonzales (b. 1947)
Gonzales is a descendant of Hispanic families who first colonized New Mexico in 1598. He was a year old when his family moved to Albuquerque in 1948. Growing up in a poor, working-class family, Gonzales showed a talent for art at the age of four. But, when his father brought magazines like the *Saturday Evening Post* home from work, he always wondered why he could find no depictions of his native culture in them. Determined to focus on everyday Hispanic life in his art, Gonzales completed his fine arts degree at UNM (following a tour of duty in Vietnam) in 1971. His nationally acclaimed art reflects his strong Hispanic roots, emphasizing the importance of families and the great value of education, including bilingual education. Since his first poster, "Su Primer Libros," appeared in 1992, his paintings and posters depicting Hispanic life and learning have been displayed in homes, including the White House, and schools across the country. He founded the annual Contemporary Hispanic Market in Santa Fe and is an award-winning author and children's book illustrator. The Edward Gonzales Elementary School has been named in recognition of his contribution to art, education, and culture. (Courtesy of Edward Gonzales.)

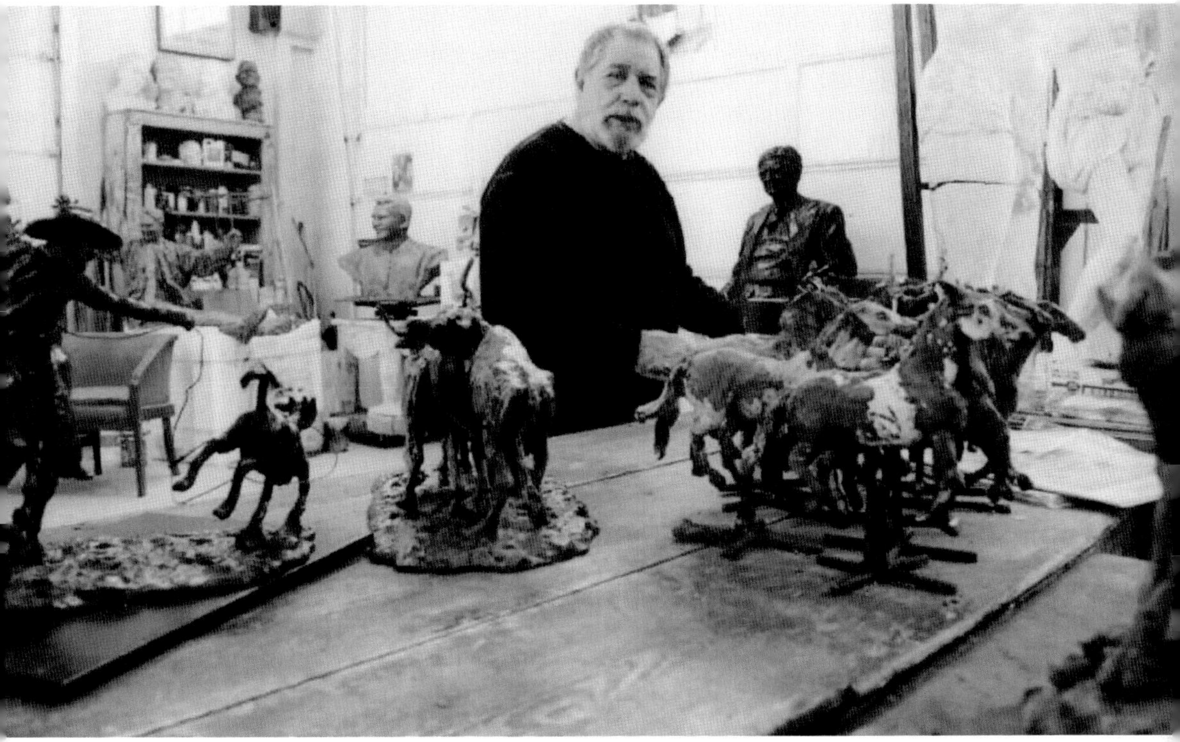

Reynaldo Rivera (b. 1938)

A native of Mesquite, New Mexico, "Sonny" Rivera joined the Navy when he was only 17. After his military service, he worked for many years as a barber until, at age 40, he studied art in Albuquerque, Chicago, Italy, and Mexico. Becoming an award-winning sculptor, he has created over 40 works of public art from his studio in Albuquerque. His works help celebrate New Mexico history and culture, with life-size bronze statues depicting Spanish settlers, a traveler on the Santa Fe Trail, author Rudolfo Anaya, Carlsbad Caverns explorer Jim White, Albuquerque mayor Harry Kinney, and two fallen soldiers, Manuel Mora and Pete Padilla, from Barelas at the National Hispanic Cultural Center. One of his sculptured Spanish settlers on the Albuquerque Museum grounds (right) is said to be Martin Chavez, the city's mayor when the sculpture was made and when Albuquerque celebrated its 300th anniversary, in 2007.

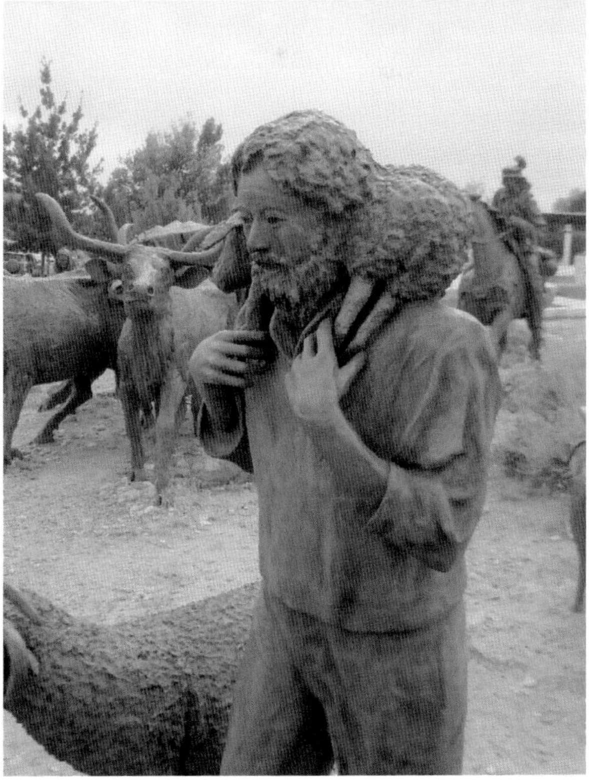

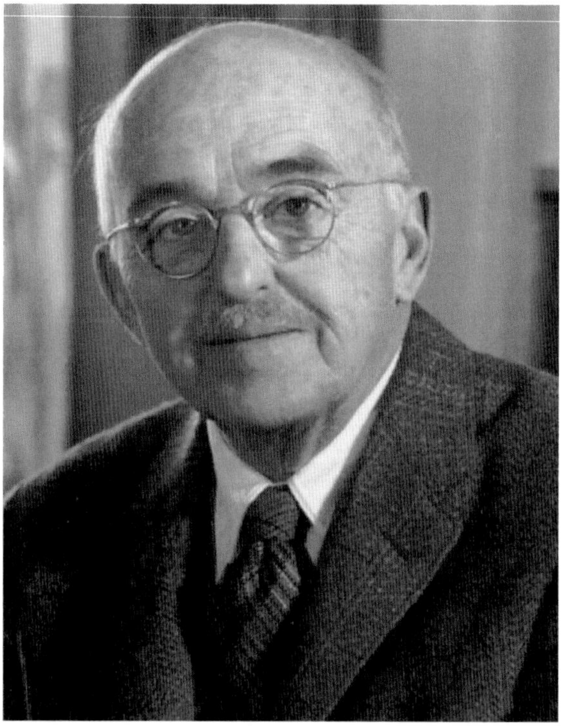

John Gaw Meem (1894–1983)
Meem was a 25-year-old engineer when he joined the army of TB refugees who came to New Mexico in search of a cure for their disease. Treated at the Sunmount sanatorium in Santa Fe, he grew to admire a Southwestern style of architecture known as Pueblo Revival. Leaving the sanatorium in the early 1920s, he remained in New Mexico and grew to become one of the most famous architects in state history. He applied the Pueblo Revival style to dozens of buildings, from homes and churches to businesses and schools. He became UNM's official architect in 1933, leading the movement to make Pueblo Revival the dominant style on campus. UNM's Zimmerman Library (below), opened in 1938, was perhaps his most famous Albuquerque work.

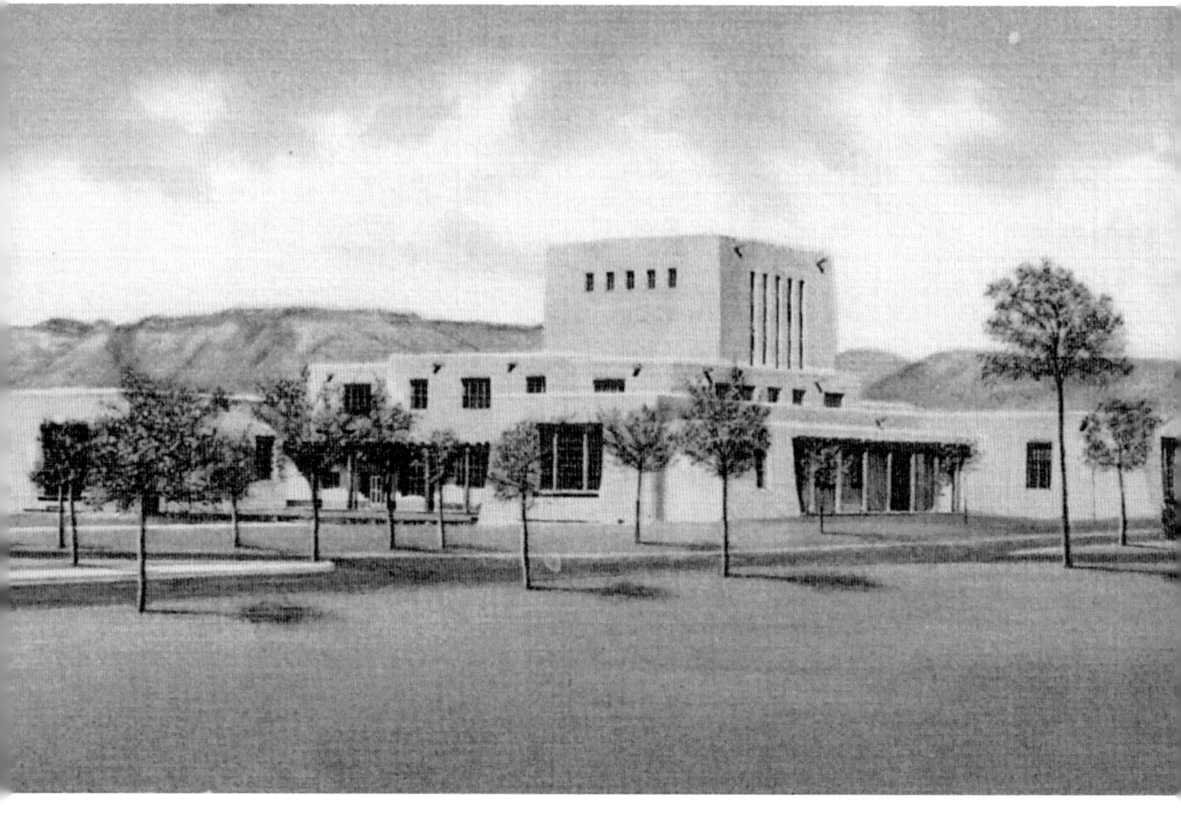

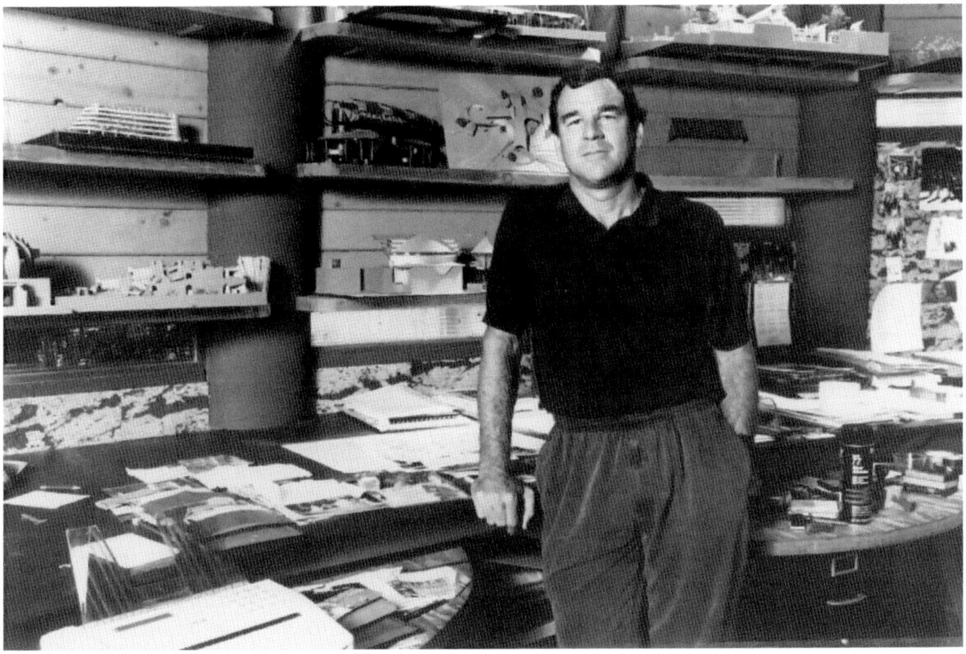

Bart Prince (b. 1947)
An Albuquerque native, Bart Prince was trained as an architect at Arizona State University. Developing an original style, Prince grew to become one of New Mexico's premier architects of the late 20th century. He is perhaps best known for the unique design of his own home and studio on 3501 Monte Vista Boulevard Northeast (below). Completed in 1984, the structure, nicknamed the "spaceship," has become a city landmark. Like all of Prince's buildings, it is a work of art. According to Prince, architecture should be a creative response to the surrounding terrain, the climate, and client interests. Buildings should be built "around and into" the New Mexico landscape, not "on top of it and in spite of it," as happens when people resort to what he refers to as "Pueblo-burger" and "Mission-burger" mass-produced styles of architecture. (Photograph of Bart Prince by Mark Kane.)

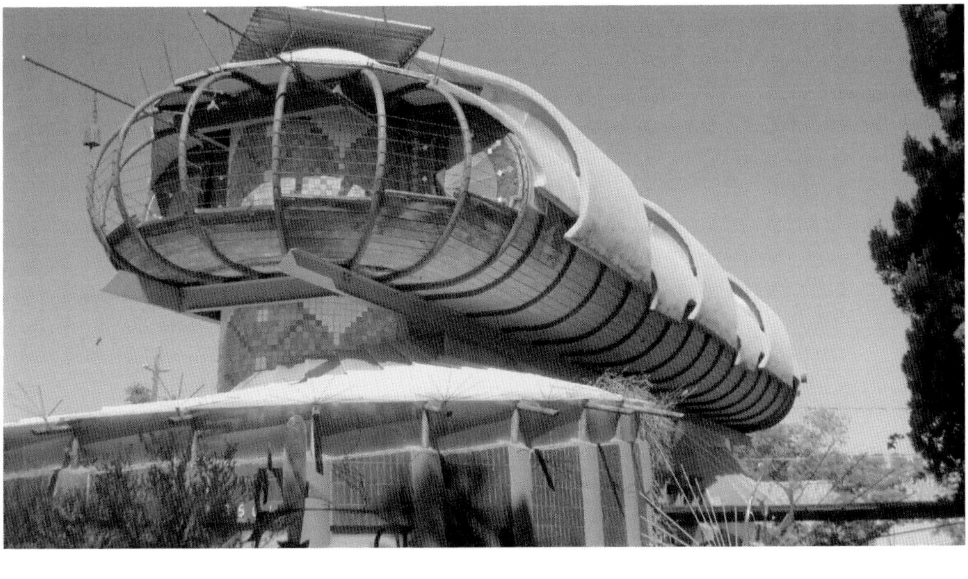

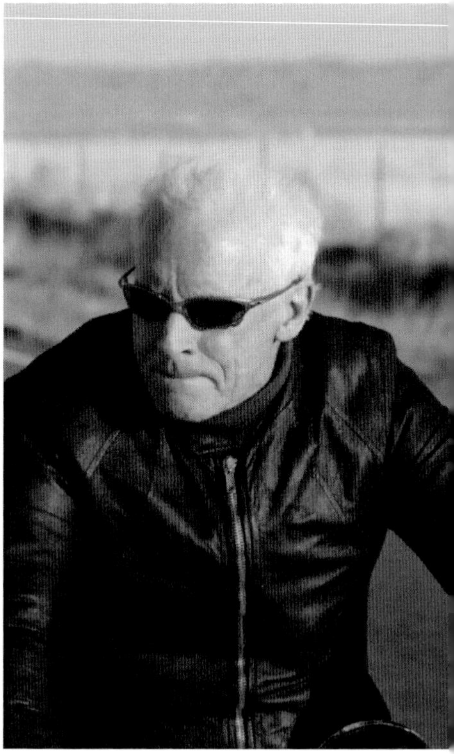

Antoine Predock (b. 1936)

An internationally acclaimed architect, Predock was educated at UNM and Columbia University. His museums, residences, resorts, libraries, and a major-league baseball park are found around the world, from Denmark to China. Many of his finest works are in Albuquerque: the Rio Grande Nature Center, UNM's School of Architecture, UNM's School of Law, the Beach Apartments, and the La Luz residential community (below). He has received countless honors and awards, including the Rome Prize in 1985, the prestigious Gold Medal from the American Institute of Architects in 2006, and the Smithsonian Design Museum Lifetime Achievement Award in 2007. In his words, "Architecture is a fascinating journey toward the unexpected. It is a ride, a physical ride and an intellectual ride." (Courtesy of Antoine Predock.)

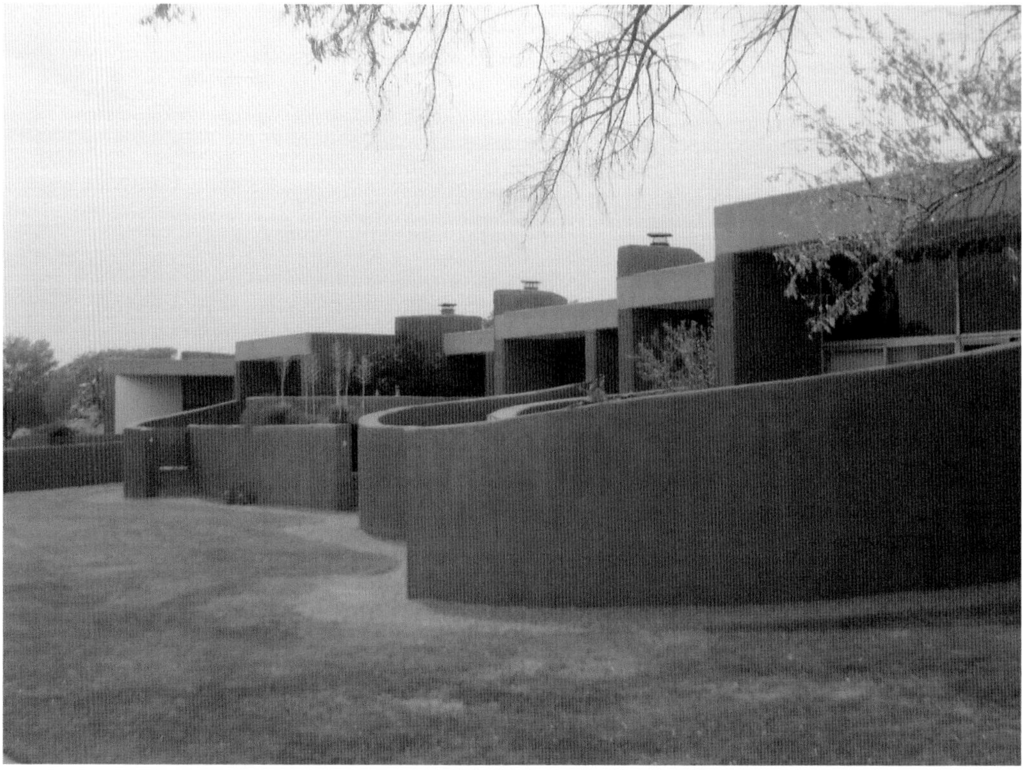

CHAPTER SIX

Cultures and Entertainment

New Mexico is justifiably famous for its three main cultures: Native American, Hispanic, and Anglo. But, Albuquerque and the entire state boasts more than these three cultures. In fact, there are many Native American cultures (including pueblos, Navajos, Apaches, and Utes), many Hispanic cultures (including Spanish American and Mexican American), and many Anglo cultures (including Italian, Greek, Jewish, and countless other ethnicities and nationalities). Although small in number, African American and Asian American populations have also thrived in the diverse city. In addition, Albuquerque can claim to have many subcultures, from the student community surrounding UNM to the agrarian culture of the Rio Grande Valley.

Most Albuquerqueans celebrate their city's cultural diversity. Individually, they are proud of their own cultures, while usually respecting and admiring all other ethnic and racial groups. In fact, many newcomers have chosen Albuquerque as their destination largely because they flourish in a community of many cultures, compared to the one-dimensional, far less interesting communities they left behind.

Sadly, there have been cases of discrimination in hiring, housing, and civil rights, and there are corners of abject poverty in the city. But most Albuquerque residents are likely to unite when traditional foods are served, traditional music is played, traditional dances are performed, traditional parades are organized, and traditional plays are staged. Just watch the great crowds at cultural events held at Old Town Plaza, the National Hispanic Cultural Center, the Indian Pueblo Cultural Center, Civic Plaza, the state fair, Tingley Coliseum, and the UNM Pit. These crowds stand in awe, smiling and proud, realizing that there is nothing quite like their city and its beautiful cultural mix in the heart of New Mexico.

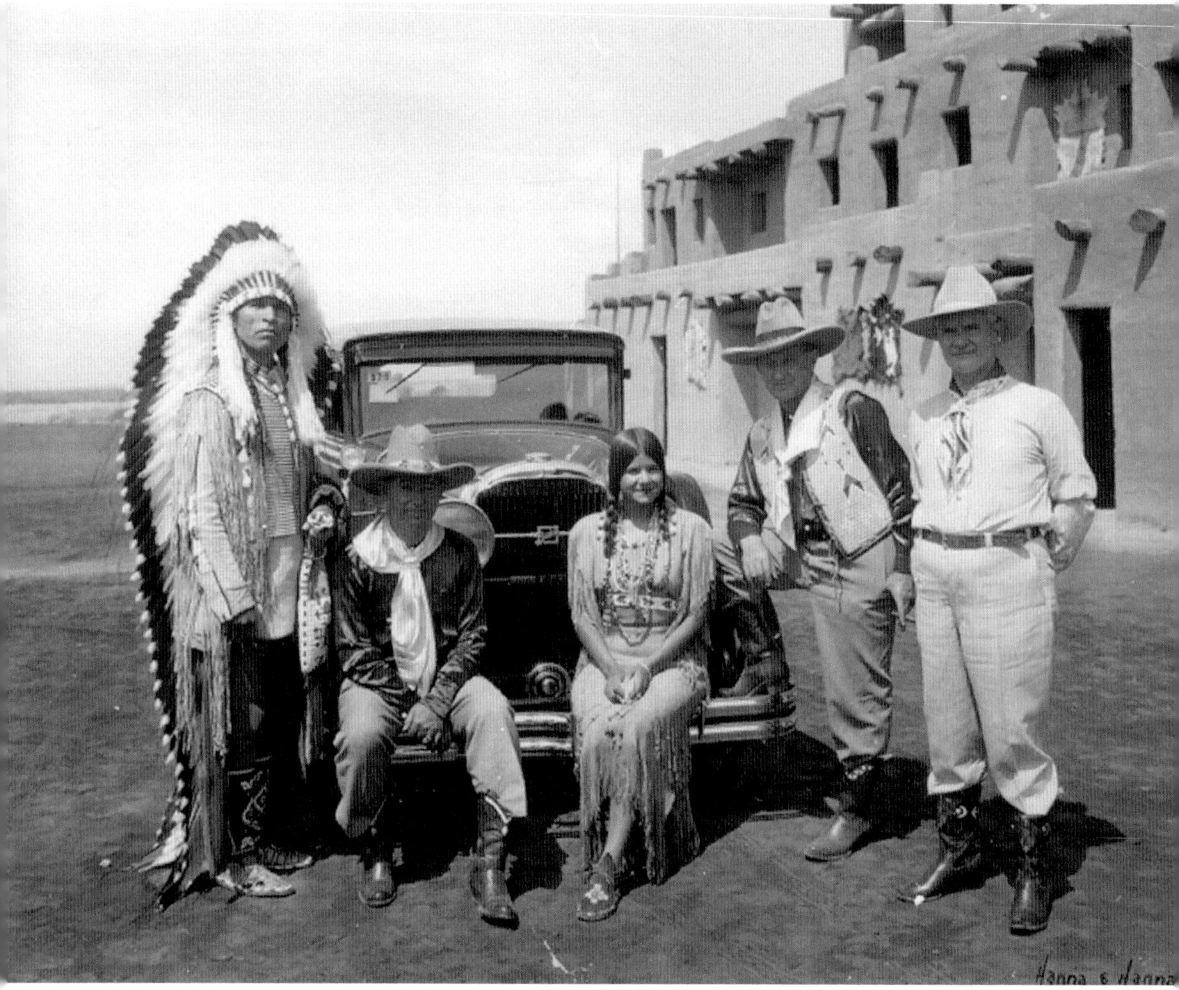

Celebrations of Culture
Indian trading-post owner Mike Kirk is usually identified as the creator of the Gallup Inter-Tribal Ceremonials in the early 1920s. Few remember that he also helped organize the First American events held in Albuquerque from 1928 to 1931. Enthusiastically supported by Clyde Tingley and other city councilmen, the Albuquerque shows were held near what is now East Central Avenue and Wyoming Boulevard. While members of many tribes participated, the show was not intended to be culturally authentic. A large facsimile of Taos Pueblo (pictured) served as a backdrop for Indian dances, trick horse-riding, and similar crowd-pleasing events. Famous Indian performers, including singer Tessie Mobley, appeared and performed. The shows were promoted by the Fred Harvey Company and the Santa Fe Railway to help bring thousands of tourists to Albuquerque each year. Shown here are, from left to right, an unidentified Native American performer, Kirk, Mobley, and two unidentified city councilmen. (Courtesy of Albuquerque Museum, PA1978-141-238.)

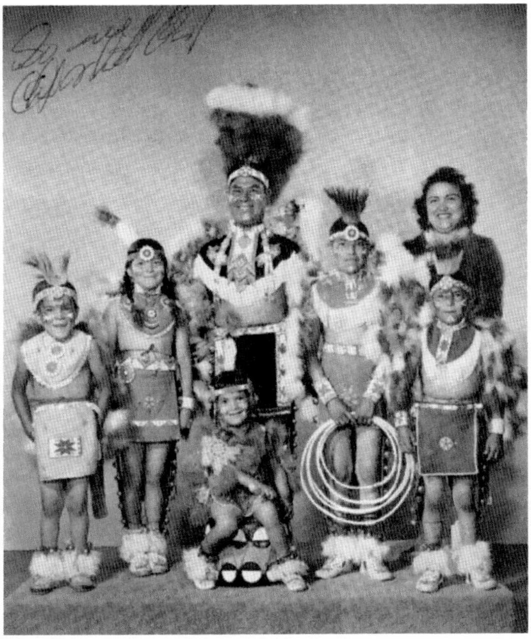

Phillip Whitecloud

Phillip Whitecloud and his family (left) performed Indian dances in Albuquerque and across the country for over 20 years. With their sons and daughters dancing from the time they were only two years old, the Whiteclouds' colorful costumes and remarkable talents were admired everywhere they traveled and, occasionally, on national television. The family performed in Albuquerque (especially in Old Town Plaza) in the winter and toured the United States, from Los Angeles to Washington, DC, in the summer. Led by Phillip (a Jemez pueblo Indian) and his wife Julia (an Apache Indian), the group performed for many dignitaries, including Pres. Dwight Eisenhower and former First Lady Eleanor Roosevelt. The Whitecloud family was even invited to Lovington to dance for rain during a particularly dry year in southeastern New Mexico. In addition to their rain dance, family members were famous for their arrow dance, hoop dance, and at least six other dances in the 1950s, 1960s, and early 1970s. On a far larger scale, nearly 3,000 Native Americans from over 700 tribes have met in Albuquerque for the Gathering of Nations (below) each April since 1983. As one of the largest powwows in the country, the gathering offers awards for performances in age categories, ranging from Tiny Tots to Elders (over 70 years old). Miss Indian World is crowned at the event each year.

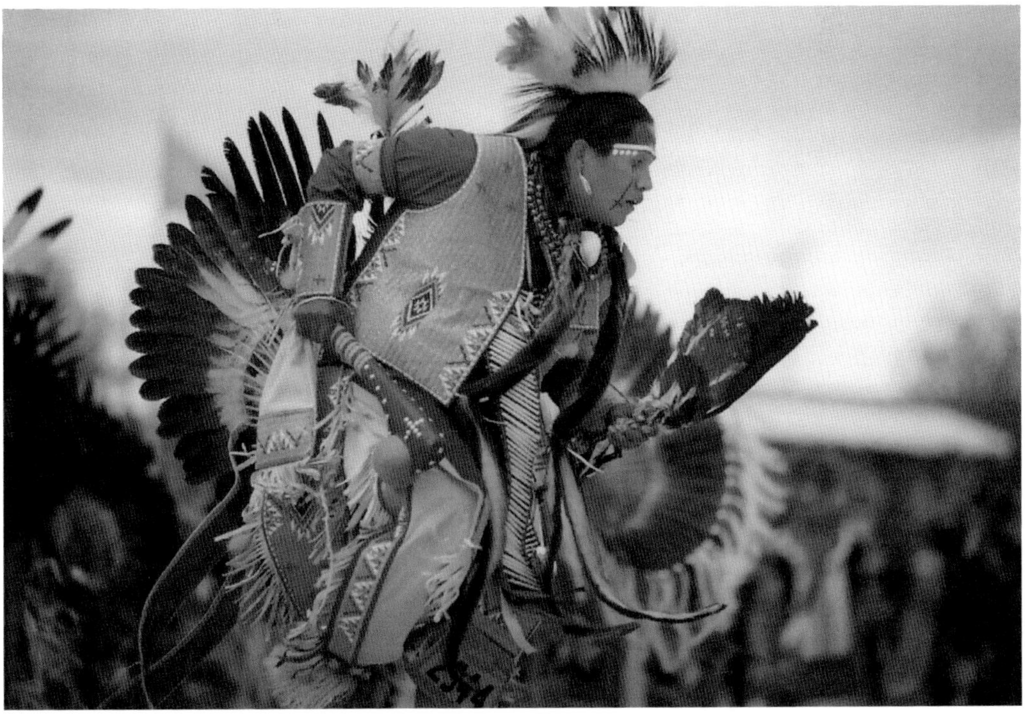

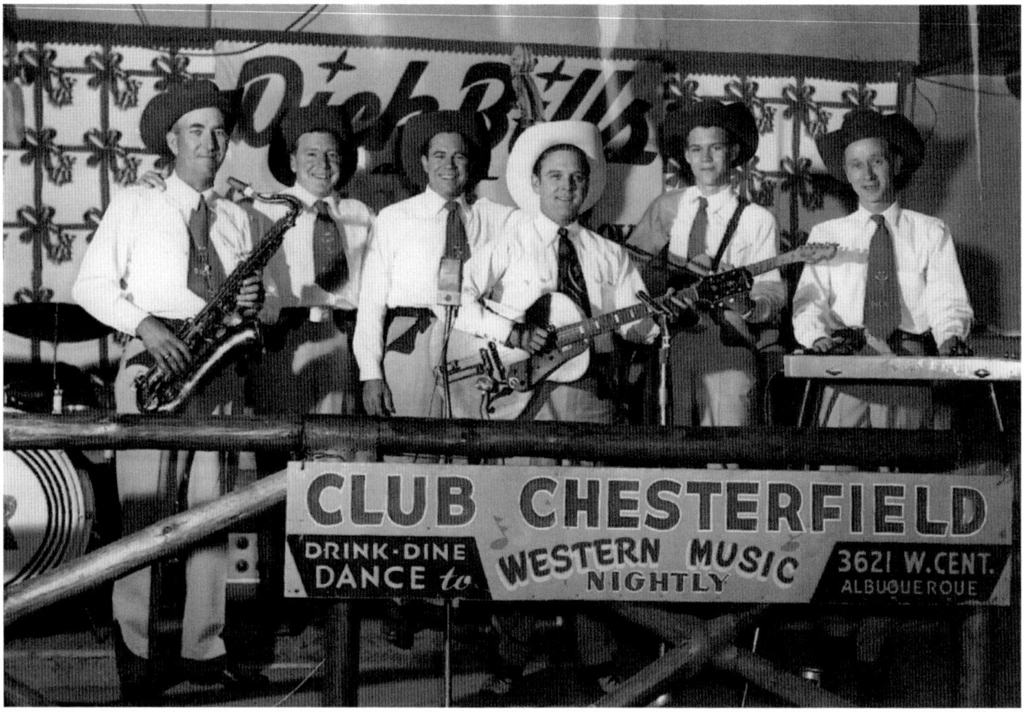

Glen Campbell (b. 1936)
Glen Campbell (second from right) began his musical career playing a $5 Sears Roebuck guitar. By 1954, he had joined his uncle's Albuquerque band, Dick Bills and the Sandia Mountain Boys. The band played at various clubs on Central Avenue as well as on local television and radio stations. Campbell formed his own band, the Western Wranglers, in 1958. He moved to Los Angeles two years later, launching a career filled with hit albums and coveted awards. (Courtesy of Albuquerque Museum, PA2003-029-002.)

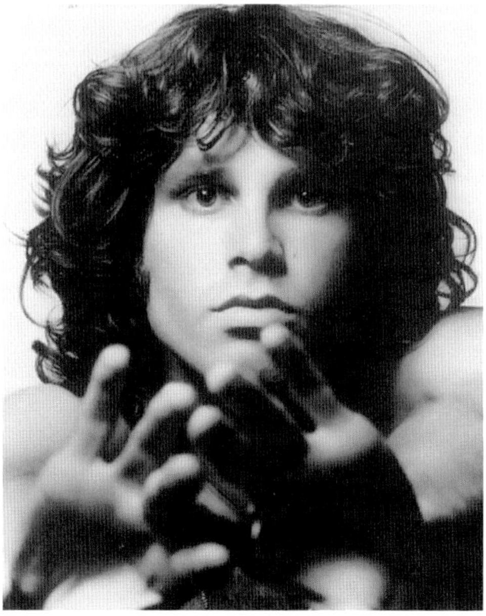

Jim Morrison (1943–1971)
The son of a naval aviator, Jim Morrison lived in several states during his childhood. His family lived on Albuquerque's Candelaria Road Northeast in 1947. On a trip to Santa Fe, the family passed the scene of a horrific accident. Morrison believed that this tragedy was the most formative event of his life. Its memory was referred to in many of the songs he wrote as the lead singer of the 1960s band the Doors.

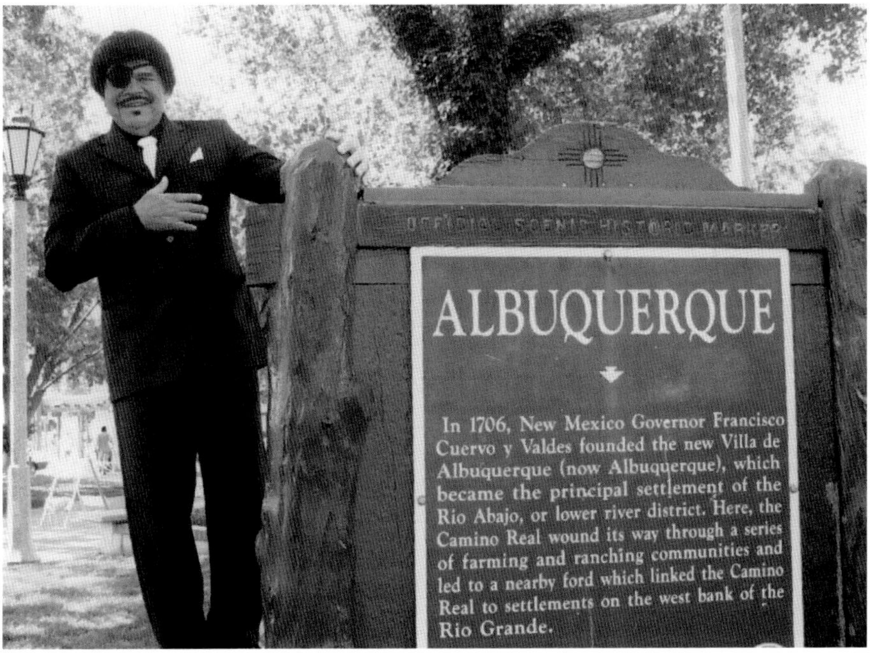

Alberto Nelson Sanchez Sr. (b. 1936)
Alberto "Al Hurricane" Sanchez and his family moved to Albuquerque from his native Dixon, New Mexico, in 1947 when he was 11 years old. His musical career began a year later, when he played his guitar for tips in Old Town's La Placita restaurant. He became famous as "Al Hurricane," a name his mother gave him because he always seemed to knock things over. His mom, Bennie L. Sanchez, became his promoter as he and his brothers Mauricio (Tiny Morrie) and Gabriel (Baby Gaby) created their unique "Albuquerque Sound." He has recorded over 50 records or CDs, many from his studio on Albuquerque's San Mateo Boulevard Northeast. He continues to record and perform with his son Al Hurricane Jr. The mural shown below, on South Fourth Street, was created by Southwest Valley community members using a color code visible at the mural's base. The finished mural reflects Al Hurricane's love of community and his community's love of him.

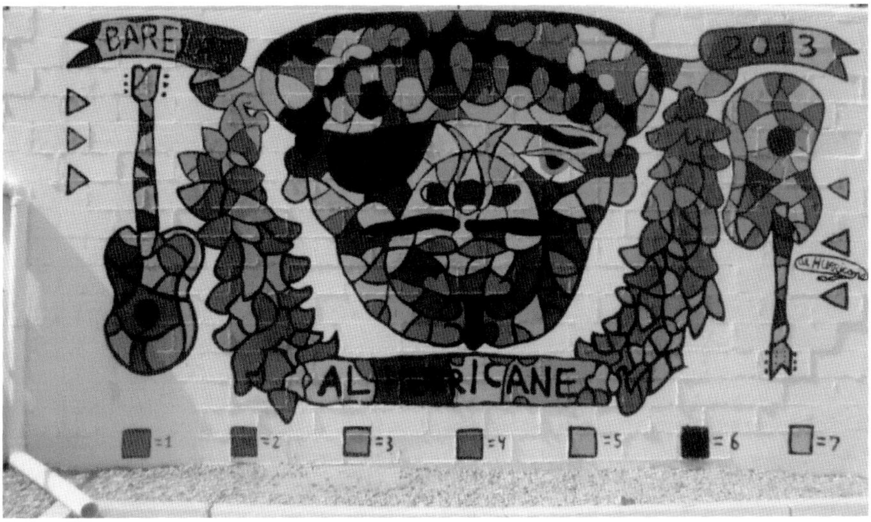

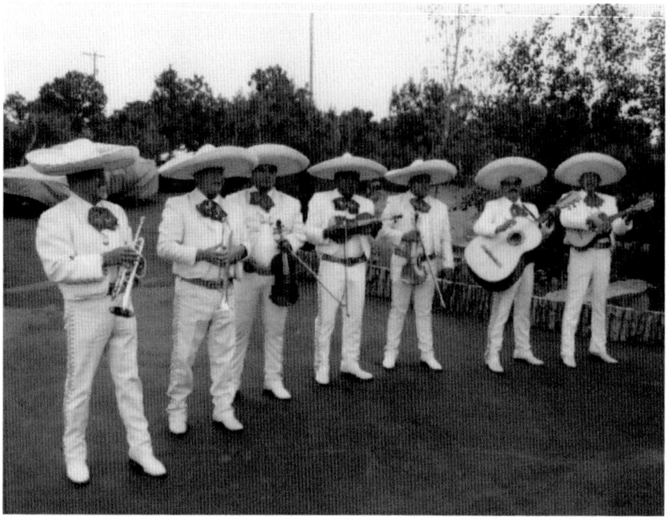

Mariachi Nuevo Sonido
With its roots in neighboring Mexico, mariachi music has become increasingly popular in New Mexico, thanks to the influence of bands like the Mariachi Nuevo Sonido. All seven members of the Albuquerque band are Mexican natives who have performed in the city—and beyond—for 25 years. The band regularly performs in the Mariachi Spectacular de Albuquerque, begun in 1991 and now one of the most important mariachi festivals in the world.

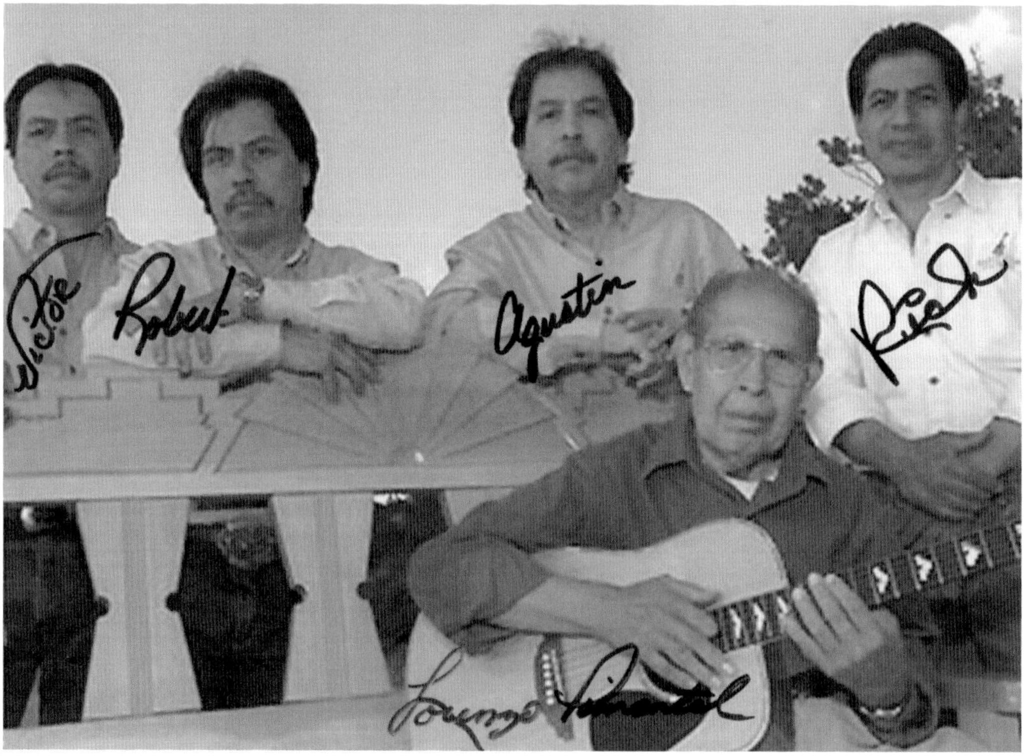

Lorenzo Pimentel (1928–2010)
When he was only 14, Pimentel (foreground) became a guitar-maker's apprentice in Mexico. Migrating to Texas and, in 1962, to Albuquerque, he became a grand master craftsman, admired around the world. Of his dozen children, four sons (shown here) have followed Lorenzo into the family business, becoming masters in their own right. Their fine handcrafted instruments are played by a wide range of artists, from local musicians to internationally acclaimed guitarists, including Pepe Romero and Ottmar Liebert. The Pimentels' Sunrise guitar became New Mexico's official state guitar in 2009. (Courtesy of Rick Pimentel.)

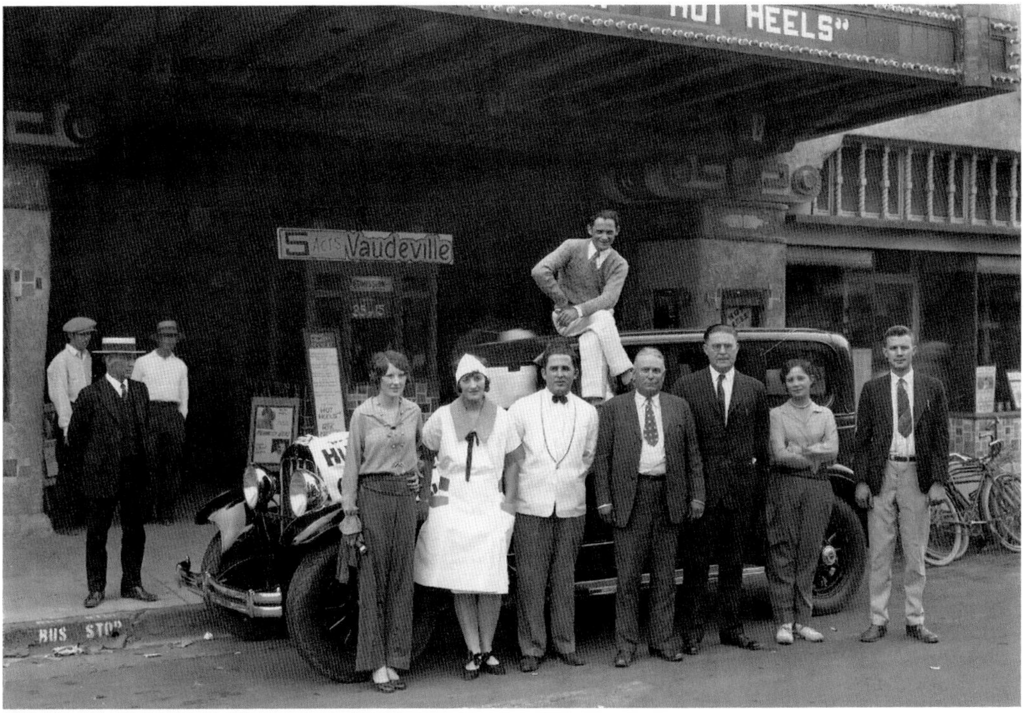

Oreste Bachechi (1860–1928)
Learning of new opportunities in New Mexico with the coming of the railroad in 1880, Oreste Bachechi migrated to Albuquerque in 1885. He succeeded in the retail and wholesale liquor business and encouraged other Italian immigrants to join him in Albuquerque's expanding community. Many followed in a serial migration, earning Bachechi the title "Father of the Albuquerque Italian Colony." Inspired by his wife, Maria, Bachechi built a new theater on Central Avenue and Fifth Street, using Pueblo Deco architecture designed by Carl Boller. In the above photograph, Bachechi (fourth from right) poses with a group of vaudeville performers in front of the theater. The KiMo was named in a contest won by Pablo Abeita of Isleta Pueblo; *kimo* means "mountain lion," or "king of its kind." The theater opened in 1927 and remains in use as a special-events center today. (Courtesy of Albuquerque Museum, PA1978-151-492.)

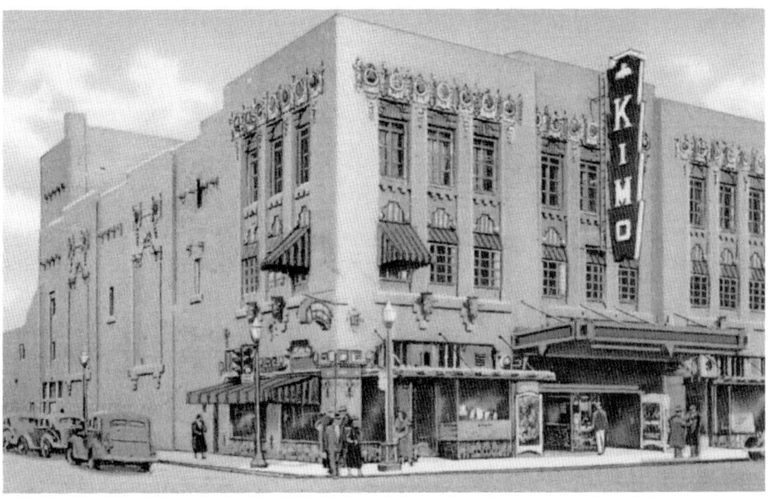

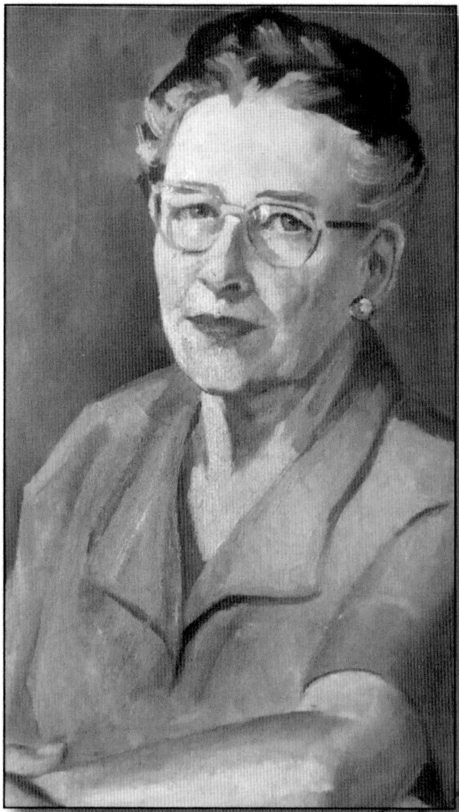

Kathryn Kennedy O'Connor (1894–1965)
O'Connor had begun her acting career on the Broadway stage when she learned that she had tuberculosis. Joining the thousands who came to New Mexico in search of a cure for TB, she arrived in Albuquerque in 1927. Three years later, she was well enough to help found the Albuquerque Little Theatre. She became its first director, producing plays at the KiMo movie theater and then at the group's WPA-built, permanent home on San Pasquale Avenue Southwest (below). She directed 207 plays in her 31-year career at the theater. O'Connor's headstone in Albuquerque's Sunset Cemetery depicts theater curtains and includes the appropriate words "Last curtain."

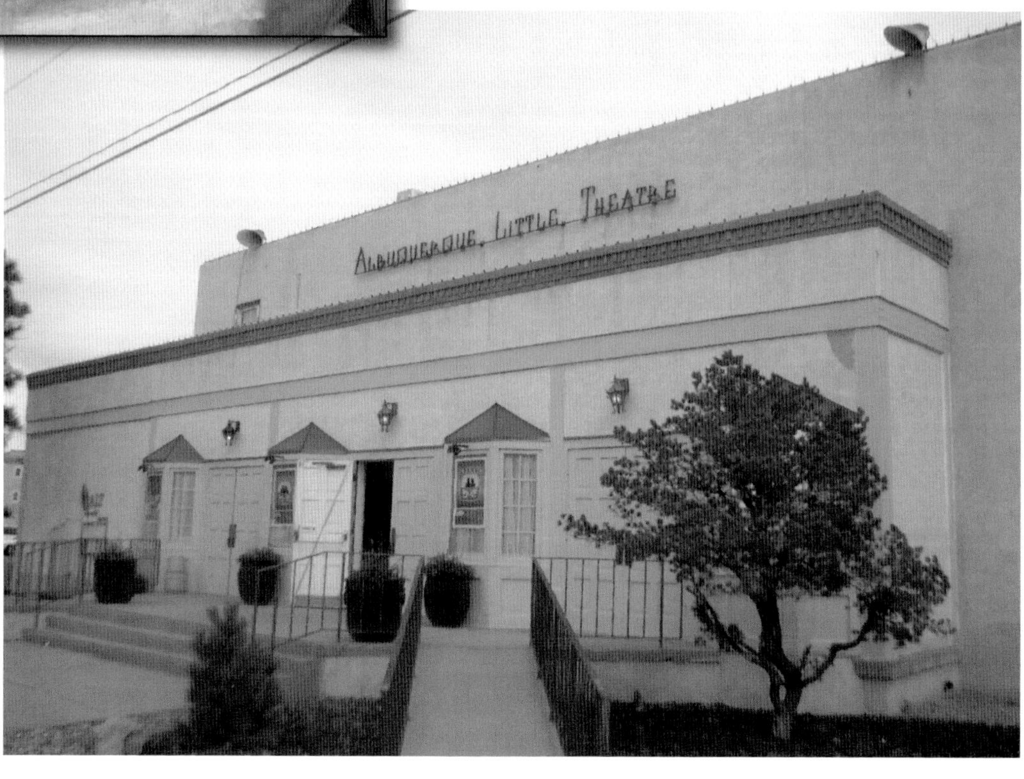

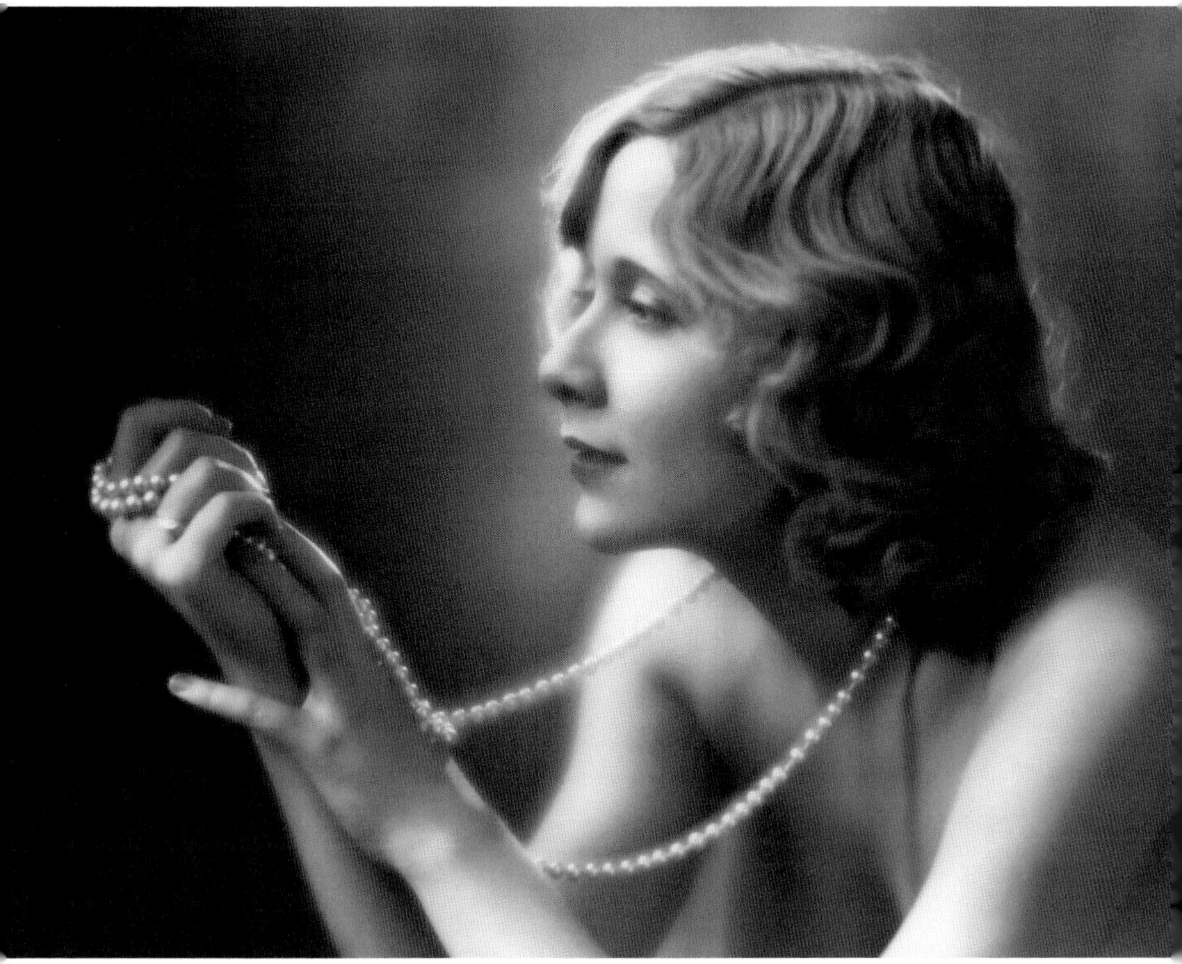

Vivian Vance (1909–1979)
Like so many Albuquerqueans, Vivian Roberta Jones moved to New Mexico because a member of her family suffered from poor health. Arriving as a teenager in 1929, "Viv" was drawn to the stage, despite her mother's opinion that acting was sinful. Appearing in the Albuquerque Little Theatre's first two seasons, she benefited not only from Kathryn Kennedy O'Connor's directing skills, but also from the money O'Connor raised to send the promising actress to New York. Calling herself Vivian Vance, she faced many early rejections; her first rejection coldly suggested that "you immediately return home." Persistent, she eventually landed supporting roles on Broadway and in several movies. In 1951, she was spotted by Desi Arnaz when he was casting actors for a new television show called *I Love Lucy*. Vance played Ethel Mertz, Lucille Ball's neighbor, in the highly successful series, which lasted over 180 episodes, from 1951 to 1957. Vivian won the first Emmy Award for Best Supporting Actress. Grateful to her friends in New Mexico, she returned to perform at the Little Theatre free of charge. Her family donated her Emmy to the theater after she died of bone cancer in 1979. A special exhibit, Everybody's Neighbor: Vivian Vance, was displayed at the Albuquerque Museum in 2014. (Courtesy of Albuquerque Museum, PA1978-153-Vance.)

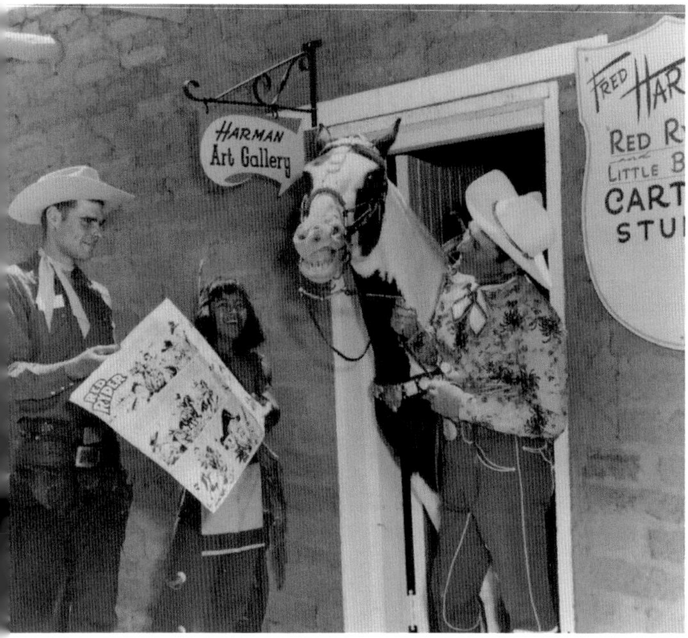

Beaver Town
Actors Fred Saunders (left), playing Red Ryder, and Troy Vincent (center), playing Little Beaver, entertained large crowds at Albuquerque's Beaver Town in the early 1960s. Based on Fred Harman's popular comic strip *Red Ryder*, the Western theme park opened in 1961. With stagecoach rides, train rides, shoot-outs, Indian dances, and dance-hall girls, the park drew both local residents and out-of-state tourists to its location off Route 66 near Tijeras Canyon. Bankrupt by 1964, the site was used as a movie set before it was abandoned and tragically vandalized. The City of Albuquerque purchased the 66-acre property in 2011 and is cleaning it up as part of the city's open-space program. (Courtesy of the Albuquerque Museum, PA1998-010-017.)

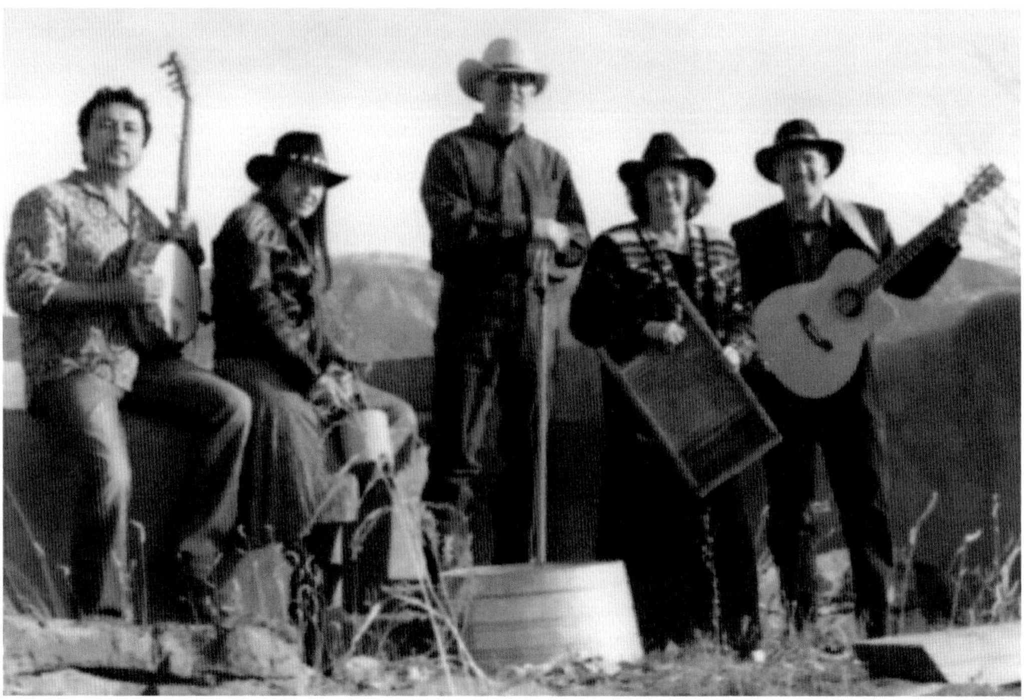

Watermelon Mountain Jug Band (1975–)
The Watermelon Mountain Jug Band was formed in Albuquerque in 1975. To the delight of thousands of their fans, band members entertain with washboards, jugs, kazoos, a washtub bass, a jaw harp, guitars, and banjos. They have performed throughout the city, including at the KiMo Theatre and the Rio Grande Zoo. Acknowledged as a "treasured natural resource," three of its members have been with the band for over 30 years. (Courtesy of the Watermelon Mountain Jug Band.)

Claire Yvonne King (b. 1946)

"Cissy" King's parents owned and operated the Fishback Studio of Dance. By 14, she and her brother John had won the National Ballroom Dancing Championship. Graduating from Highland High, she attended UNM, where she became a cheerleader, a gymnast, and a member of the synchronized swim team. Spotted at a dance competition in 1967, she performed as Bobby Burgess's dance partner on the nationally televised *Lawrence Welk Show* for a dozen years. She is seen here with Burgess (right) and Welk in a publicity photograph.

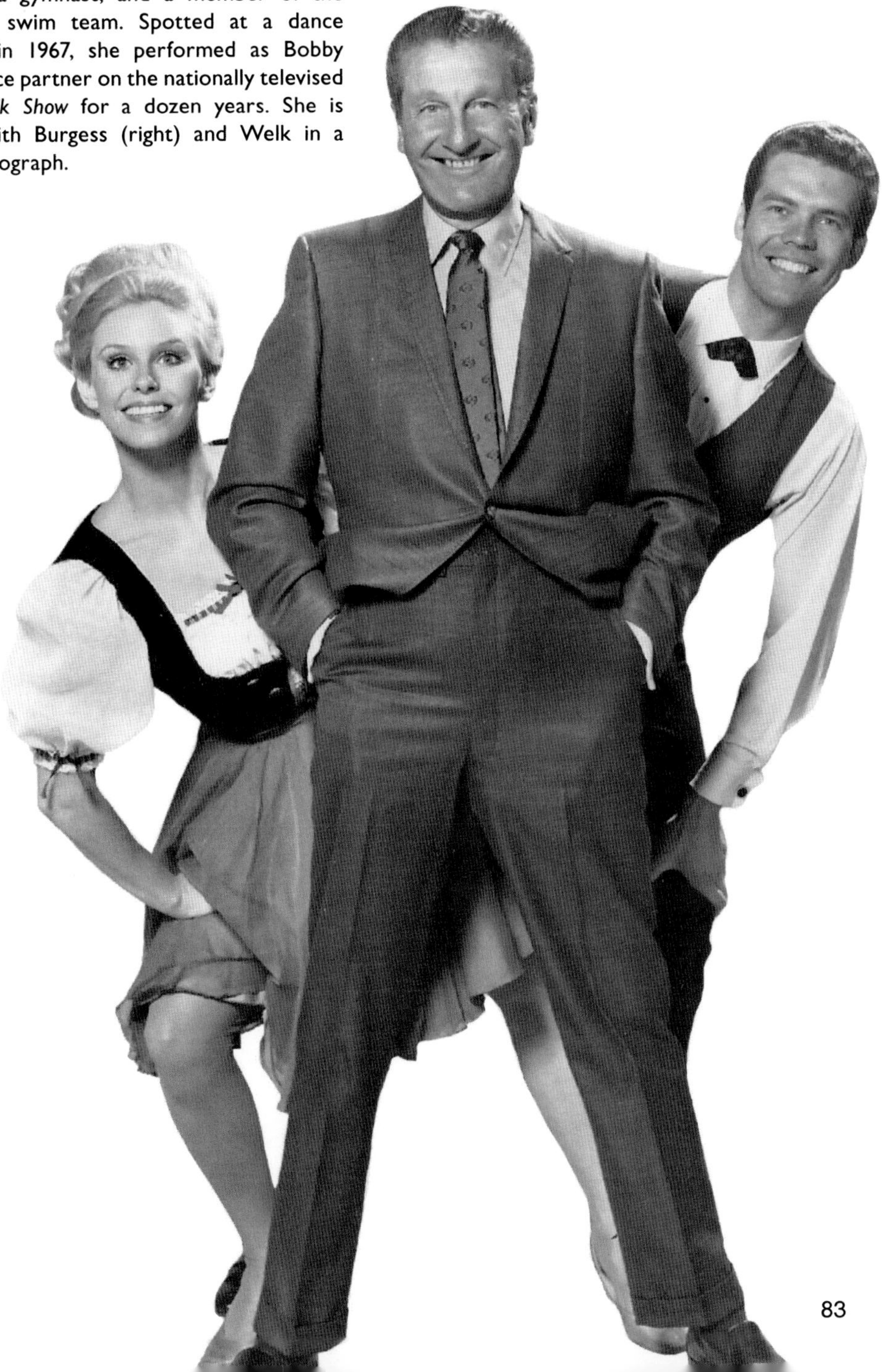

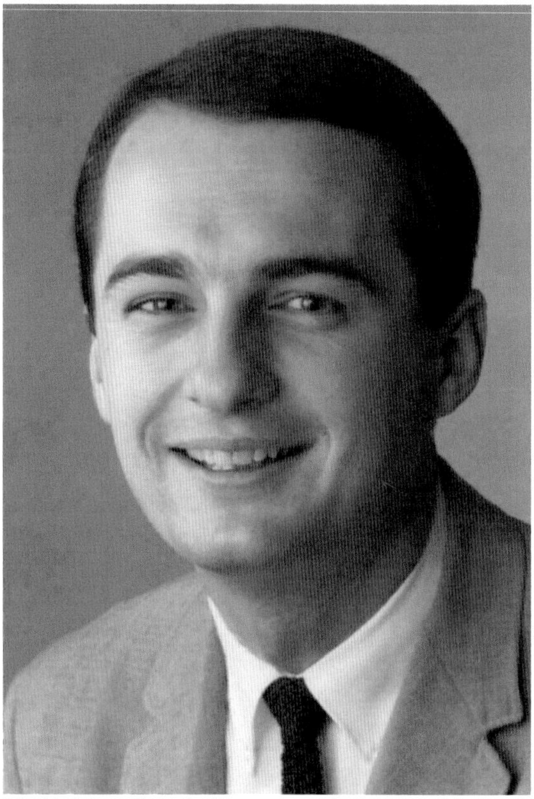

Dick Knipfing (b. 1942)

Knipfing began his career in television news in July 1963 as a $60-a-week reporter at Albuquerque's CBS affiliate KGGM (now KRQE). He became a highly paid news anchor, eventually working at all three major network affiliates. The veteran newsman became so well-regarded that he was rated No. 1 in a statewide poll of celebrities. After 51 years, his final broadcast aired on July 13, 2014.

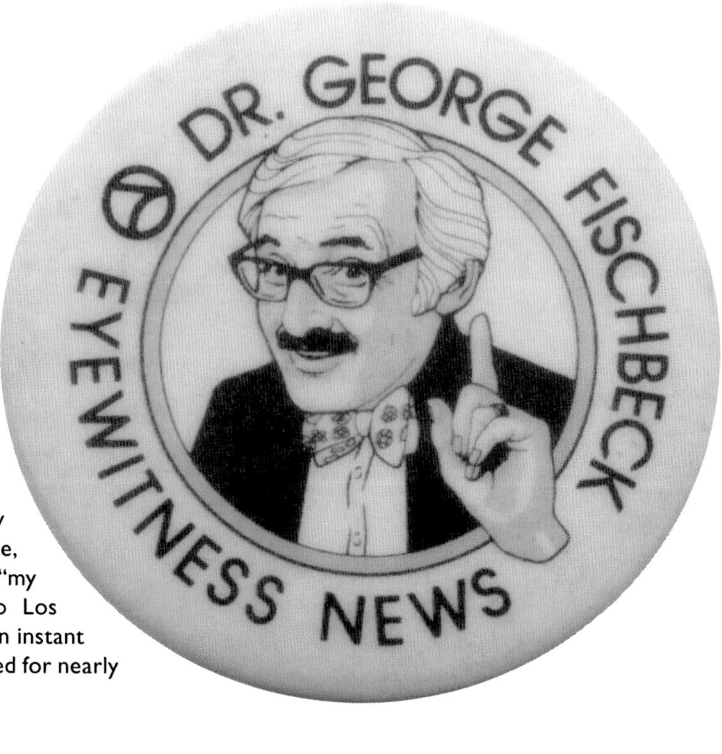

George Fischbeck (1922–2015)

Famous for his mustache, bow tie, and humor, Fischbeck taught science in the classroom and on Albuquerque's KNME for many years. Becoming a local television weatherman, he reported the weather largely by teaching it to his audience, which he collectively called "my friends." Taking his skills to Los Angeles in 1972, he became an instant hit on KABC, where he worked for nearly 20 years.

Neil Patrick Harris (b. 1973)
Albuquerque-born Neil Patrick Harris attended La Cueva High School, where he performed in many plays and musicals. He landed the starring role in the television series *Doogie Howser, MD*, at age 16. He later starred in the even more successful series *How I Met Your Mother.* In 2006, he announced that he was "quite proud to say that I am a very content gay man living my life to the fullest."

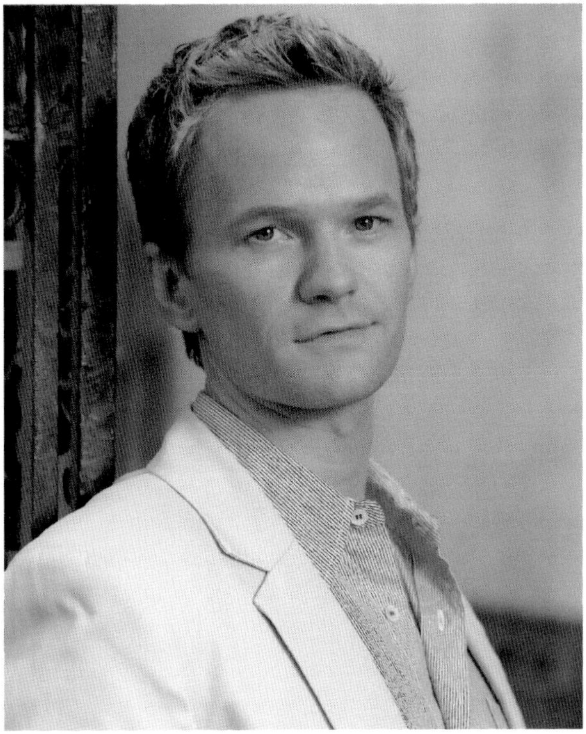

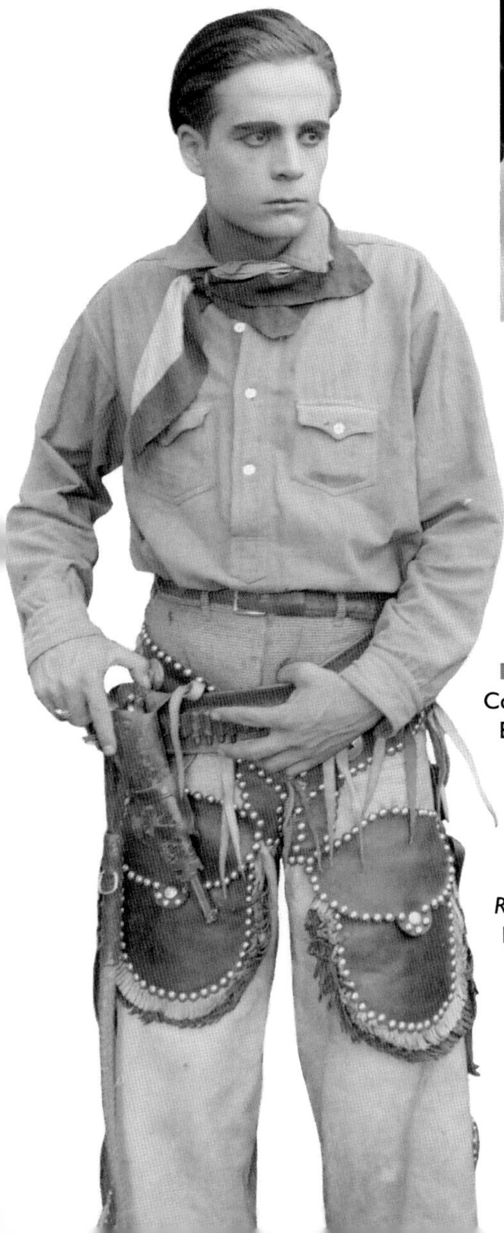

Edmund Cobb (1892–1974)
Cobb was born in Albuquerque, the son of William and Edmundie "Eddie" Cobb, two of the city's most successful early photographers. Leaving home when he was 18, Edmund arrived in Los Angeles and began to appear in silent movies in the 1910s and 1920s. He made the transition to "talkies" and appeared in about 415 movies, over half of which were Westerns, like *Renegades of the Rio Grande* (1945). (Courtesy of Albuquerque Museum, PA2011-003-734.)

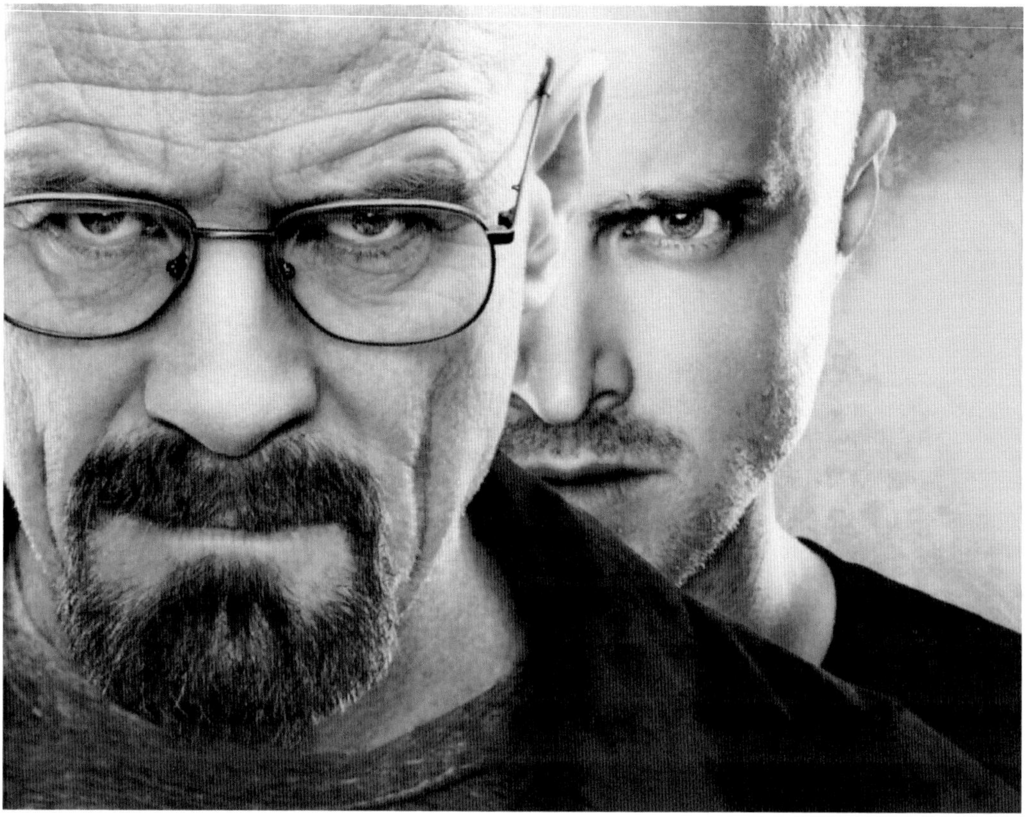

"Walter White" (1961–2013)
Walter White, played by actor Bryan Cranston, was the lead character in the television series *Breaking Bad.* Filmed in Albuquerque, the series featured White's career as a former high school chemistry teacher turned ruthless drug lord. White was such a popular character that, when he died in the show's last episode in 2013, his fans placed an obituary in the *Albuquerque Journal* (right) and a gravestone in a local cemetery.

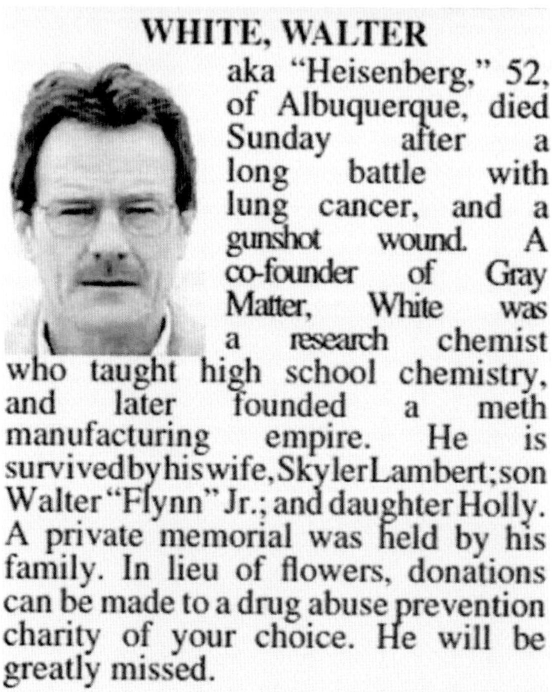

WHITE, WALTER

aka "Heisenberg," 52, of Albuquerque, died Sunday after a long battle with lung cancer, and a gunshot wound. A co-founder of Gray Matter, White was a research chemist who taught high school chemistry, and later founded a meth manufacturing empire. He is survived by his wife, Skyler Lambert; son Walter "Flynn" Jr.; and daughter Holly. A private memorial was held by his family. In lieu of flowers, donations can be made to a drug abuse prevention charity of your choice. He will be greatly missed.

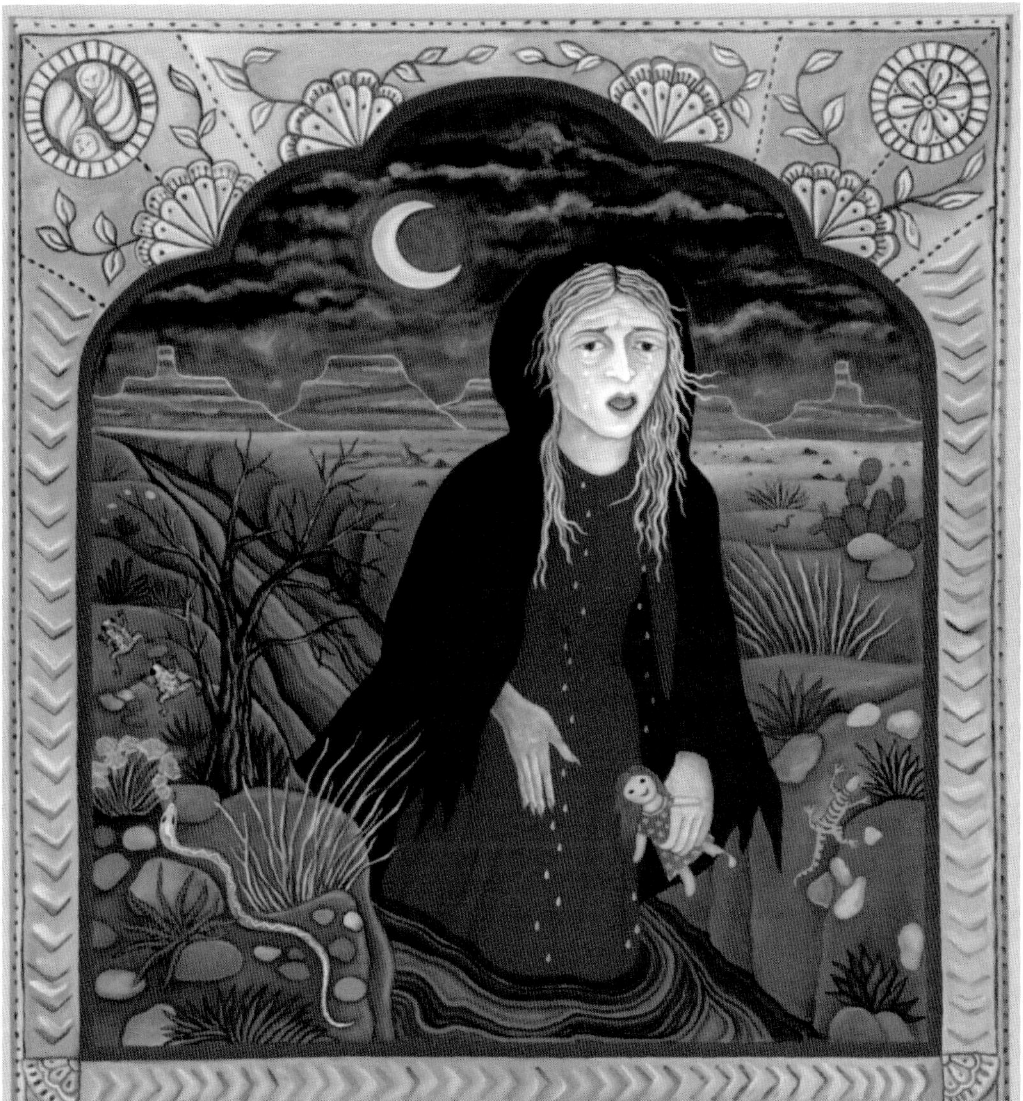

La Llorona (The Weeping Woman)
La Llorona is the main character in Albuquerque's—and New Mexico's—most famous folktale. The tragic story features a young mother who killed her children by drowning them in a ditch to somehow satisfy her lover. Heartbroken, she wanders up and down the ditch banks, weeping for her lost children. Some believe that her children represent traditional Hispanic culture, which has been lost to modern Anglo society, symbolized by the lover. (Courtesy of the artist, Diana Bryer.)

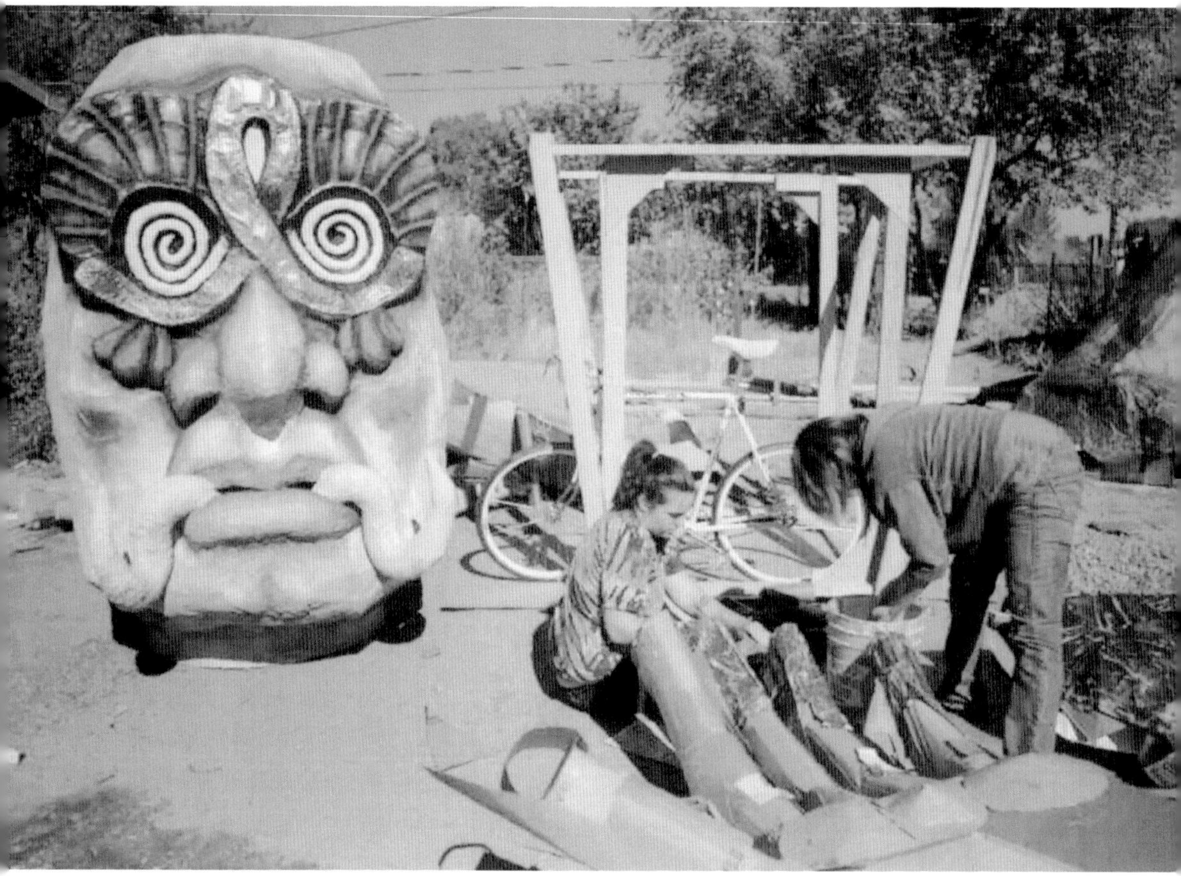

El Kookooee (1989–)
New Mexicans are well aware of Zozobra, the effigy that is burned at the start of the Santa Fe Fiesta each year. Fewer people know of Albuquerque's El Kookooee, which has burned each Halloween night since 1989. Those who come to witness the event are encouraged to write their fears on pieces of paper that are stuffed into El Kookooee before the large effigy—and everyone's fears—go up in smoke.

CHAPTER SEVEN

Business and Tourism

Albuquerque was a small, agricultural community for most of its early history. Centered in Old Town, a handful of shopkeepers supplied the basic needs of farmers and sheep ranchers in the surrounding Rio Grande Valley. A few affluent Hispanic families, known as *ricos*, dominated the local economy, while most families remained poor but productive.

All changed with the American conquest of 1846 and the coming of the railroad in 1880. In a decision that forever shaped Albuquerque's future, the Atchison, Topeka & Santa Fe Railroad chose Albuquerque (over Bernalillo) to be the center of its operations in New Mexico. As a result, a whole new section of Albuquerque, called New Town, blossomed, bringing modern ideas, values, and businesses two miles (and many centuries) from Old Town and its traditional ways. Businesses opened in New Town to serve the railroad, its workers, and the flood of newcomers who came to visit, settle, or, in the case of health-seekers, remain for as long as it took to recover their health. Several sanatoriums built for the care of patients with tuberculosis became major hospitals, the foundation of Albuquerque's modern healthcare industry.

World War II brought a new wave of economic activity to supply the needs of Kirtland Army Air Field (named in honor of Col. Roy C. Kirtland), later renamed Kirtland Air Force Base, southeast of Albuquerque. Sandia National Laboratories, the state's top employer by the 1950s, added to Albuquerque's status as an important part of the nation's so-called military-industrial complex.

If Albuquerque's economy stands on four legs, starting with the railroad, healthcare, and the military-industrial complex, tourism represents the city's vital fourth source of support. Arriving by trains, cars, buses, and planes, tourists come for the city's natural beauty, cultural diversity, and ideal weather. Restaurants, hotels, street vendors, art galleries, tour-guide companies, the Sandia Peak Tram, and other enterprises have profited from the money spent by tourists, most of who return home with glowing reports about the colorful, interesting discoveries they make in Albuquerque.

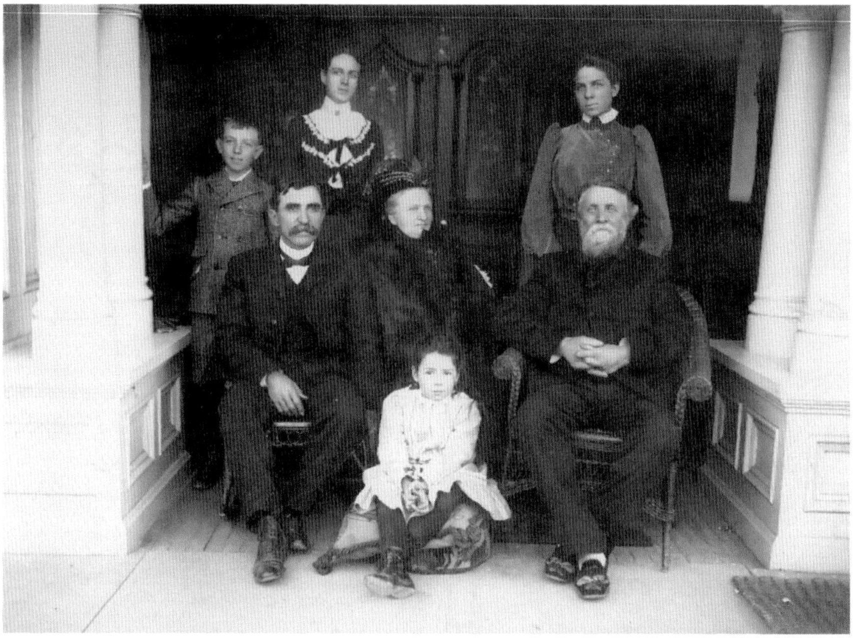

Franz Huning (1827–1905)

Franz Huning and three of his brothers immigrated to New Mexico from their native Hanover, Germany, about 1860. Franz opened a mercantile store as well as profitable flour mills and sawmills in Old Town Albuquerque. He also profited by selling land for the construction of the Santa Fe Railroad and by selling residential lots in what became known as the Huning-Highland neighborhood east of Albuquerque's new railroad tracks. He built his own famous house on Railroad (now Central) Avenue and Fourteenth Street in 1883. In the above photograph, Franz (seated at right) poses with his family at the entrance to his house, known as the Huning Castle (below). The 14-room, Bavarian-style building became the Manzano Day School after Huning's death in 1905; it was demolished in 1955. Modern apartments designed in a similar architectural style have recently been built near the castle's original site. (Courtesy of Albuquerque Museum, PA2011-001-057.)

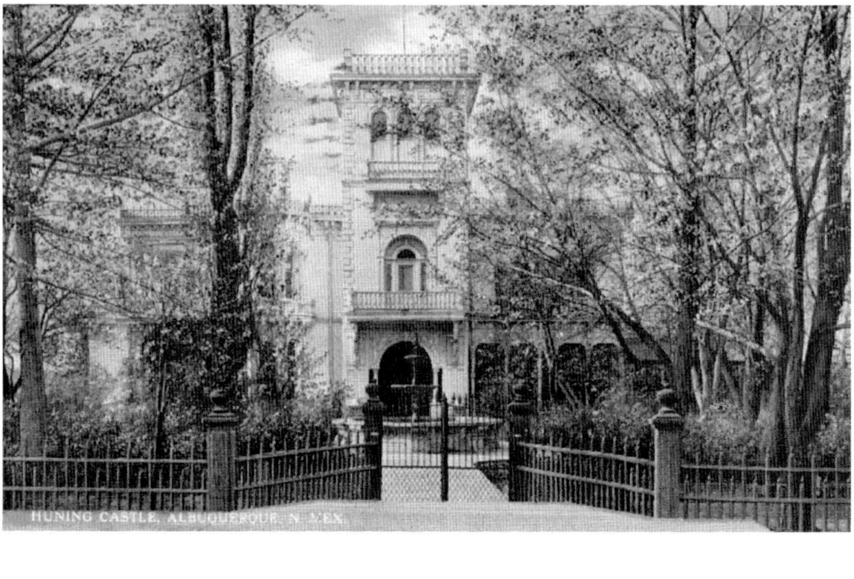

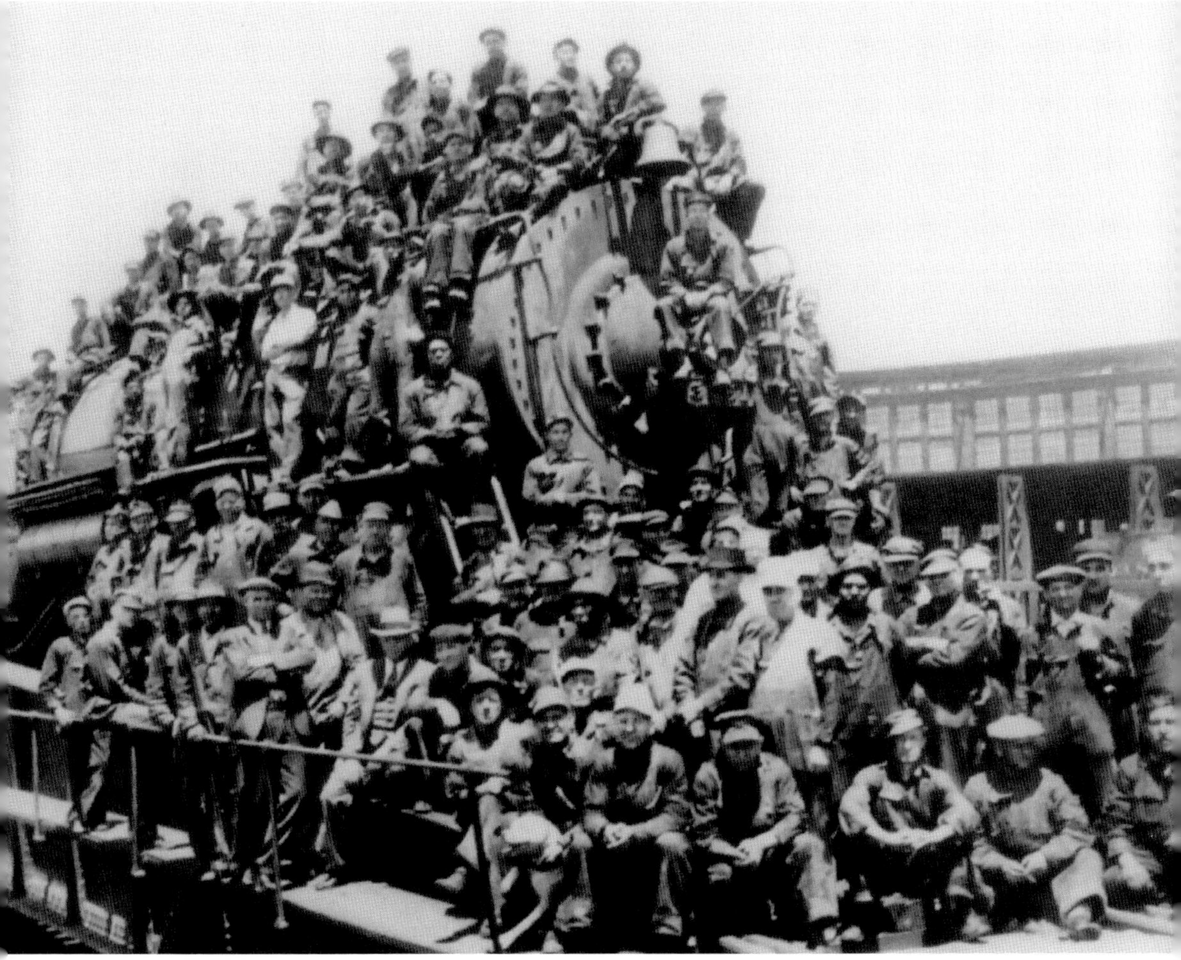

Santa Fe Railway Workers

Railroad tracks arrived in Albuquerque on April 5, 1880. The Atchison, Topeka & Santa Fe Railroad made the city its central headquarters for New Mexico, building dozens of offices and shops while employing thousands of men and women in jobs like welders, machinists, boilermakers, blacksmiths, carpenters, painters, car inspectors, and paymasters. Employees and their often large families lived in nearby neighborhoods, like Barelas. Railroad workers performed essential tasks, especially during World War II, when transportation was vitally important to the country's war effort. But railroad work was often dangerous, leading to career-ending or even fatal accidents. In 1926, the Santa Fe built a hospital at 806 Central Avenue Southwest to treat its employees. Generations of family members worked for the railroad, one of Albuquerque's largest, most valuable industries. Then, the conversion from steam to diesel engines sealed the Albuquerque yards' fate. The workers' legacy and the general impact of the railroad are honored in Albuquerque's new Wheels Museum, located where the railroad shops once hummed with life and activity. (Courtesy of the Wheels Museum.)

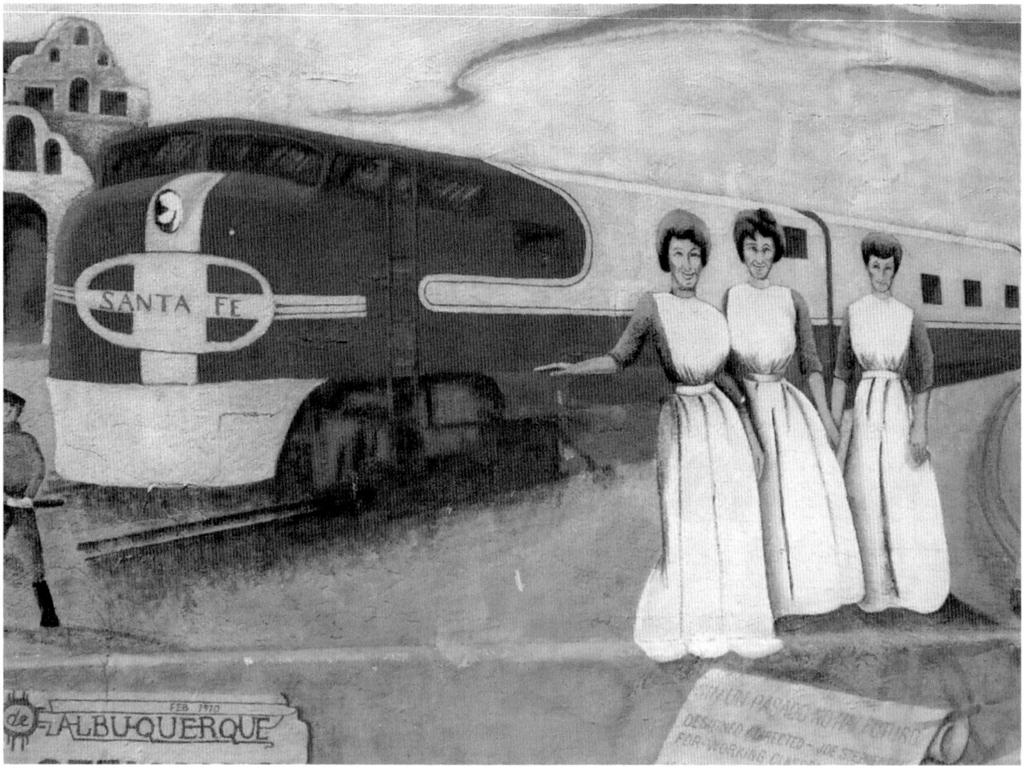

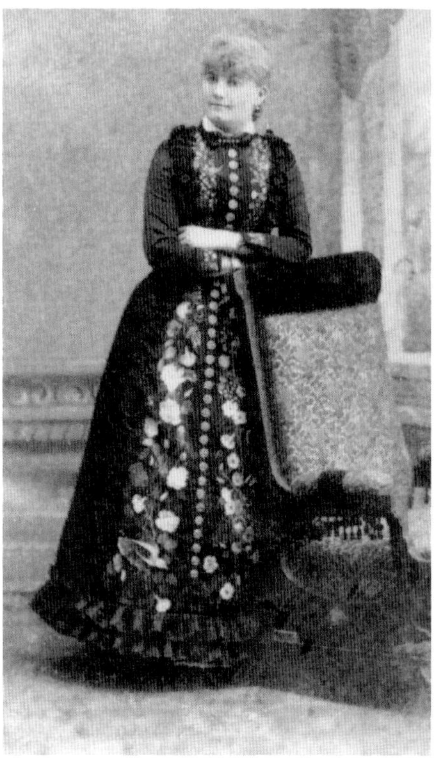

Harvey Girls

Harvey Girls worked at Fred Harvey's Alvarado Hotel in downtown Albuquerque from its opening in 1902 until its closing in 1970. Harvey Houses were famous for employing attractive, intelligent young women who were dedicated to providing exceptional service to hungry passengers traveling on the Santa Fe Railway. As eligible young women, Harvey Girls often married local residents. Humorist Will Rogers quipped that Fred Harvey kept the West in good food and young brides. This mural is located at South Second Street and Gold Avenue Southwest.

Elizabeth McGrath (1861–1921?)

"Lizzie" McGrath was only 21 when she arrived in Albuquerque in 1882. A "lady of the night," McGrath worked at houses of ill repute until 1885, when she opened her own establishment at 312 West Copper Avenue. She served as the city's most famous madam for about 40 years. Albuquerque's exclusive Hyatt Regency Hotel, with its elegant Lizzie McGrath restaurant, was built at Lizzie's old address. The eatery closed with a mock funeral in 2013. (Courtesy of Albuquerque Museum, PA1984-014-001.)

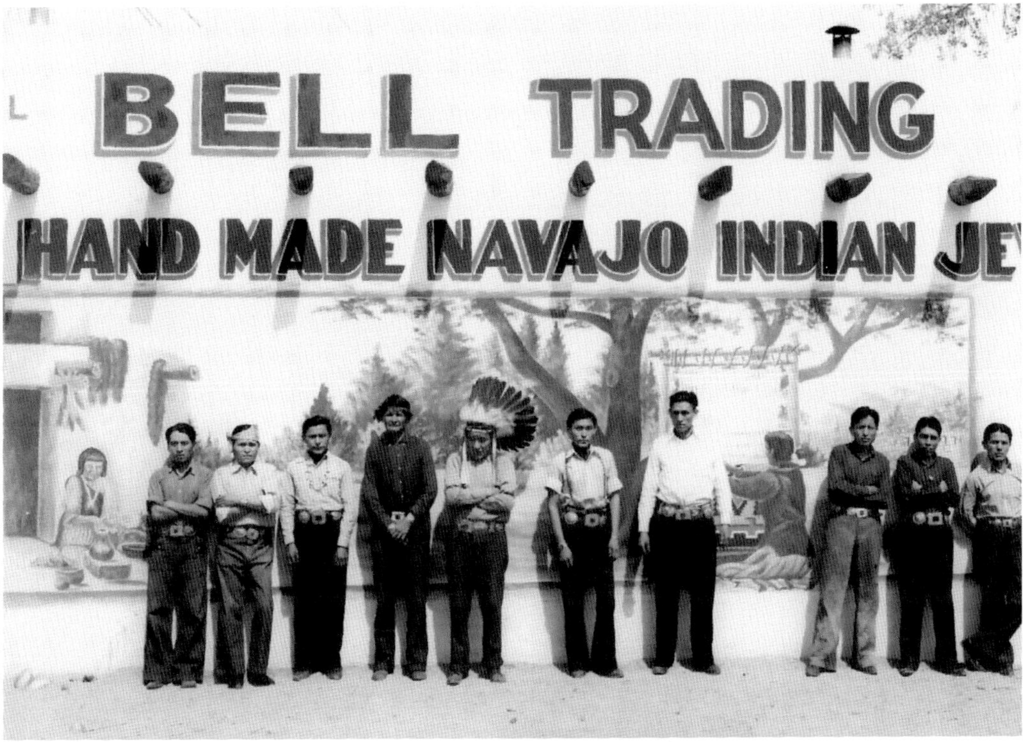

Indian Craftsmen

Many Native American craftsmen worked at home on their reservations. Others lived in Albuquerque and worked in the city's Indian Room at the Alvarado Hotel and at large trading posts, demonstrating their skills and helping to prove that their finished products were in fact Indian made. Maisel's, Wright's, and Bell's were among the most famous of these trading posts in downtown Albuquerque, along Central Avenue.

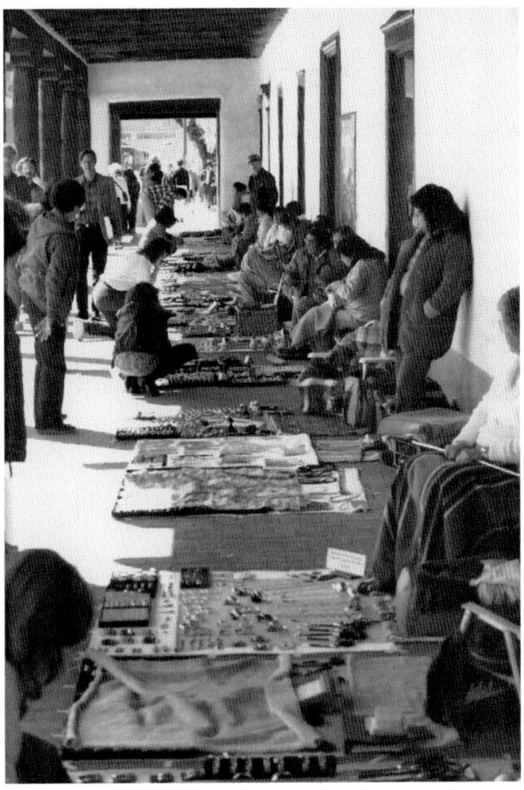

Indian Vendors

Displaying their beautiful jewelry on colorful rugs, Indian vendors have long been a fixture at the Santa Fe Railway depot and Old Town Plaza. But, vendors have faced controversy. Many Indian vendors objected to being photographed. Later, Old Town merchants opposed their sidewalk competition. Controversy has also centered on whether only Indians could sell their wares as vendors. Most issues have been resolved, preserving one of Albuquerque's oldest, most important tourist attractions. (Courtesy of Albuquerque Museum.)

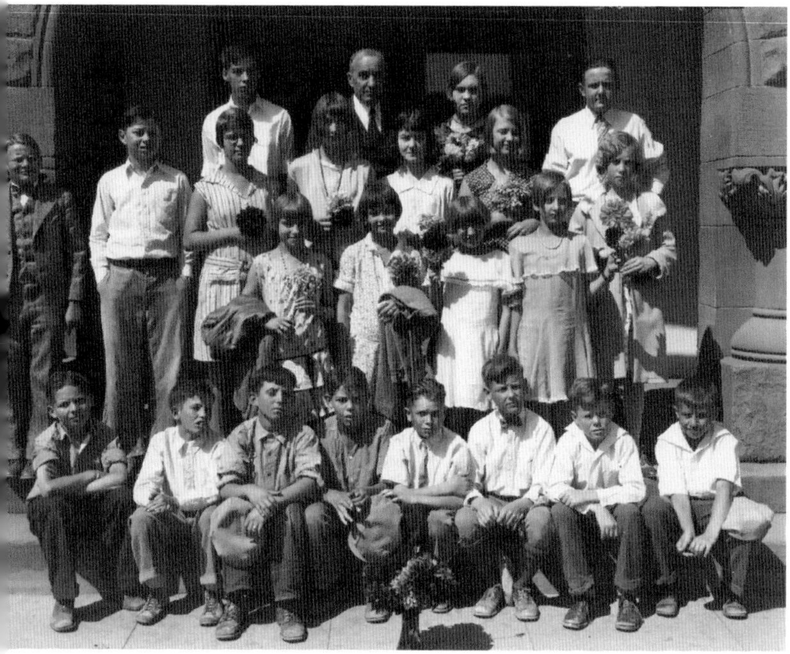

Chester T. French (1882–1966)
In 1904, Chester French (back row, center) accompanied his brother Jesse to Albuquerque when his sibling suffered from TB. Jesse died, but Chester remained to open the French-Fitzgerald Mortuary, soon one of the most successful establishments of its kind in the city. He also opened Sunset Memorial Park in 1929. Always eager to help his community, French worked with children, transported TB patients to events, and planted flowers along Albuquerque's streets. (Courtesy of Albuquerque Museum, PA1978-151-372.)

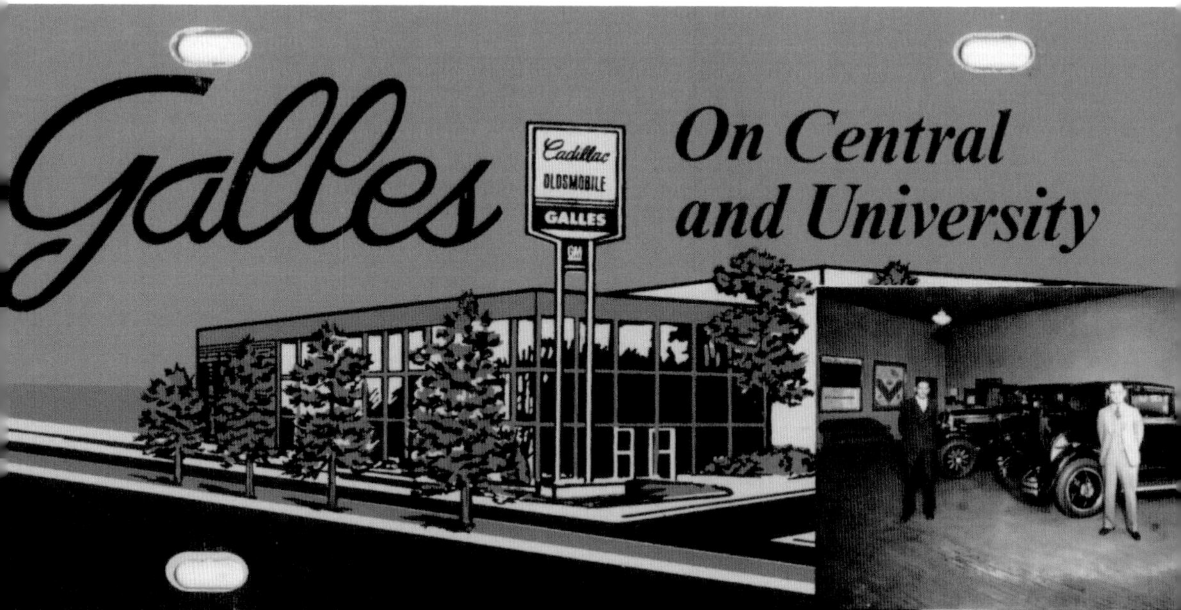

H.L. Galles Jr. (1912–2007)
The Galles Motor Company was founded by H.L. Galles Sr. in 1908. H.L. "Hickum" Galles Jr. (shown at right in the insert) joined his family's car dealership in 1928, taking over its management in 1951. A great success in business, Hickum Galles also financed a winning racecar team, founded the UNM Lobo Booster Club, and chaired the committee that built the Albuquerque Sports Stadium. Galles worked until the Saturday before his death at age 95.

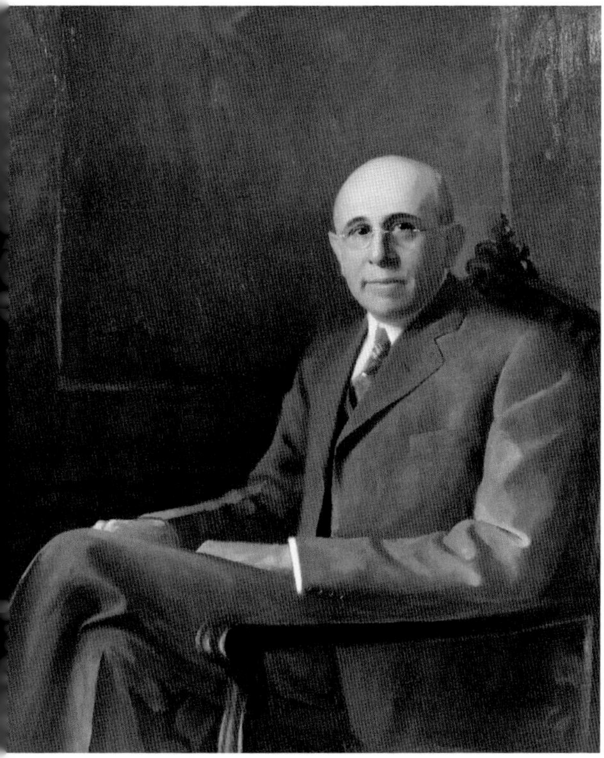

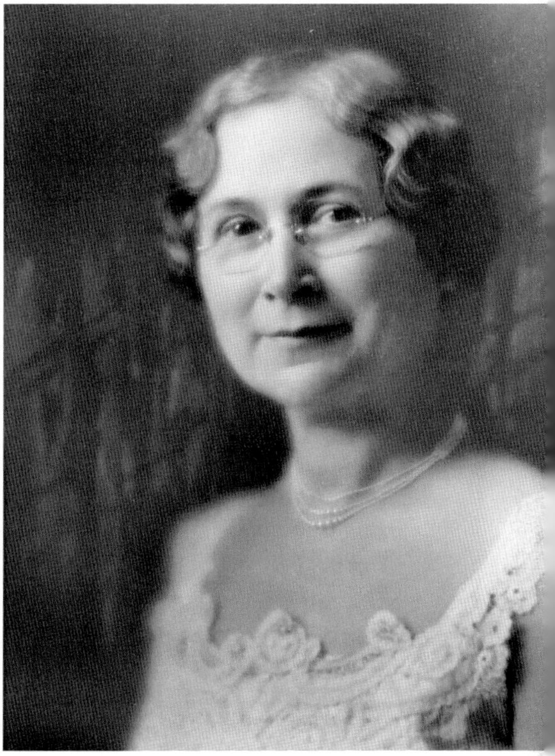

George Kaseman (1868–1938) and Anna T. Kaseman (c. 1875–1964)
The founder of Albuquerque National Bank in 1924, George Kaseman also had extensive investments in the fuel industry, owning the Albuquerque & Cerrillos Coal Company in Madrid, New Mexico, and the Defiance Coal Company near Gallup. Kaseman and seven other men were killed in a terrible explosion at an oil rig near Hobbs in June 1938. He was survived by his wife, Anna T. Kaseman, who lived at the family home, designed by John Gaw Meem, until her death in 1964. Most of the Kasemans' large estate was willed to Albuquerque's St. John's Episcopal Church and the Presbyterian Hospital. The hospital used its share of the estate to construct Anna Kaseman Hospital, a 67-bed satellite facility in northeast Albuquerque. Its single-story architecture provided views of nature from every patient's room. The $3 million health center opened in September 1970. The Kasemans' portraits hang in the vastly expanded hospital today. (Courtesy of the Albuquerque Museum, PA1982-180-109 and PA1992-005-935.)

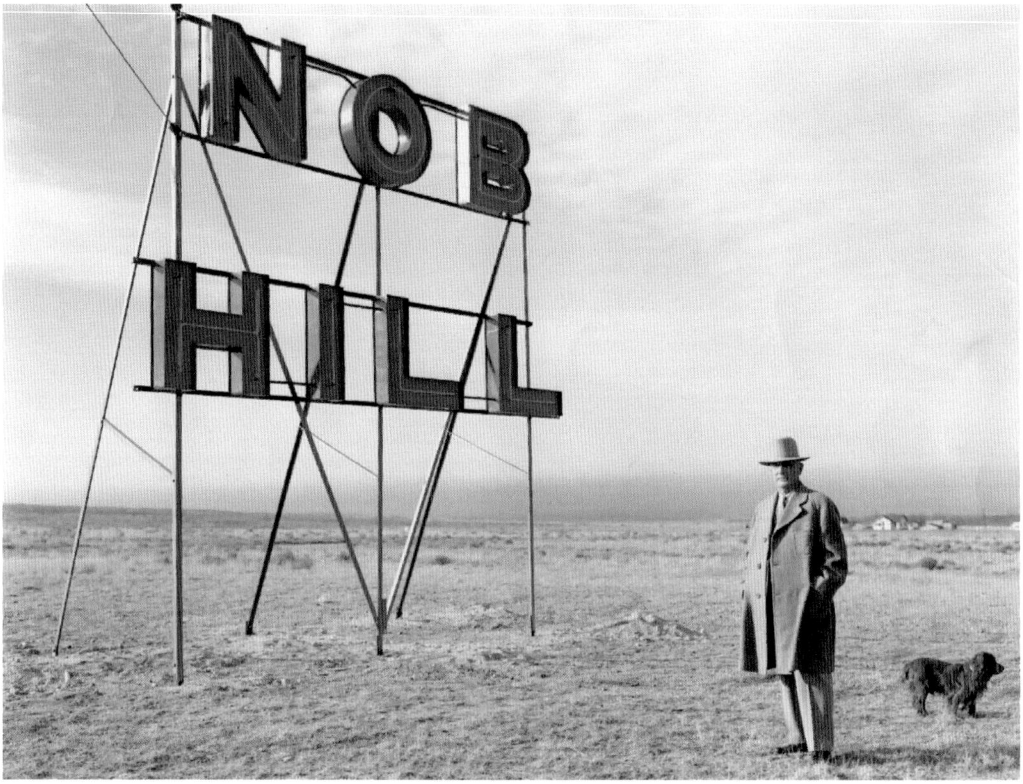

D.K.B. Sellers (1861–post 1950)
Arriving in Albuquerque in 1901, D.K.B. Sellers quickly made an impact on his new community. By 1903, he was the president of the New Mexico Territorial Fair. A Democrat, he served as the city's mayor (1912–1913). He was largely responsible for changing the name of Albuquerque's main street from Railroad Avenue to Central Avenue. Sellers is best remembered for helping to develop today's thriving Nob Hill neighborhood, originally thought to be too remote to succeed. (Courtesy of the Albuquerque Museum, PA1978-141-282.)

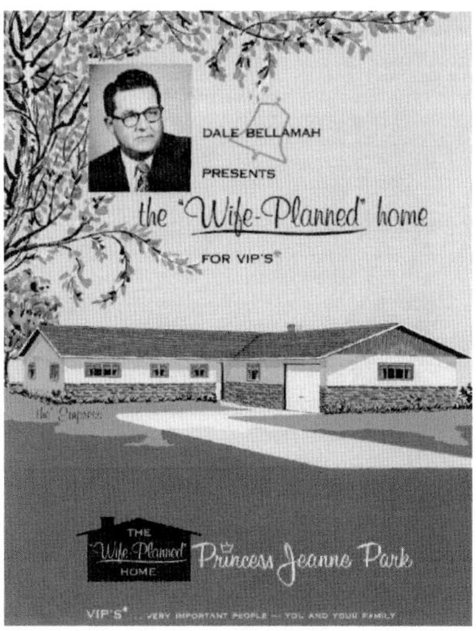

Abdul Hamid Bellamah (1914–1972)
Starting from humble roots in the village of Veguita, New Mexico, "Dale" Bellamah moved to Albuquerque, attended UNM, served in World War II, and worked for the railroad. Recognizing the tremendous demand for housing after the war, he began constructing large subdivisions in Albuquerque, including the 1,600-house Princess Jeanne subdivision (pictured), named after his wife. By 1961, his corporations built 1,000 homes a year, making him one of the largest homebuilders in the country. (Courtesy of Dale Bellamah Homes Records, Box 1, Folder 1, Center for Southwest Research, University Libraries, University of New Mexico.)

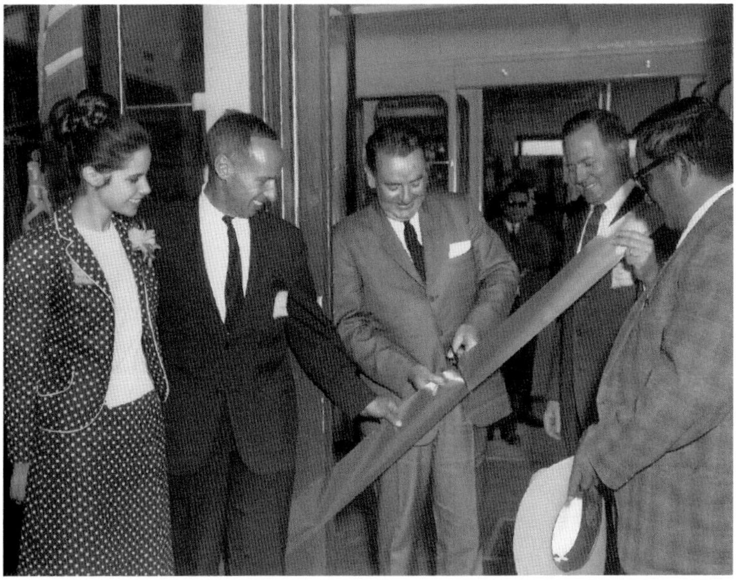

Robert J. Nordhaus (1909–2007)

Robert J. Nordhaus spent much of his childhood in Albuquerque before leaving to complete his education at Yale University. Returning to Albuquerque in 1935, he and his friends cleared runs in the Sandia Mountains, installed a primitive rope tow, and formed a ski club. During World War II, he was a member of the 10th Mountain Division, which gave him the opportunity to see several of Europe's most famous tramways. After the war, he practiced law, focusing on important cases involving Indian land and water rights. He also helped install a T-bar lift for skiers in the Sandias and, with Ben Abruzzo, constructed the 2.7-mile Sandia Peak Tramway, the longest aerial tramway in the world. The above photograph shows the tram's opening day in 1966, with, from left to right, Elizabeth Nordhaus Messeca, Robert J. Nordhaus, Gov. Jack Campbell, Ben Abruzzo, and a leader of Sandia Pueblo. Nordhaus took the tram up the mountain for lunch about once a week until his final days. The New Mexico Ski Museum, with a plaque in his honor, was dedicated in 2008. (Above, courtesy of Elizabeth Nordhaus Messeca; below photograph by Jay Blackwood.)

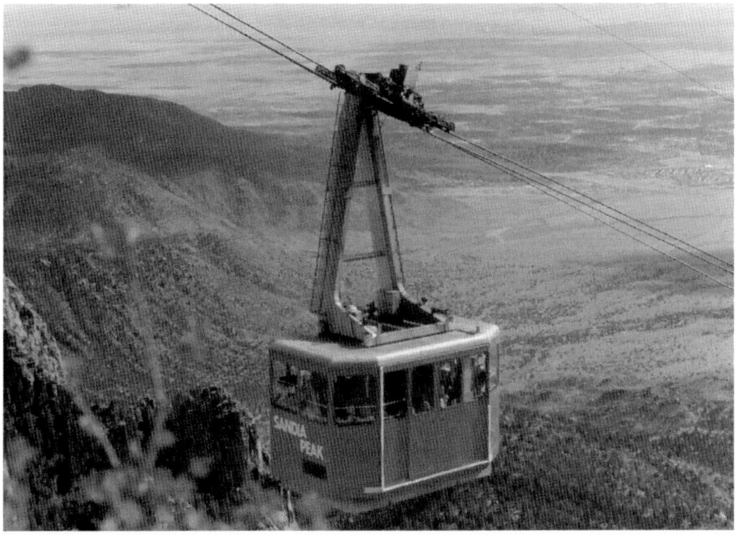

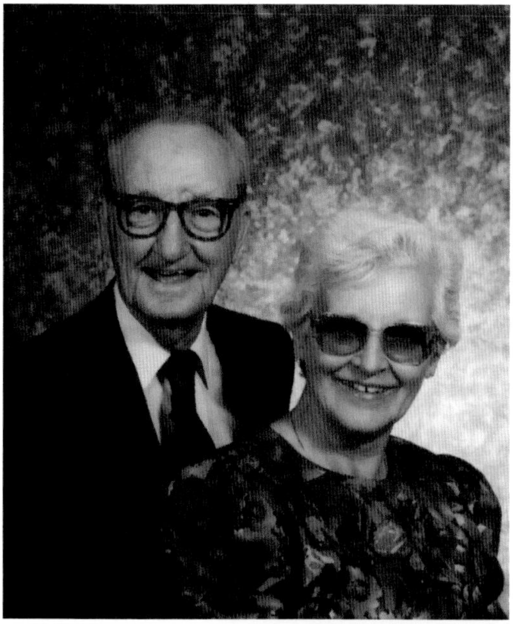

Cliff Hammond (1915–2012)
The Hammond family survived the Great Depression with the help of Cliff's earnings as a member of Franklin Roosevelt's Civilian Conservation Corps (CCC). In 1959, Cliff and his wife, Zella (left), moved to Albuquerque, where they opened Uncle Cliff's Kiddieland on 7600 Lomas Boulevard Northeast. In 1963, the Hammonds moved their amusement park to 4800 Osuna Road Northeast, then an isolated spot far from most homes and businesses. Thousands of families have enjoyed the park's many thrill rides, including the popular Cliff Hanger. Now known as Cliff's Amusement Park, the business remains a landmark in Albuquerque, with 23 rides and an average of 300,000 guests per year. The park also employs 500 local youths each year, giving many teens their first opportunity to work and earn money. (Courtesy of the Hammond family.)

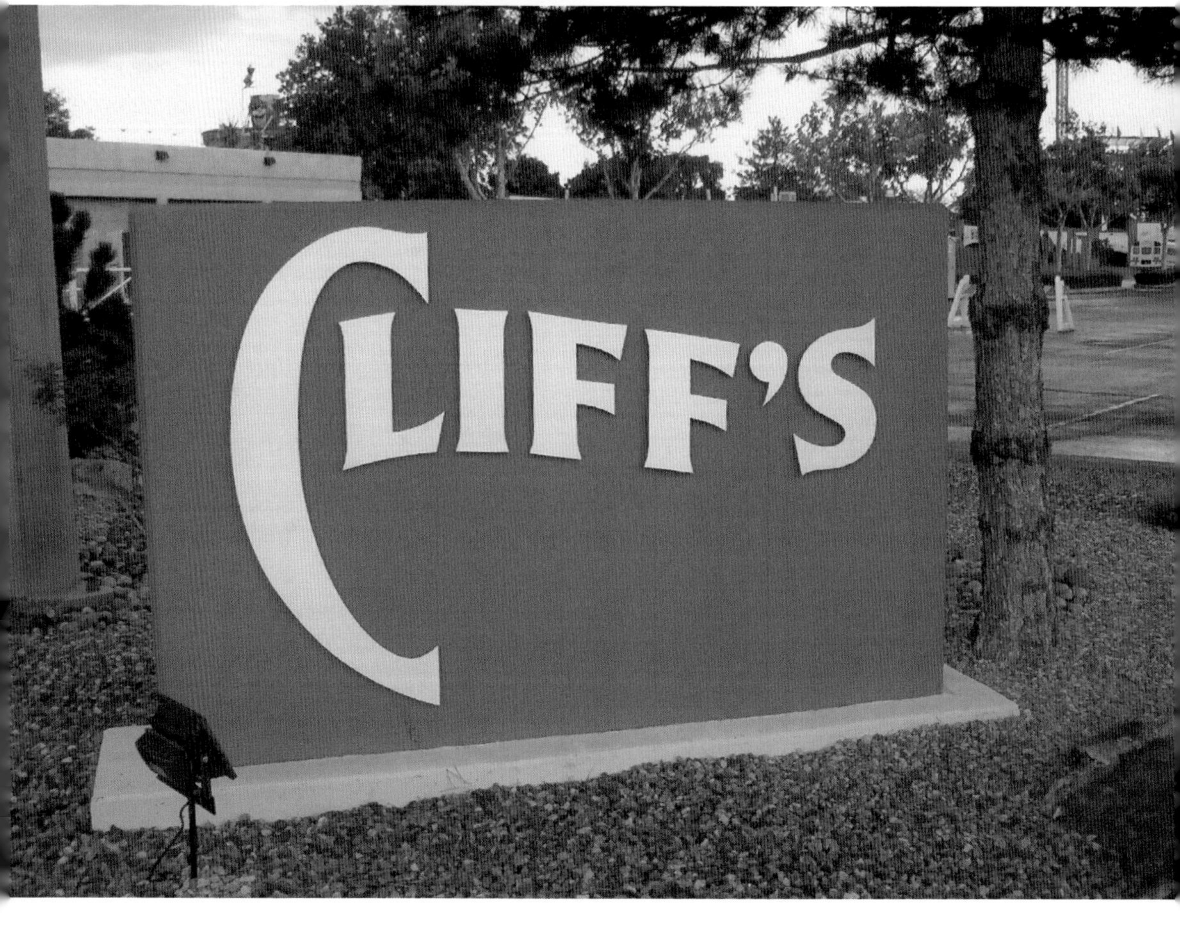

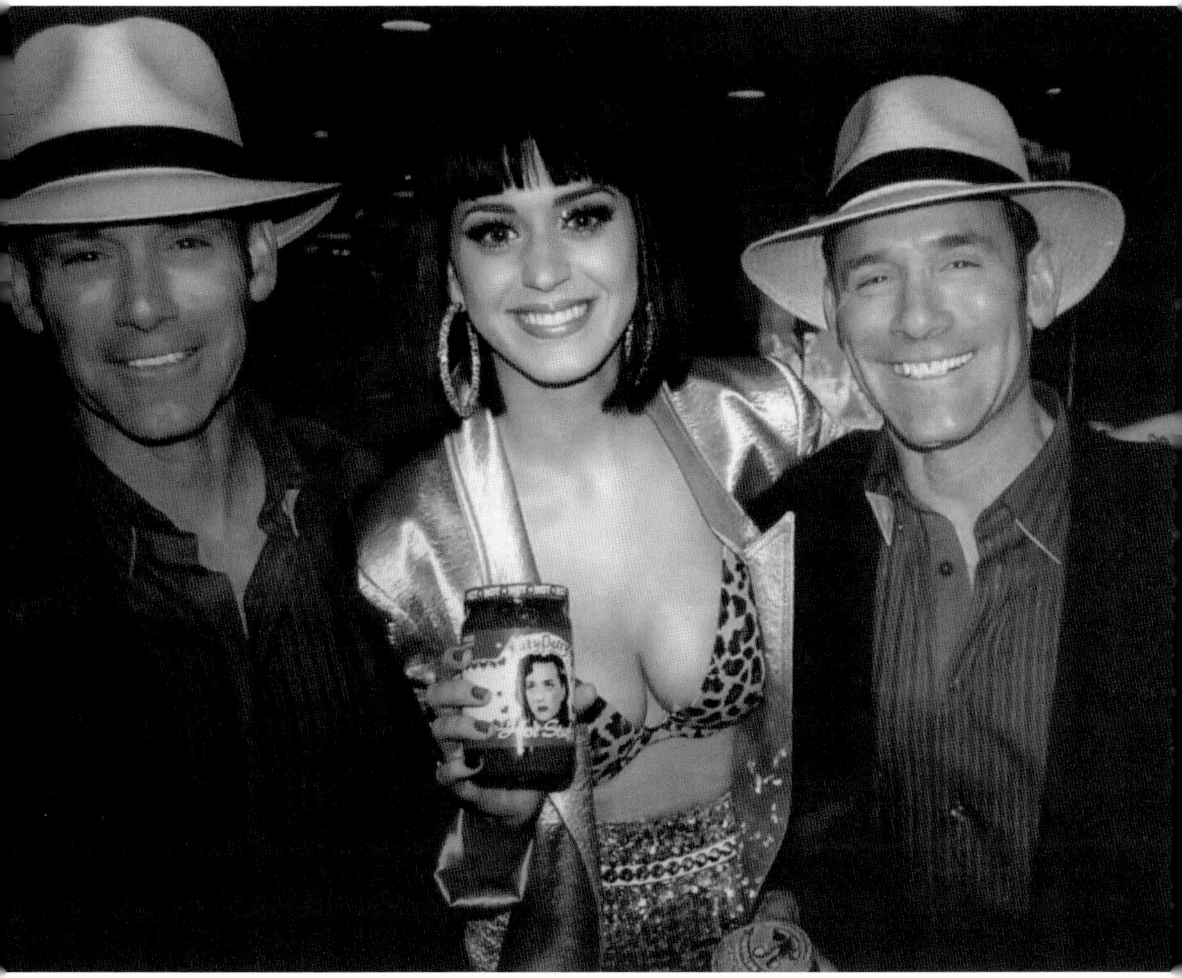

Jim and John Thomas (b. 1959)
In 1962, Jack and Connie Thomas opened northwest Albuquerque's El Pinto restaurant, using Connie's mother's recipes and philosophy: "*Panza llena, corazon contento*" ("Full stomach, happy heart"). The Thomases' six children helped with the business, but their twins, Jim and John, became so involved in El Pinto that they bought it in 1994 and have managed the business ever since. El Pinto, which seats 1,000 guests, is the largest restaurant in the city. Jim and John's salsa became so famous that they have marketed it nationwide and have become known as the "salsa twins." El Pinto's salsa has been served on Cinco de Mayo at the White House and onboard the naval submarine USS *Albuquerque*. Photographs of Jim (left) and John (right) with celebrity guests, like singer Katy Perry (center), line the walls of El Pinto's lobby.

Mike Gonzales (b. 1957)

Mike Gonzales and his brother James opened the Barelas Coffee House on 1502 South Fourth Street Southwest on Valentine's Day 1978. The restaurant soon became popular not only with its local neighbors, but also with politicos, from mayors to presidents. Serving about 500 customers a day, Mike (seen here with Gerry Lucero) likes to call his place "Cheers without the liquor." Some satisfied customers eat nearly all of their meals at the popular restaurant.

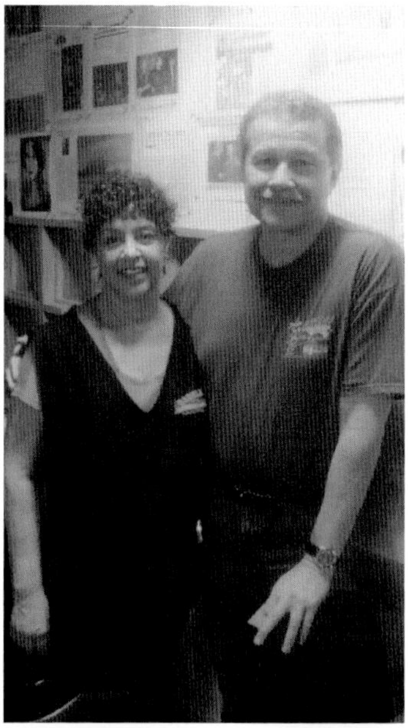

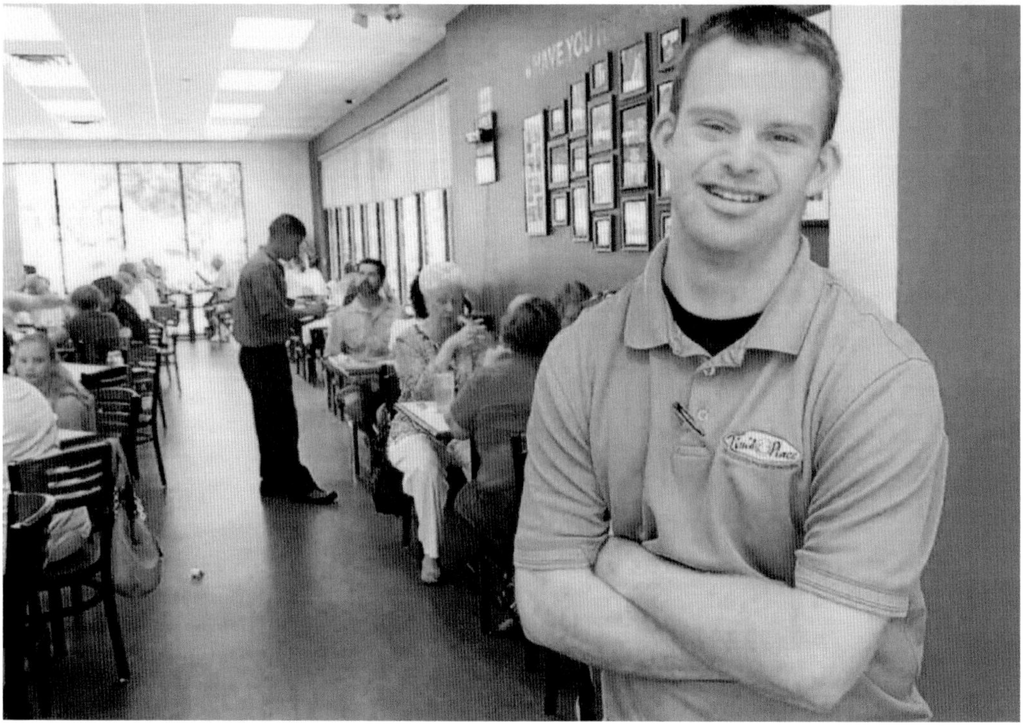

Tim Harris (b. 1986)

An Albuquerque native born with Down syndrome, Tim Harris graduated from Eldorado High School in 2004. Defying expectations, he went to college, sailed the Caribbean, won Special Olympics gold medals, and, as of 2010, owned his own restaurant. Tim's Place is famous for its good food and Harris's warm hugs. He has even visited the White House, where he was recognized by Pres. Barack Obama. Harris, of course, gave the chief executive an enthusiastic hug.

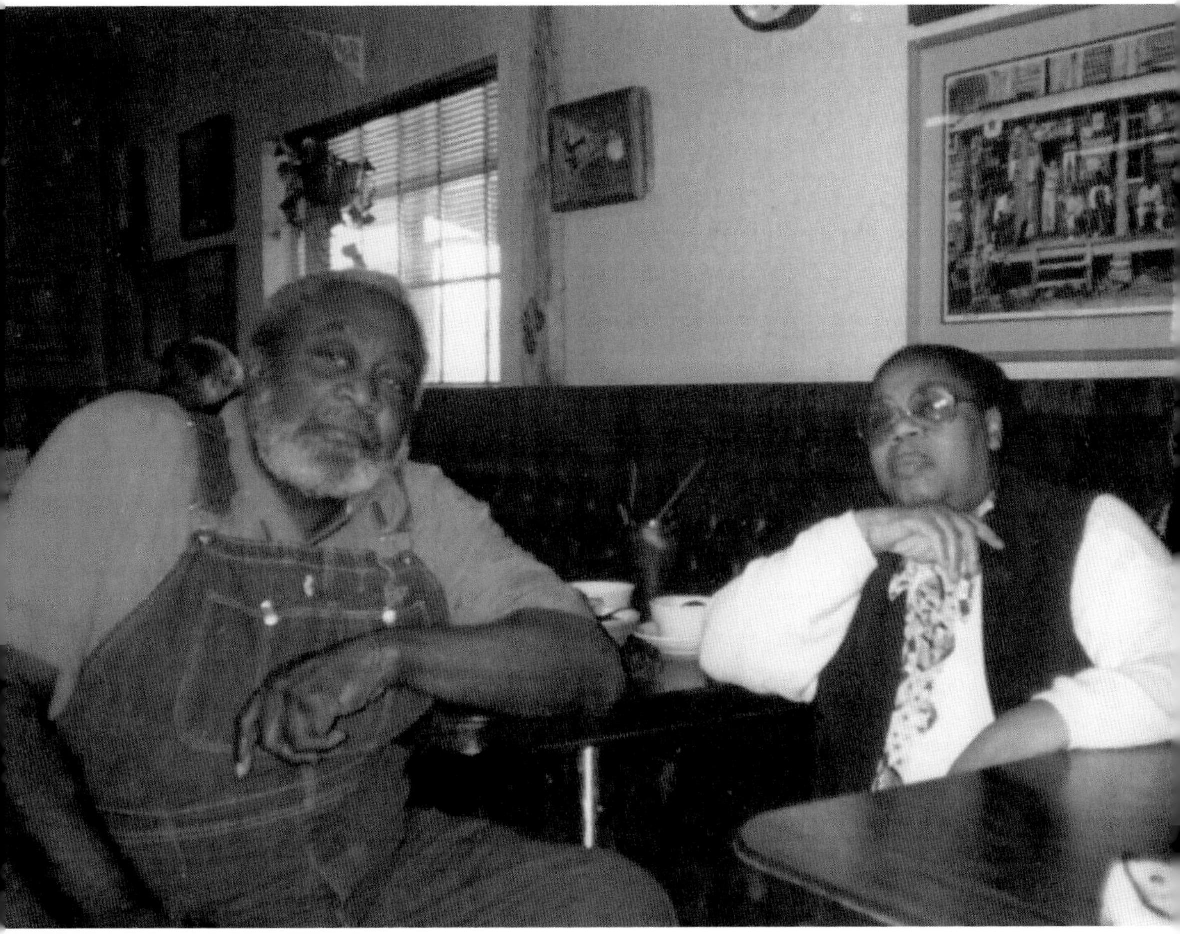

Pete Powdrell (1921–2007) and Catherine Powdrell (1925–2004)
Driving a station wagon and an old pickup, Pete and Catherine Powdrell and their 11 children moved from Texas to Albuquerque in 1958. The couple brought a strong work ethic, lots of experience in the restaurant business, and an old family recipe for sauce and barbecue. In 1962, they opened Powdrell's Barbecue, a restaurant that became so successful that they "went from making barbecue sauce out of a pot to using fifty-gallon vats," in Pete's words. The family catered parties, birthdays, weddings, graduations, political victories, and even divorces. Pete claimed that their success came from an important attitude: "Be honest, put out a good product consistently, and be joyful." (Courtesy of the Powdrell family.)

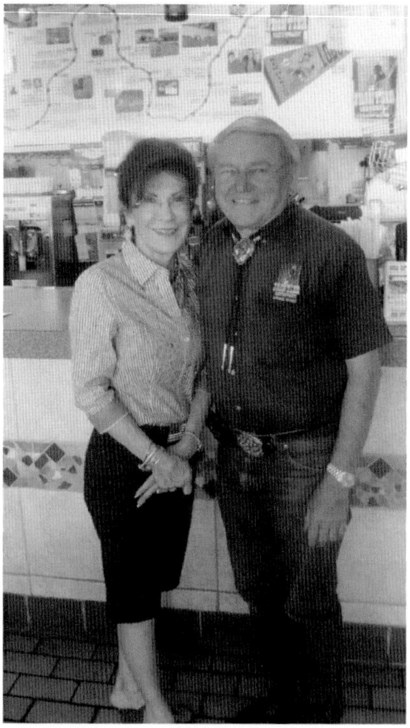

Larry and Dorothy Rainosek

When Larry and Dorothy Rainosek arrived in Albuquerque from Austin, Texas, in 1970, they thought they had arrived on the frontier, so they naturally called their new restaurant The Frontier. Located across from the UNM campus at 2400 Central Avenue Southeast, The Frontier soon became a favorite destination for students, faculty, and staff. It also became a popular eatery for many families in the community, especially for weekend breakfasts. Starting with one room and a 99-person seating capacity, by 1984 The Frontier had expanded to four rooms and a 320-person capacity. Thousands of college students have worked at The Frontier, dutifully serving its famous sweet rolls and green chili hamburgers. The Rainoseks' customers have included mayors, governors, congressmen, senators, television stars, and an archbishop. Like Mike Gonzales of the Barelas Coffee House, Larry Rainosek describes his award-winning establishment as a "bar without the booze." The Frontier has become a Central Avenue icon.

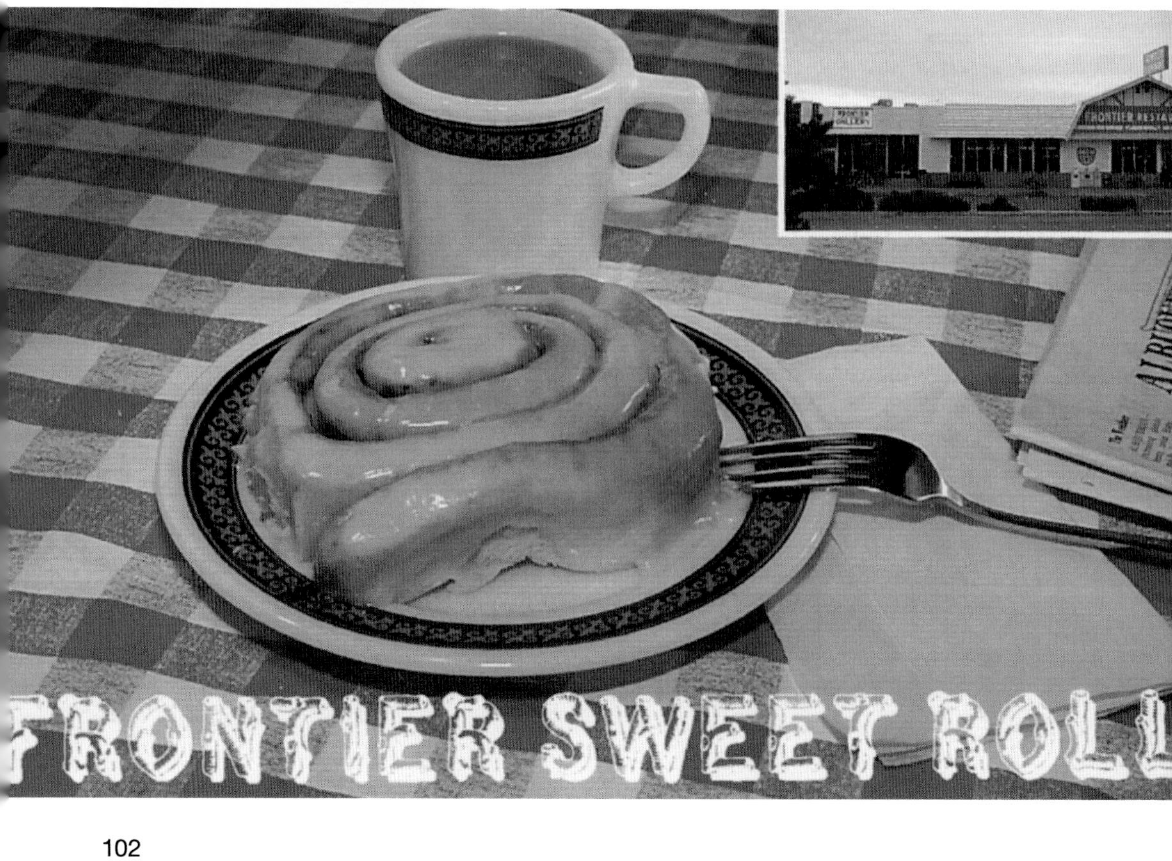

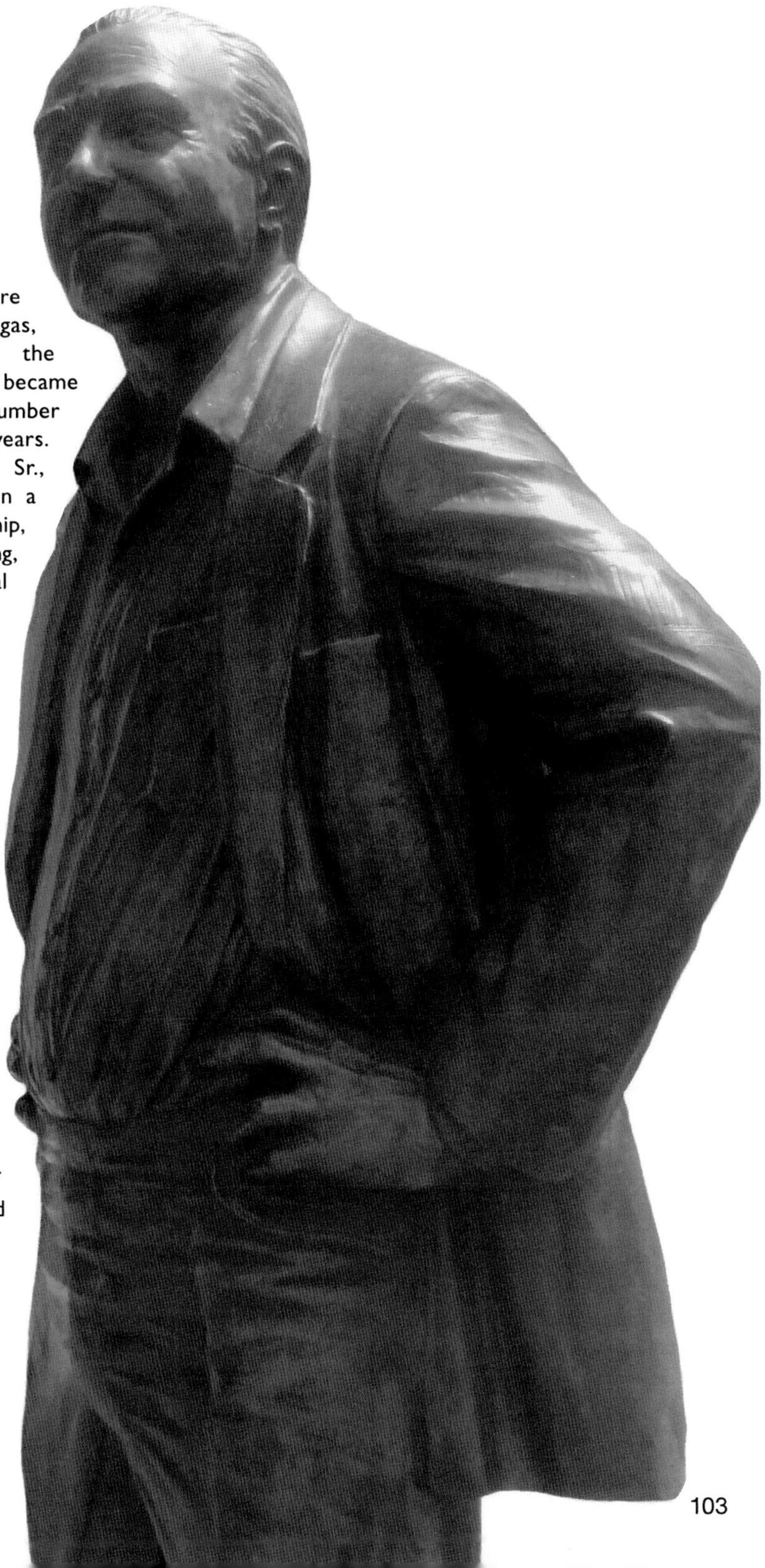

George Maloof Sr. (1923–1980)
Starting with a general store they opened in Las Vegas, New Mexico, in 1892, the Lebanese Maloof family became incredibly successful in a number of businesses over the years. Led by George Maloof Sr., their fortune was made in a Coors beer distributorship, a trucking business, banking, hotels, and professional basketball teams. By 1995, the Maloofs were said to be the richest family in New Mexico. By 2000, they were worth over $1 billion. Most recently, the family has chosen Albuquerque to release a "dietary supplement" called Never Hungover. The drink, which comes in two-ounce bottles and retails for $2.99, seems oddly in keeping with the Maloofs' beer distribution business, which the family sold in 2010. Paul Moore's sculpture of George Maloof Sr. (pictured) stands at the corner of North Third Street and Tijeras Avenue Northwest.

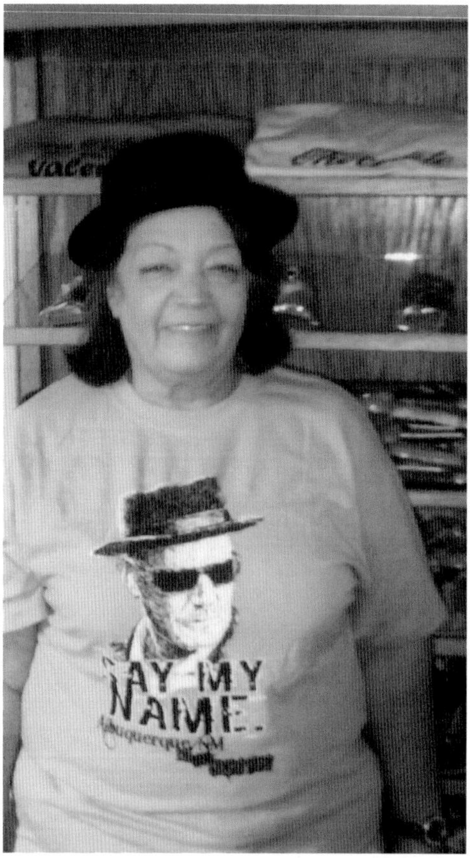

Debbie Ball (b. 1952)

The descendant of an original Spanish family in New Mexico, Debbie Ball started by selling her homemade candy at craft shows. She eventually opened a small shop of her own in Old Town, selling a few varieties of fudge and licorice. Everything changed in 1982, when the *Albuquerque Tribune* reported that she was selling X-rated candy. Some who objected to her risqué candy picketed her shop with signs declaring, "Pornography is sin." Their opposition backfired as stories about the controversial candy spread on news outlets across the country, giving Ball tons of free publicity. "The more people try to take down a business," Debbie says, "the more people want it because they want to see what all the hype is about." More recently, "The Candy Lady" enjoyed the rewards of another controversial product. With the hit television series *Breaking Bad* filmed in Albuquerque, Ball has produced "blue meth candy," a takeoff on the blue methamphetamine produced by the bad guys in the show.

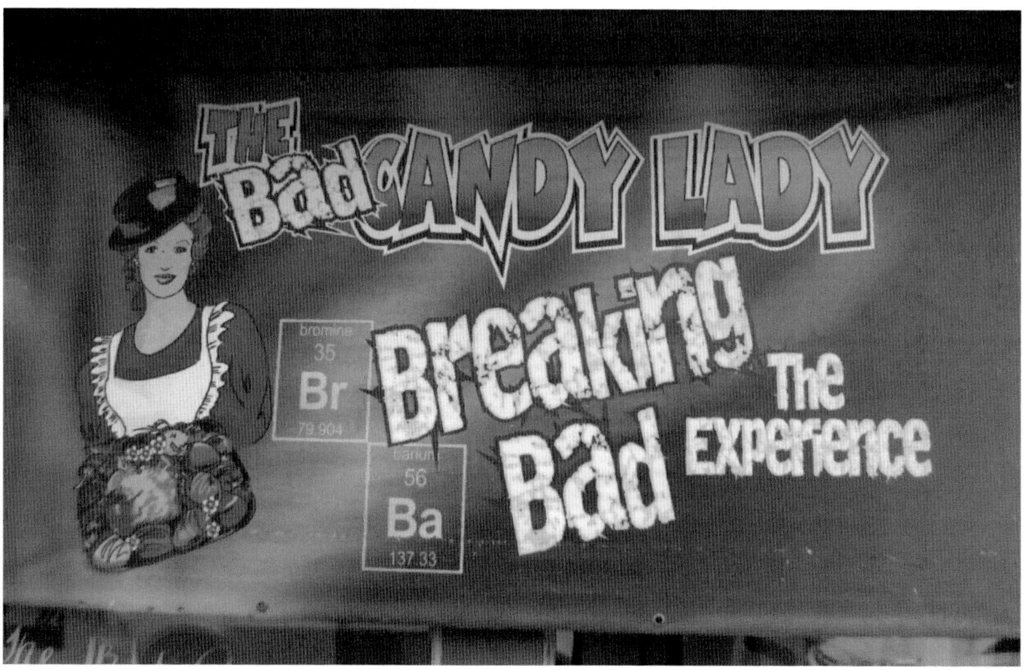

CHAPTER EIGHT

Health, Science, Technology, and Space

Albuquerque's reputation as a mecca for health-seekers began with the spread of a terrible disease: tuberculosis. Thousands of victims arrived in Albuquerque, attracted by its mild climate and clean air, long considered essential to recovery from TB. Sanatoriums that specialized in the treatment of TB thrived in the early 20th century. So many sanatoriums were built along Central Avenue that the road was nicknamed "Lungers Alley." Several sanatoriums, including Presbyterian and St. Joseph, became general hospitals and the center of the city's thriving healthcare industry.

Albuquerque's reputation as a scientific research center began in the 1930s with the atmospheric studies of a young UNM physics professor named E.J. "Jack" Workman. During World War II, Workman joined the top-secret Manhattan Project at Los Alamos, working at the project's important Site Z on Albuquerque's Sandia Army Base. Site Z evolved into Sandia National Laboratories by 1949 and the outset of the Cold War. The labs have been the center of scientific research of many kinds, especially nuclear weapons essential to American defense systems.

Albuquerque engineer H. Edward Roberts invented the first commercially successful personal computer in 1975 and is deservedly known as the "father of the personal computer." Scientists at Sandia Labs have also become leaders in technological progress, developing some of the most powerful computers in the world. Thanks to the work of Sandia's Willis Whitfield, "clean rooms" have led to revolutionary advancements in microelectronics. The Intel Corporation plant in neighboring Rio Rancho could not produce its valuable microchips without such technology. And personal computer software, developed by Bill Gates and Paul Allen in Albuquerque, would not have been possible without microchips first. Personal computers, clean rooms, advanced microchips, and personal computer software—essential parts of the modern technological revolution—all have their origins in Albuquerque.

Albuquerqueans have also made major contributions in space travel. The United States' earliest astronauts underwent thorough testing at the city's Lovelace Clinic under Dr. Randy Lovelace II, a pioneer in aviation medicine. A trio of astronauts with Albuquerque ties has traveled into space: Sidney Gutierrez, Richard Mullane, and Laurel Clark. While 13 women were tested at Lovelace Clinic as part of the Mercury 13 program, no women were selected as American astronauts until Sally Ride traveled into space in 1983. Albuquerque's Laurel Clark was the 32nd female astronaut to fly for NASA.

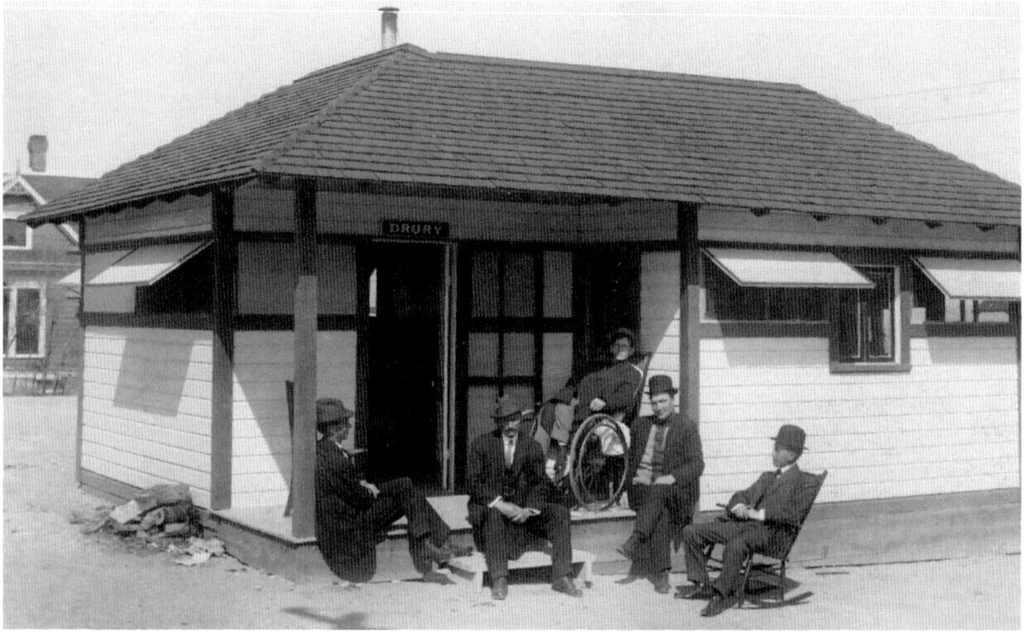

Tuberculosis Patients

Tuberculosis was the nation's leading cause of death in the late 19th and early 20th centuries. Eastern doctors often urged their TB patients to attempt to recover in New Mexico, where the clean, dry air was believed to be beneficial. Thousands took this medical advice, often arriving in Albuquerque via its excellent railroad connections. By 1920, so many victims of TB (called "lungers") populated the city that someone suggested that a sign should be placed in each of their yards. Another observer quipped that it would be easier to place signs in the yards of places that did *not* house a lunger. The recovering patients lived in everything from tents to sanatoriums, including the Presbyterian Sanatorium (below). Lungers were at first welcomed to the city by the businesses they frequented, but a reaction soon set in when local residents feared that TB would spread, which it did. New drugs to cure the dreaded disease were finally discovered in the 1940s and early 1950s. (Courtesy of the Presbyterian Hospital, PC 59 and PC 122.)

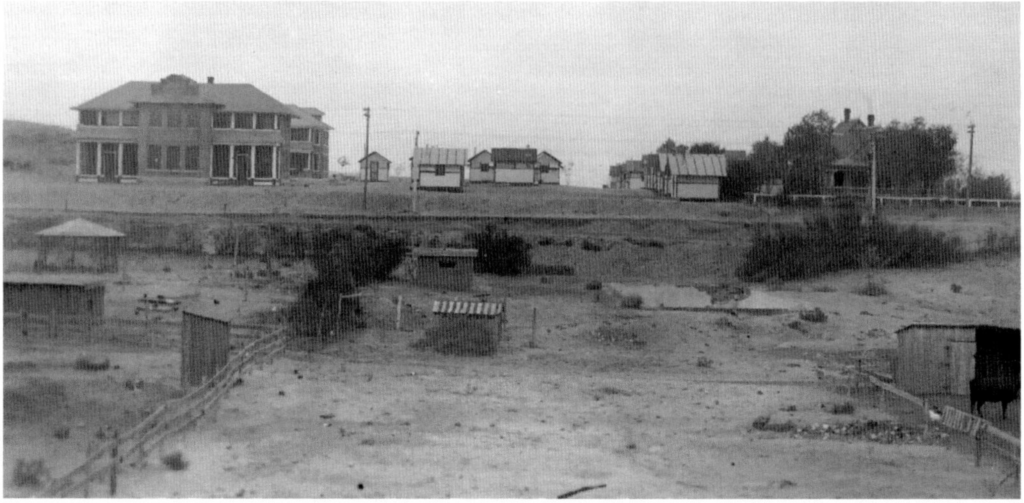

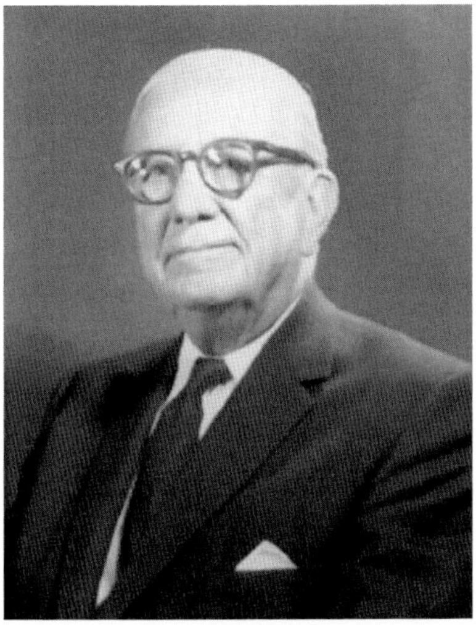

William Randolph Lovelace I (1883–1968)
Like many of New Mexico's most famous physicians, William Lovelace came to the Southwest as a patient suffering from tuberculosis. After opening a practice in Sunnyside (now Fort Sumner), Lovelace moved to Albuquerque, where he opened a medical clinic with Dr. Edgar Lassetter in 1919. Modeled after the famous Mayo Clinic, Lovelace Clinic expanded and eventually merged with the adjacent Bataan Memorial Methodist Hospital, becoming one of the largest medical health centers in Albuquerque. (Courtesy of the Lovelace Health System.)

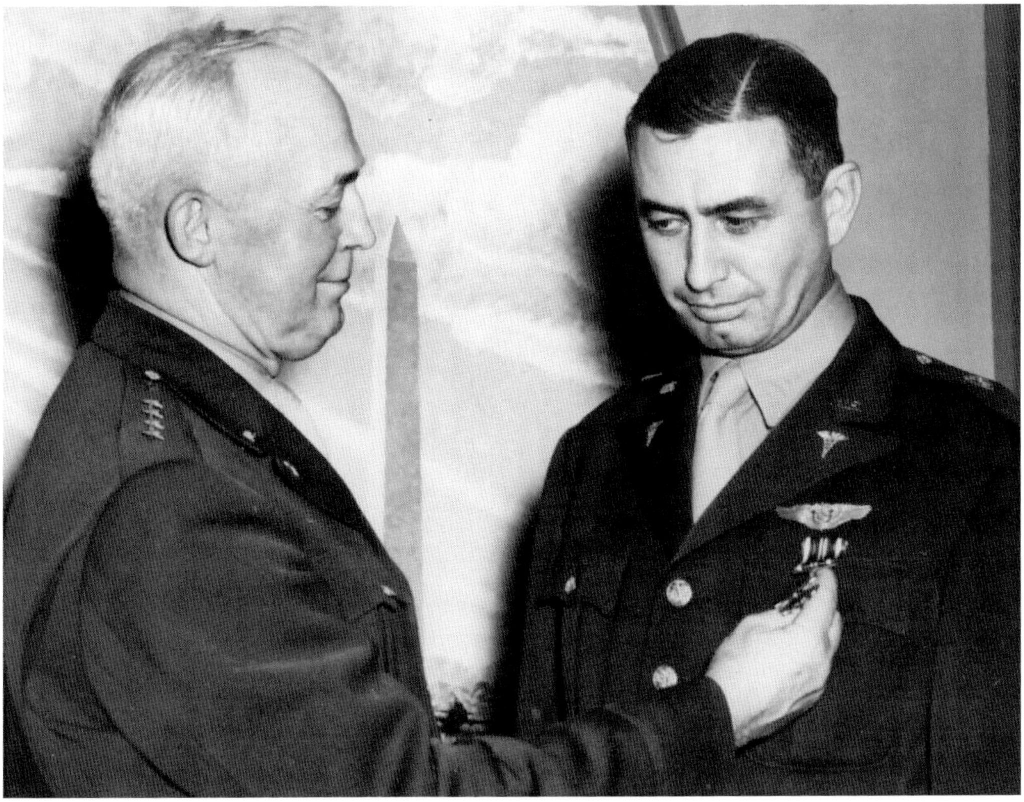

William Randolph "Randy" Lovelace II (1907–1965)
Dr. William Lovelace I had no children, but he treated his nephew Randy much like a son. Educated at Harvard University, Randy became a pioneer in aviation medicine during World War II, when he tested modern oxygen equipment by jumping out of a plane from an altitude of over 40,000 feet. Here, Lovelace (right) receives the Distinguished Flying Cross from Gen. "Hap" Arnold for this remarkable feat. He joined his uncle's Albuquerque clinic and was chosen to perform complete medical evaluations of the United States' first seven astronauts.

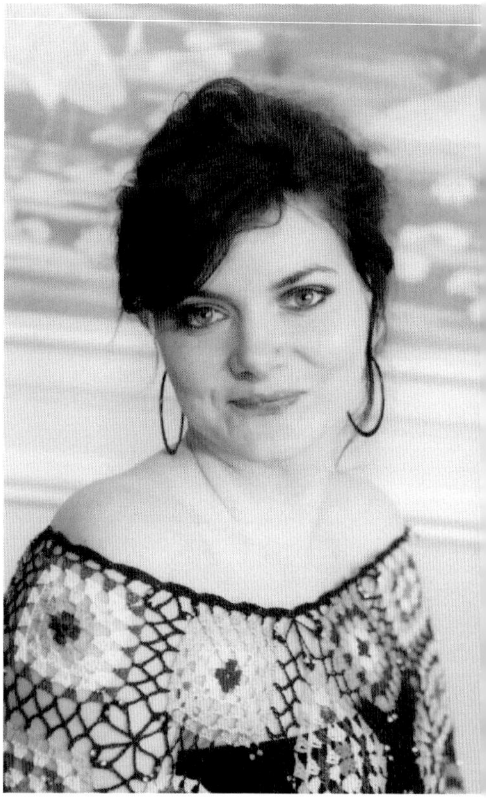

Cody Unser (b. 1987)

On February 5, 1999, sixth-grader Cody Unser was practicing basketball when she began to feel excessively tired. The daughter of racecar champion Al Unser Jr. and his wife, Shelley, Cody experienced mysterious symptoms that were diagnosed as a rare neurological disorder known as transverse myelitis (TM), which left her paralyzed from the waist down. In true Unser tradition, Cody refused to let her paralysis slow her down. She became a tireless advocate, producing an award-winning documentary, testifying at legislative sessions, and delivering speeches to educate thousands about TM. She also created the Cody Unser First Step Foundation to help raise research funds to fight paralysis and build awareness of TM. Realizing the personal benefits of scuba diving, Cody helped create Adaptive Scuba to help other paraplegics, including military veterans. She is a champion like no other Unser, on or off the racetrack. (Courtesy of Cody Unser.)

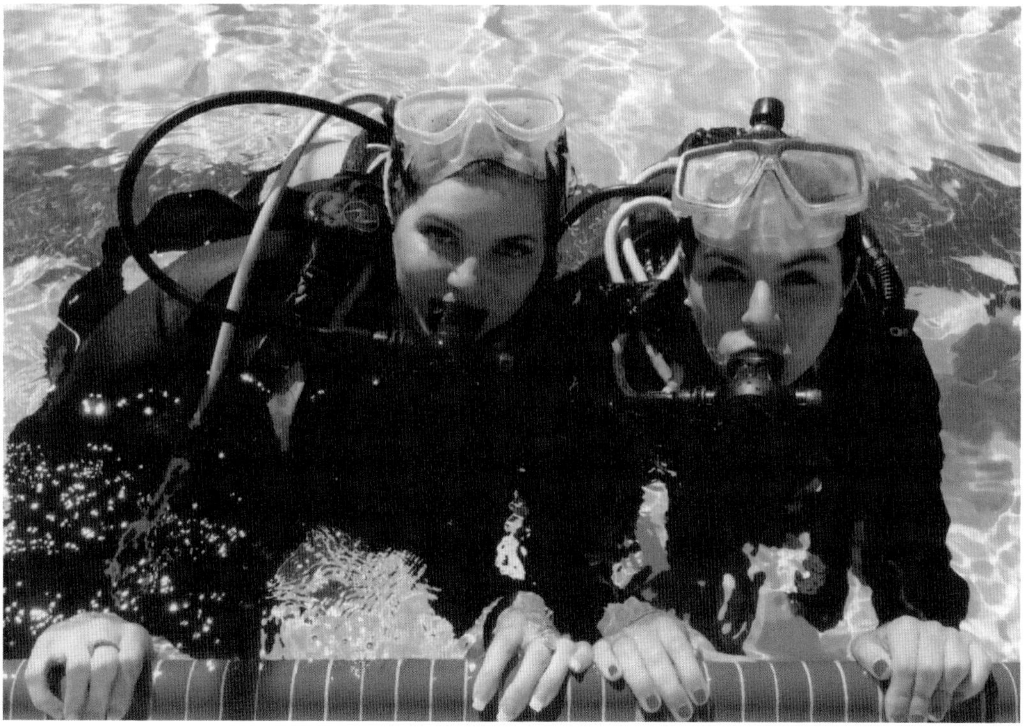

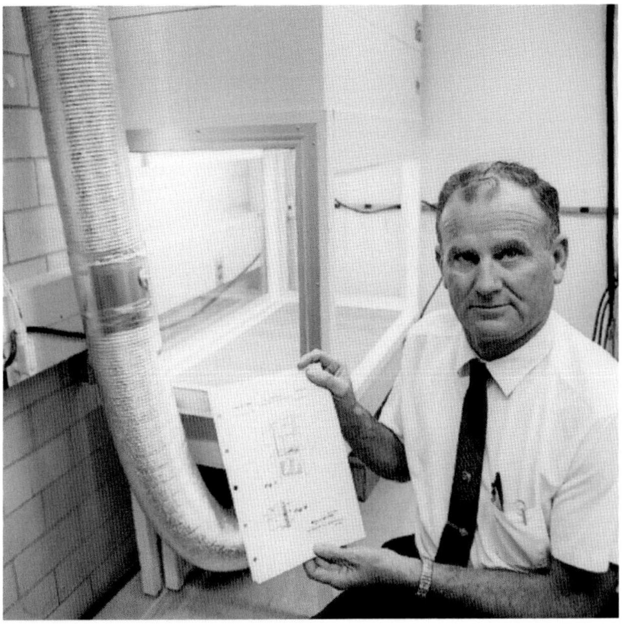

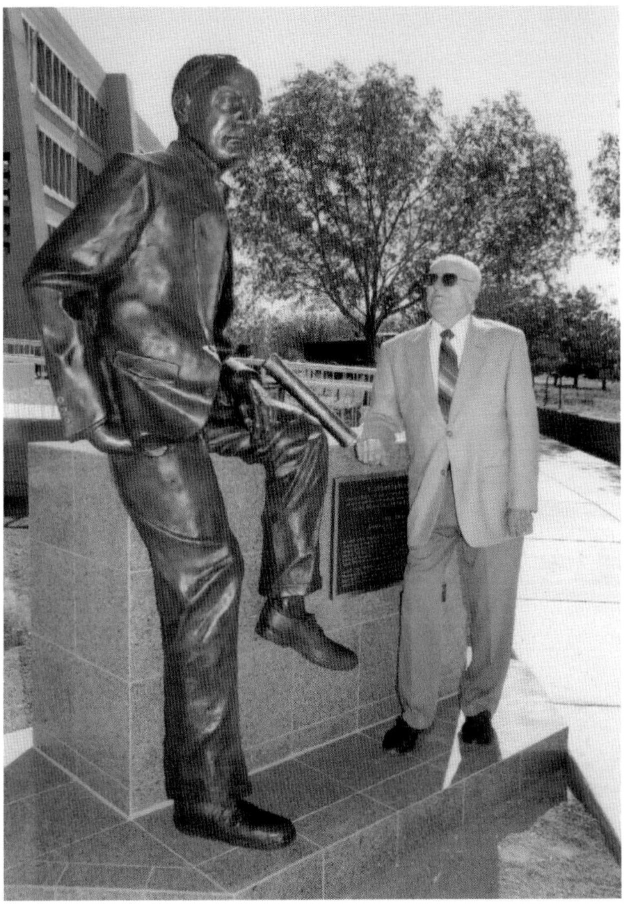

Willis Whitfield (1919–2012)
Born on a Texas cotton farm, Willis Whitfield produced one of the most important inventions of the modern world. A Sandia National Laboratories employee from 1954 to 1984, he invented the "clean room," which allowed for revolutionary advancements in microelectronics, hospital operating rooms, and space exploration. Whitfield was called "Mr. Clean" by *Time* magazine, and his invention could completely replace the air in a room 10 times every minute. He received many honors for his groundbreaking achievement, but he remained humble to the end of his life at age 92. Ironically, his wife confessed that Mr. Clean was not always tidy. As she told a *New York Times* reporter, Willis did not always put his shoes away at home. Below, he is shown with his sculpture, by Neal McEwen, which stands on the Sandia National Labs' campus. (Courtesy of the Sandia National Laboratories.)

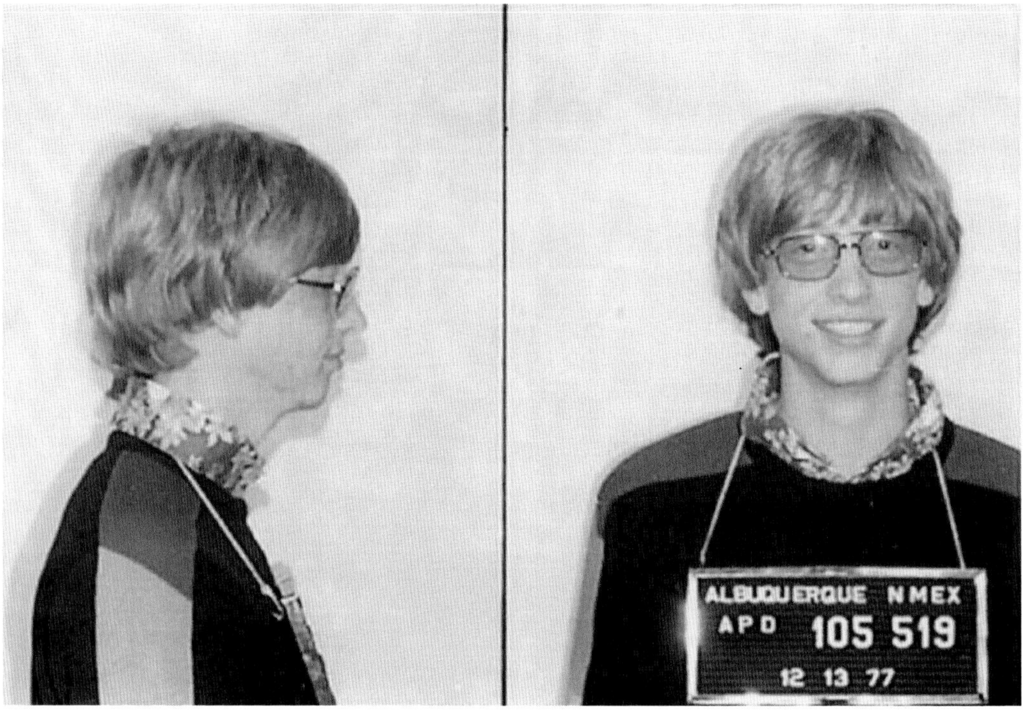

Bill Gates (b. 1955)
Young Bill Gates and his business partner, Paul Allen, founded Microsoft, Inc., which soon became the country's dominant software company, while living in Albuquerque in the 1970s. With a small office located near the State Fair Grounds, the new company employed less than 20 young men and women. Gates and Allen lived at the Sundowner Motel at 6101 Central Avenue. On April 29, 1975, Gates was arrested in Albuquerque for speeding and failure to provide a driver's license.

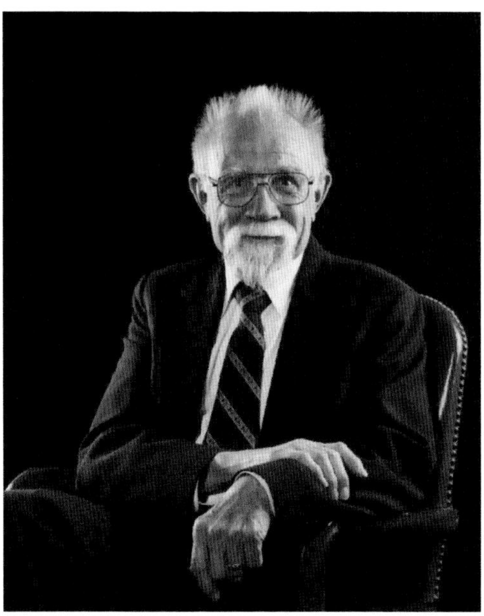

Gustavus J. Simmons (b. 1930)
With a doctorate in mathematics from UNM, Gustavus Simmons became a world-famous cryptographer. Employed at Sandia National Laboratories, he is known as the "father of authentication theory," a mathematical method used to send encrypted messages that could be trusted by both senders and receivers. He has received many honors, including the Ernest Orlando Lawrence Award, the highest government award given to an American scientist. (Photograph by Randy Montoya, courtesy of the Sandia National Laboratories.)

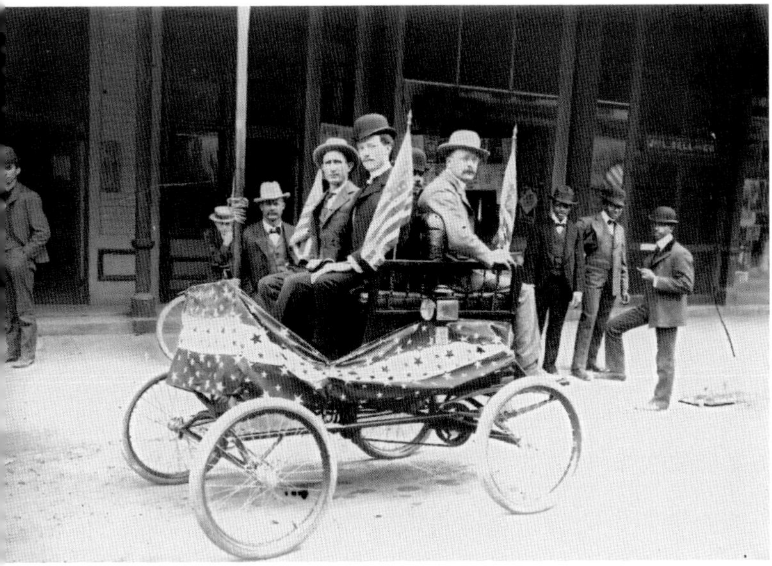

J.L. Dodson

Dodson, an Albuquerque bicycle dealer, purchased the city's first automobile in late 1897. Although he often became lost on unmarked dirt roads, Dodson drove his Locomobile home from Denver, Colorado, in five days. Horses panicked at the strange vehicle's loud sound and dark shape. Dodson had to order gasoline sent by train so it would be ready for him to refuel in towns en route. Once in Albuquerque, he (pictured here in a dark bowler hat) urged others to purchase cars, although some residents worked to ban the disturbing "devil wagons" from city streets. Gradually accepting the newfangled machines, Albuquerqueans owned 32 cars by 1910. Conditions dramatically changed by the 1950s, when cars crowded city streets, especially Central Avenue (below). (Courtesy of the Albuquerque Museum, PA1990-013-240.)

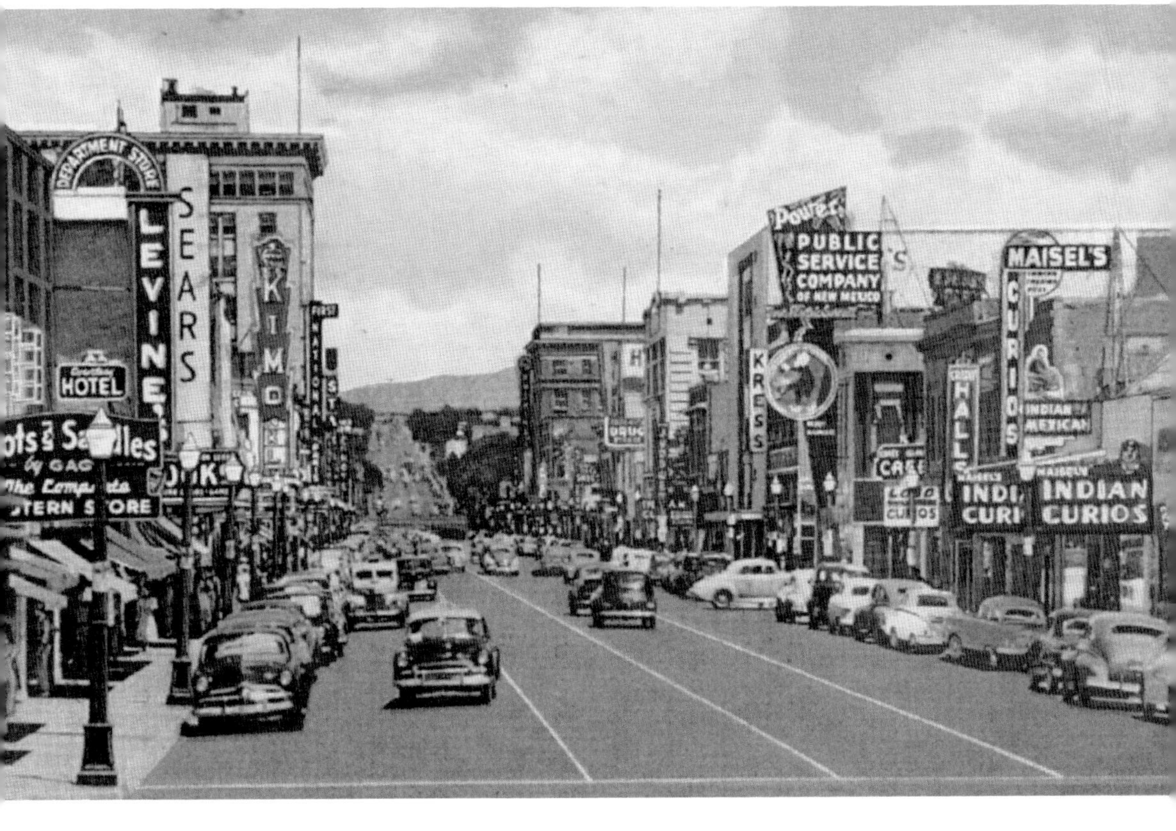

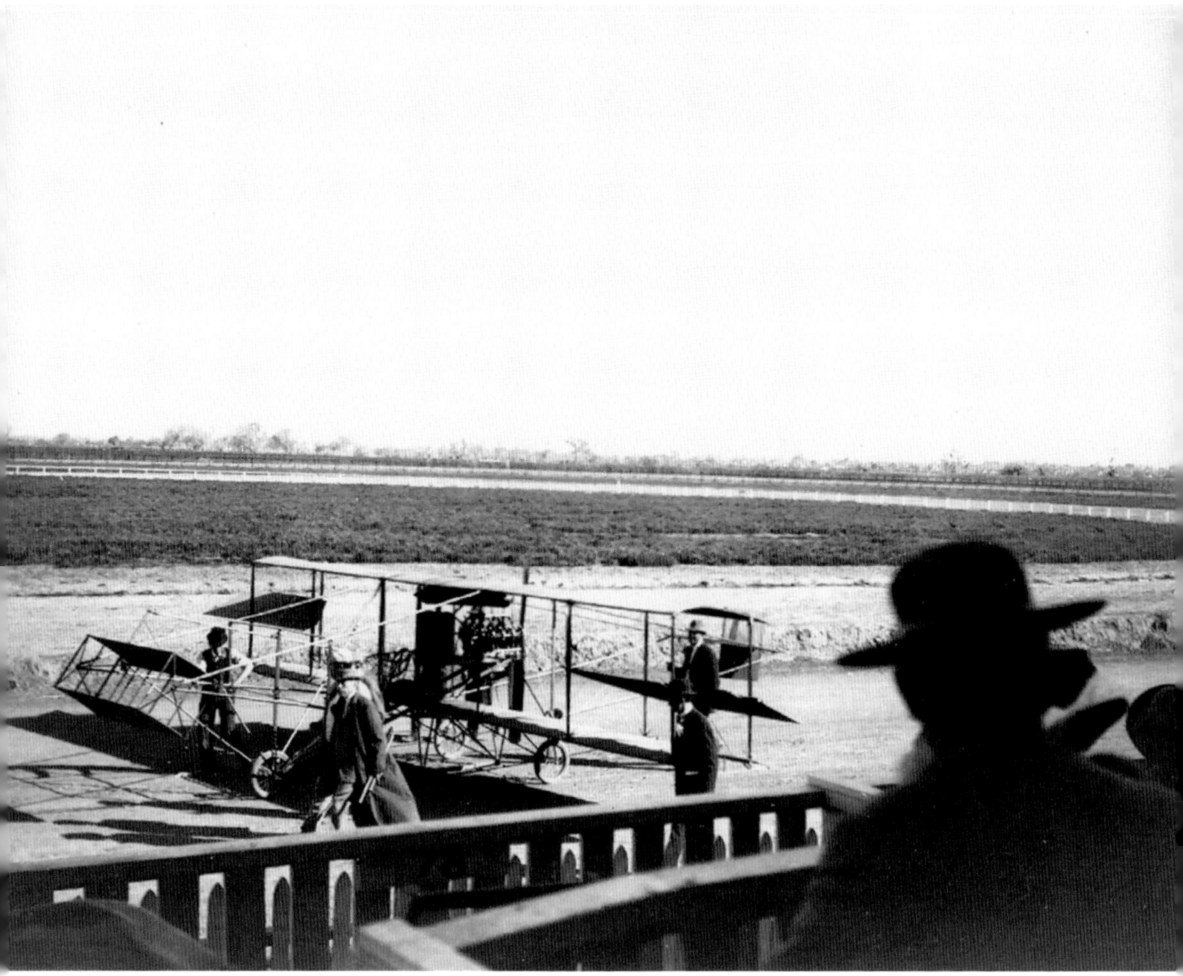

Charles Walsh (1877–1912)
Building his own plane and learning to fly it, Charles Walsh received California Pilot's License No. 1, issued on August 8, 1911. He reportedly flew the first plane in New Mexico history, taking off before a large crowd at the Territorial Fair on October 11, 1911. To the amazement of all, he flew his single-propeller Curtiss Model "D" biplane for 15 minutes before completing a successful landing. He returned to fly in Albuquerque the following year, reaching an altitude of over 5,000 feet. He flew at similar events in the United States, Canada, and Cuba until his tragic death in October 1912. Performing before a crowd of 65,000 at the New Jersey State Fair in Trenton, the 34-year-old Walsh crashed while attempting a dangerous spiral descent. An attending doctor confirmed that every bone in his body had been broken in the fall. The train carrying Walsh's remains home to California stopped in Albuquerque for a moment in his honor. A replica of his plane hangs from a high ceiling at the Albuquerque International Sunport. (Courtesy of the Albuquerque Museum, PA1978-001-013.)

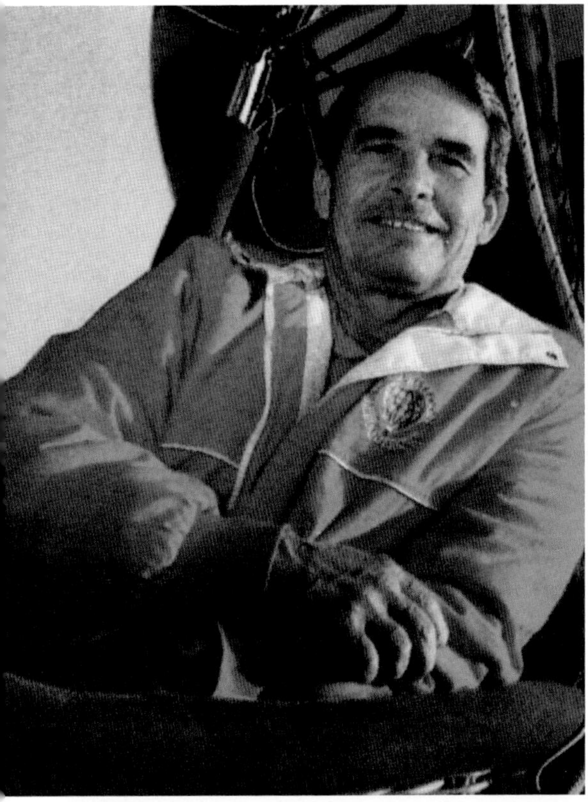

Sidney Cutter (1934–2011)
A grandson of Gov. Richard C. Dillon, "Sid" Cutter was born and raised in Albuquerque, where he developed an early interest in aviation. He received his private pilot's license when he was 17 and flew both jets and cargo planes as an officer in the US Air Force. He became interested in hot-air ballooning and was asked to organize Albuquerque's first hot-air balloon fiesta on April 8, 1972, as part of KOB radio's 50th-anniversary celebration. Known as the father of Albuquerque's balloon fiesta, he remained active in the gala event for many years. By the time of his death in 2011, Cutter had logged over 22,000 hours in planes and 5,000 hours as a balloon pilot.

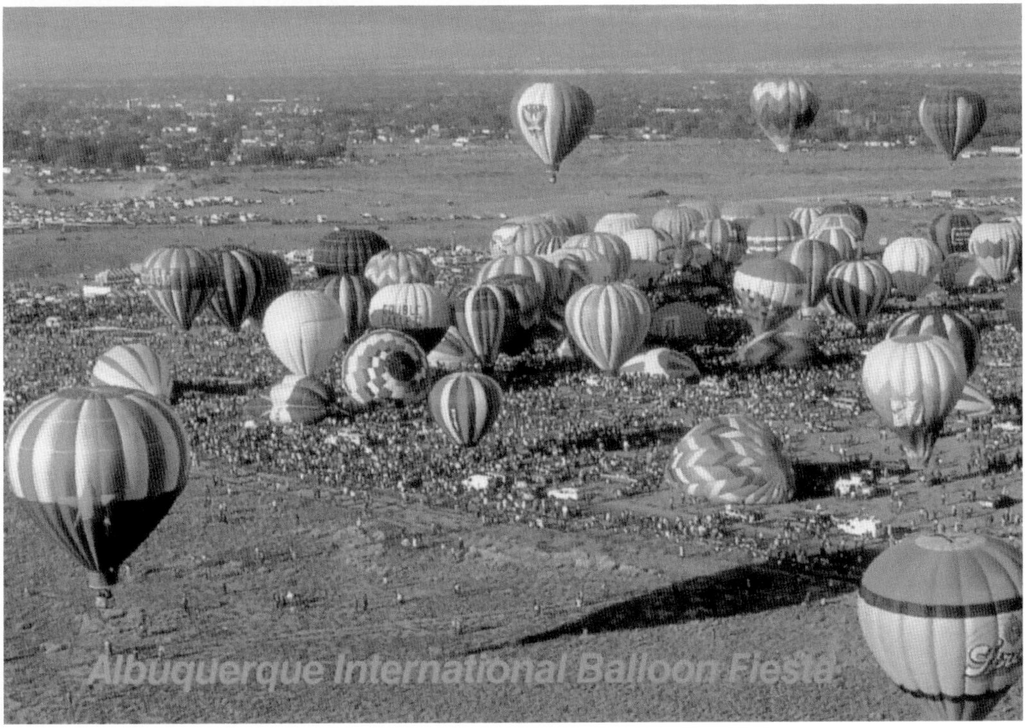

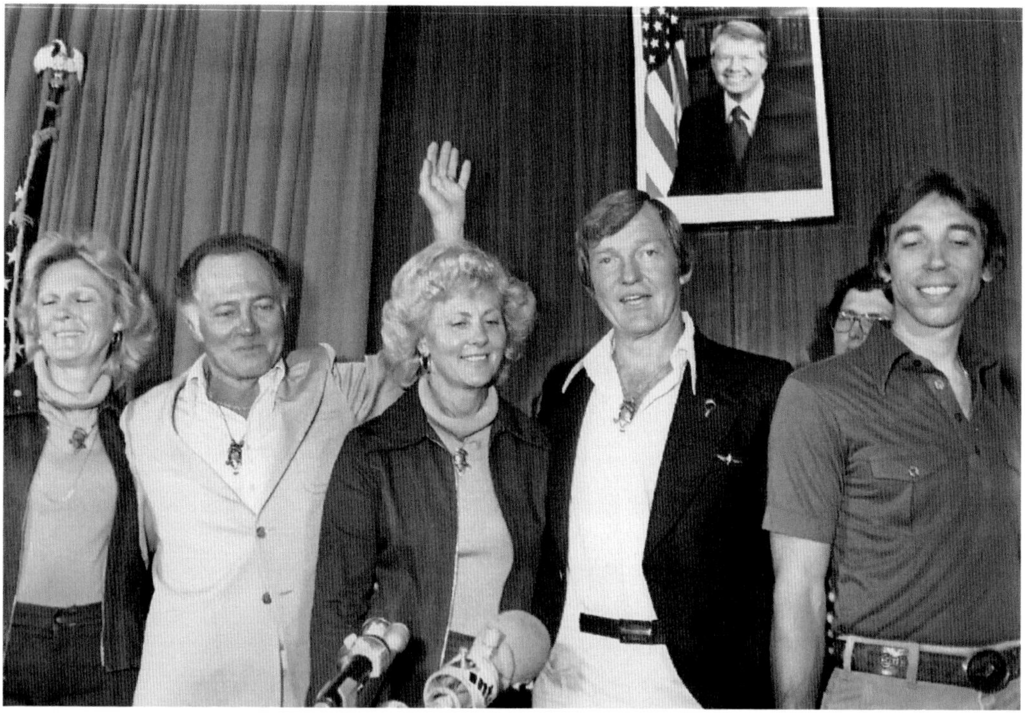

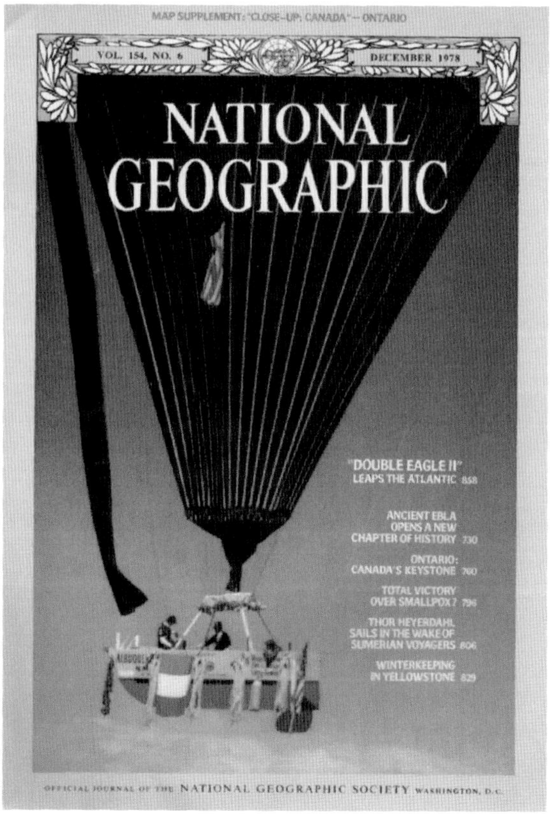

Ben Abruzzo (1930–1985)

Abruzzo first came to Albuquerque when he was assigned to Kirtland Air Force Base in the early 1950s. Remaining when his military service ended, he eventually joined Bob Nordhaus to build the Sandia Peak Tramway, from 1964 to 1966. In 1978, Abruzzo teamed with Maxie Anderson and Larry Newman to become the first crew to fly across the Atlantic Ocean in a hot-air balloon, the *Double Eagle II*. Their dramatic story was featured in *National Geographic* magazine (left). He accomplished a similar feat by flying across the Pacific in the *Double Eagle V* three years later. Albuquerque's Anderson-Abruzzo International Balloon Museum was named in his and Maxie Anderson's honor when it opened in 2005. Shown above are, from left to right, Patricia Abruzzo, Ben Abruzzo, Patty and Maxie Anderson (center), and Larry Newman (right).

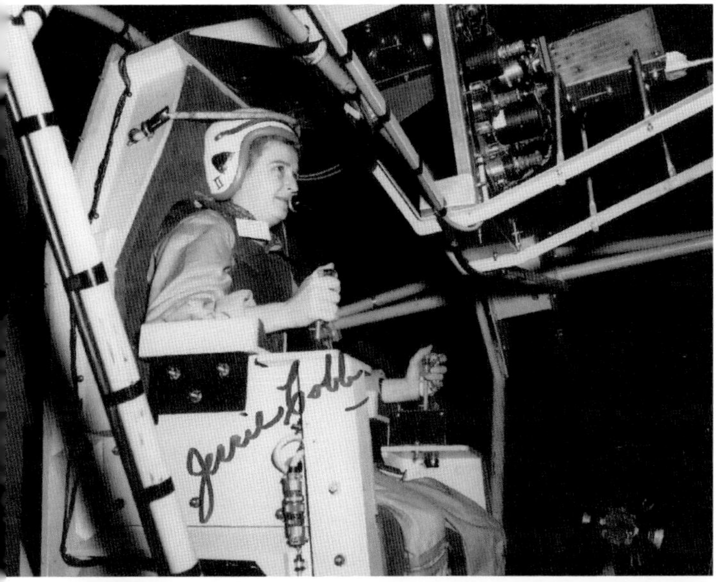

The Mercury 13

The United States competed with the Soviet Union for the distinction of sending the first human being into space. America tested male astronauts at Albuquerque's Lovelace Clinic. The clinic also tested 13 well-qualified women in a program known as the Mercury 13. Every woman, including Jerrie Cobb (pictured), successfully completed the program, but none were selected for further testing. As a result, the first woman in space was Russia's Valentina Tereshkova, in 1963.

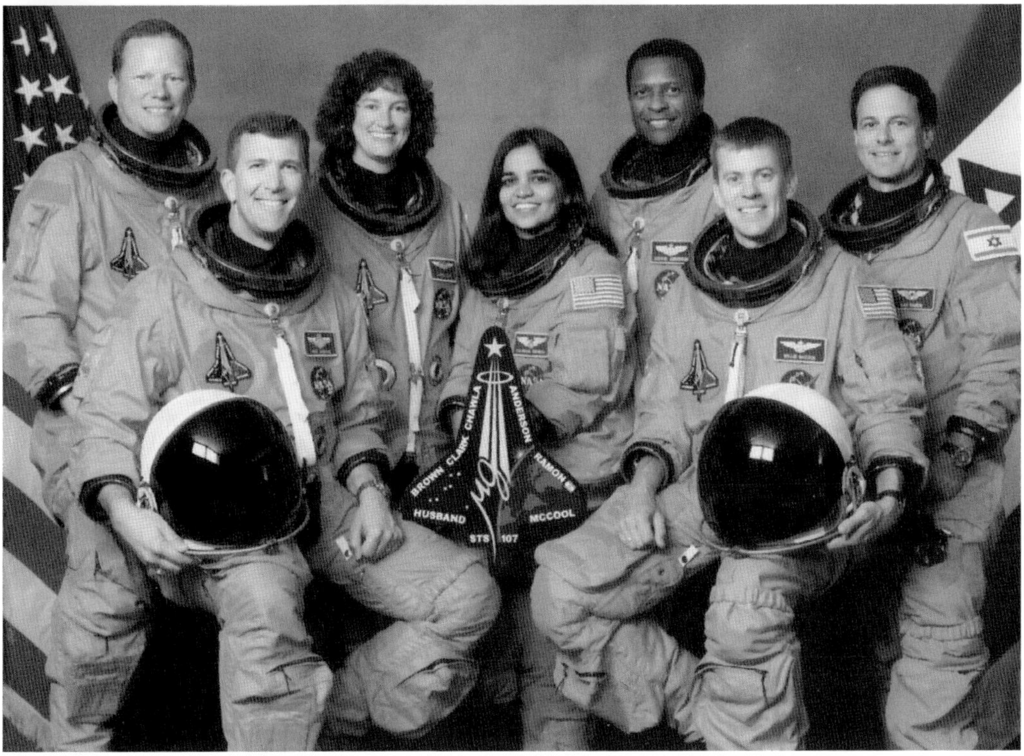

Laurel Clark (1961–2003)

Laurel Clark (third from left) spent several years of her childhood in Albuquerque, attending Hodgin Elementary School and Monroe Middle School. Trained as a naval physician, she became a NASA astronaut and joined the *Columbia* space shuttle crew on its 2003 mission. Tragically, the craft exploded within minutes of its planned landing in Florida, killing Clark and her six fellow crew members. The entire crew (pictured here) posthumously received the Congressional Space Medal of Honor.

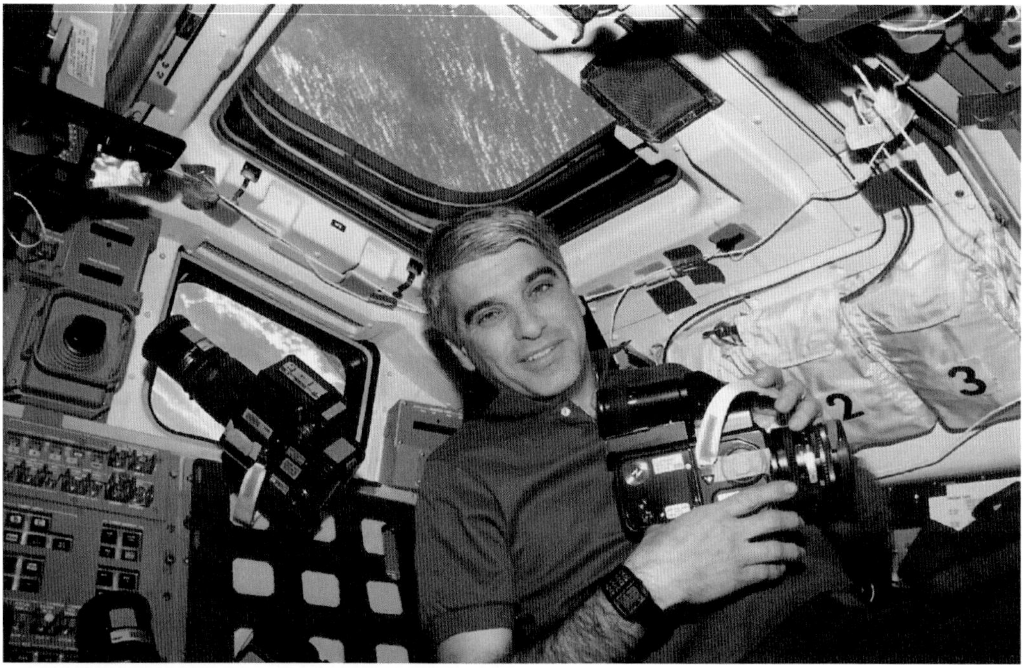

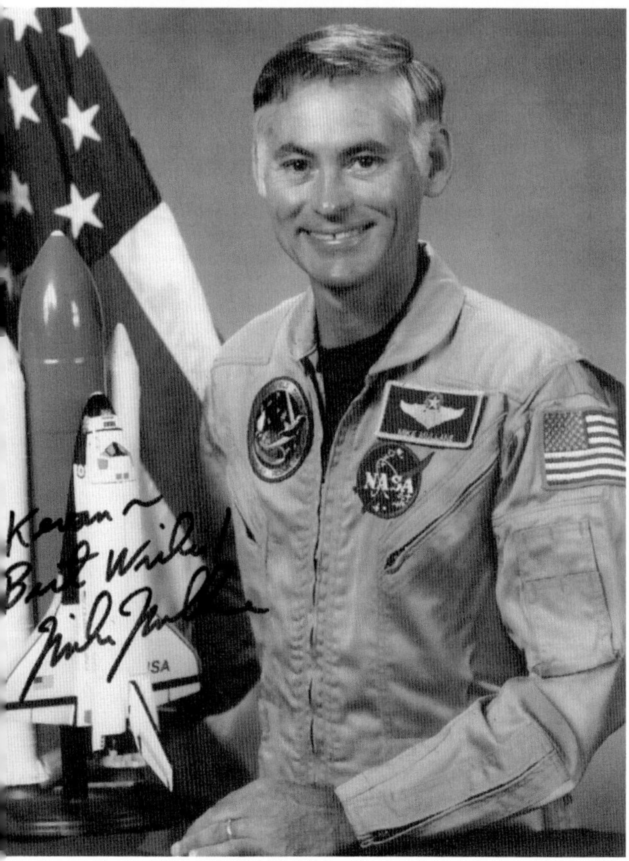

Sidney "Sid" Gutierrez (b. 1951)
Albuquerque native Sidney Gutierrez graduated as the valedictorian in Valley High School's class of 1969. Graduating from the US Air Force Academy in 1973, he became a NASA astronaut in 1984. A veteran of two space flights, he logged over 488 hours in space. Retiring in 1994, he joined Sandia National Laboratories and was inducted into the International Space Hall of Fame the following year. An Albuquerque middle school is named in his honor. (Courtesy of NASA-JSC, STS059-19-004.)

Richard Mullane (b. 1945)
A 1963 graduate of Albuquerque's St. Pius X High School, Mullane has been interested in space since childhood. He experimented with rockets on the mesa near his home. A West Point graduate, he was selected as a member of the first group of space shuttle astronauts. Mullane completed three space missions aboard the shuttles *Discovery* and *Atlantis*. His memoir is titled *Riding Rockets: The Outrageous Tales of a Space Shuttle Astronaut* (2007).

CHAPTER NINE

Sports

The men, women, and children of Albuquerque have long enjoyed the challenge and excitement of competitive sports. Racing, on foot or on horseback, has been a favorite sport since Spanish colonial days. Races became even more popular during the annual New Mexico Territorial Fair, long held at what is now the northwest corner of Central Avenue and Rio Grande Boulevard. By the 1890s, bicycle races were also held at the fairground's quarter-mile track or on longer, rougher routes. Roy Stamm, who grew up in Albuquerque, recalled that liberal betting, accompanied by large quantities of hard liquor, were typical at most racing events.

Team sports became popular by the turn of the 20th century. Often improved with the signing of professional players, local baseball teams played on diamonds, including one inside the racetrack at the territorial fairgrounds. Football games also drew large crowds, although the sport was so rough that many of its early formations were later banned. Both baseball and football games were played by teams fielded by Albuquerque High School, UNM, and the Albuquerque Indian School. Kenneth Balcomb, author of *A Boy's Albuquerque, 1898–1912*, remembered that the *Albuquerque Journal* posted scores of important out-of-town games (especially the World Series) on its street window. Large crowds waited for changing scores with great anticipation.

Basketball is arguably the most popular team sport in Albuquerque, especially after UNM began fielding winning men's teams in the 1960s. The school's enthusiastic fans cheer their Lobos in UNM's basketball arena, better known as The Pit, which is considered one of the most attractive, yet intimidating venues in the country.

Albuquerque's fans have strongly supported their professional teams, especially the baseball Dukes and Isotopes, long affiliated with the Los Angeles Dodgers and now in the Colorado Rockies' farm system. All-star major leaguers like Ron Cey, Davey Lopes, Pedro Martinez, Mike Piazza, and Orel Hershiser got their starts at the ballpark on University Avenue and César Chávez Boulevard Southeast.

Other sports gained large followings in the 20th century. The city produced many champion boxers, including Bob Foster, Johnny Tapia, and Holly Holms. Golfer Notah Begay III, gymnast Trent Dimas, and the car-racing Unser family have been proud to call Albuquerque home.

Roy W. Johnson (1892–1989)

Becoming UNM's athletic director in 1920, Roy Johnson coached nearly every sport on campus, while also working as the athletic department's business manager, equipment manager, and groundskeeper. He retired after 39 years of dedicated service to the university. UNM's gymnasium (where this photograph hangs) was named in his honor when it was completed in 1957. Also interested in drama and music, Coach Johnson performed at the Albuquerque Little Theatre, lending his rich bass voice to several musicals.

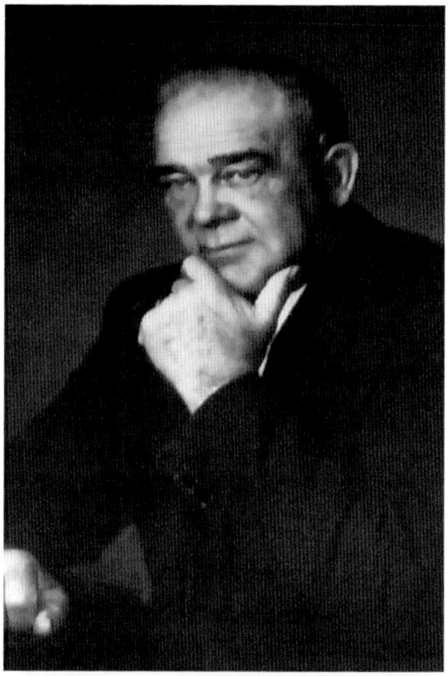

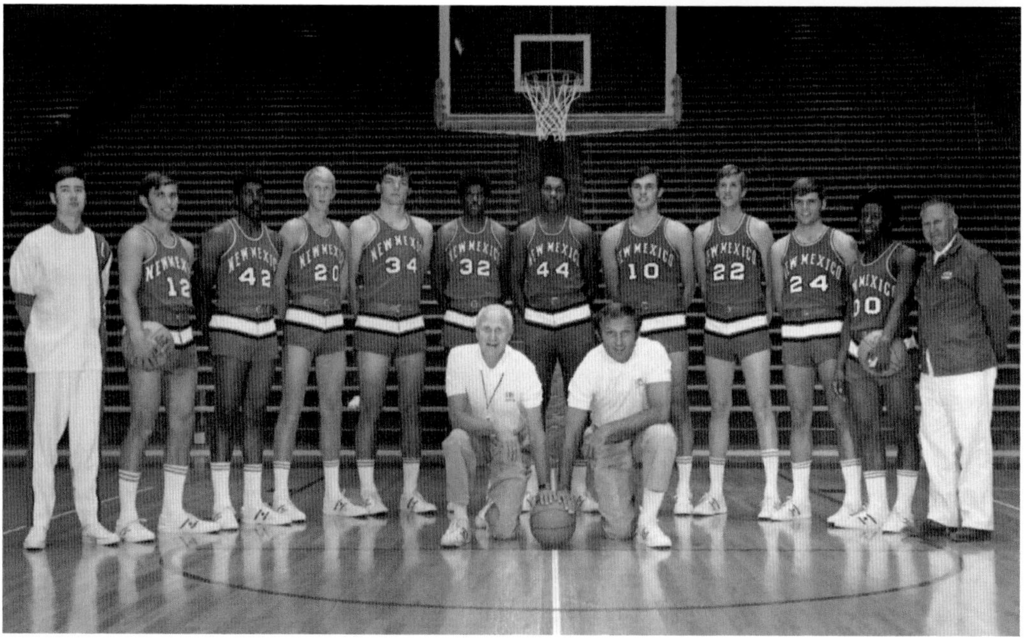

Bob King (1923–2004)

Named the University of New Mexico's head basketball coach in 1962, Bob King proceeded to put UNM on the map as a national power during his 10 years at the program's helm. King's teams were often ranked in the top 10 nationally. His Lobos opened the new, 14,831-seat Pit arena on December 1, 1966. Posing with the 1970 Lobos are King (kneeling, left), assistant coach Norm Ellenberger (kneeling, right), and athletic trainer Tow Diehm (far right). In 1992, UNM named the Pit's floor "Bob King Court." (Courtesy of UNM Athletics Department Records, Box 4, Center for Southwest Research, University Libraries, University of New Mexico.)

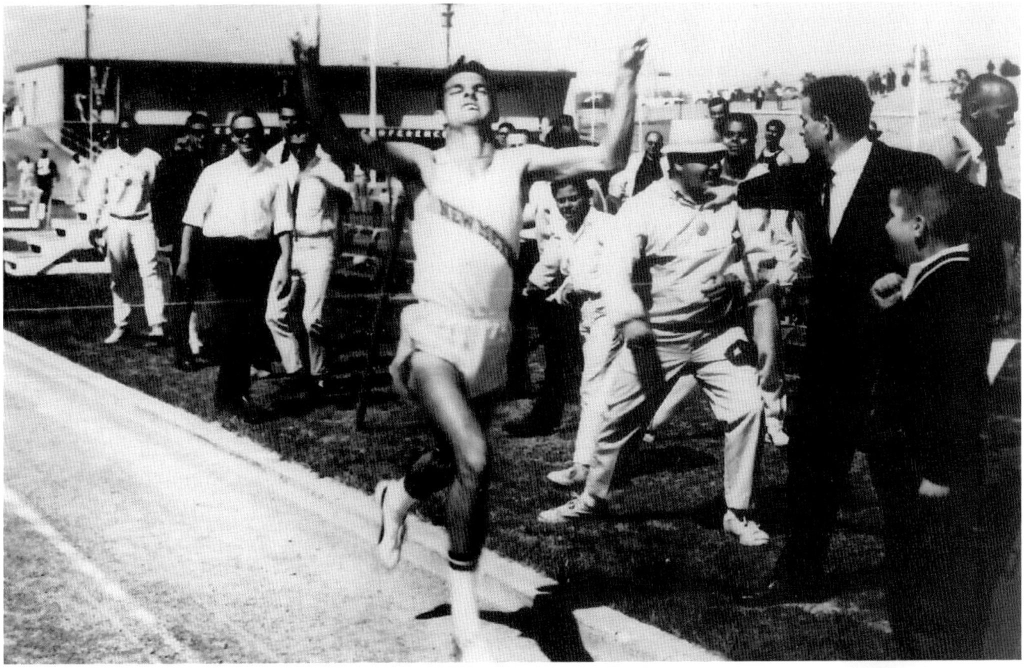

John Baker (1944–1970)
John Baker was never considered much of an athlete as a child. By the time he graduated from Manzano High in 1962, however, he was ranked as the best mile runner in New Mexico. After college at UNM, he coached the Duke City Dashers and the track team at Aspen Elementary School. Despite a heroic struggle, Coach Baker died of cancer on Thanksgiving Day, 1970. Aspen Elementary was renamed John Baker Elementary School in his honor.

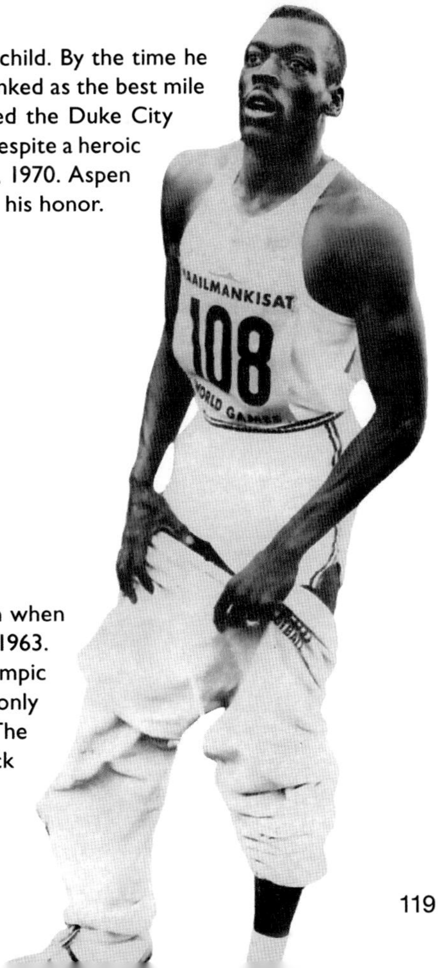

Adolph Plummer (b. 1938)
Plummer was a member of the UNM track-and-field team when he broke the world record in the 440-yard dash on May 25, 1963. Plummer won the race by several yards over future Olympic gold medalist Ulis Williams. Plummer later said that his only memory of the race was when the starter called "set." The rest was just a blur. It is considered the most famous track race in UNM history.

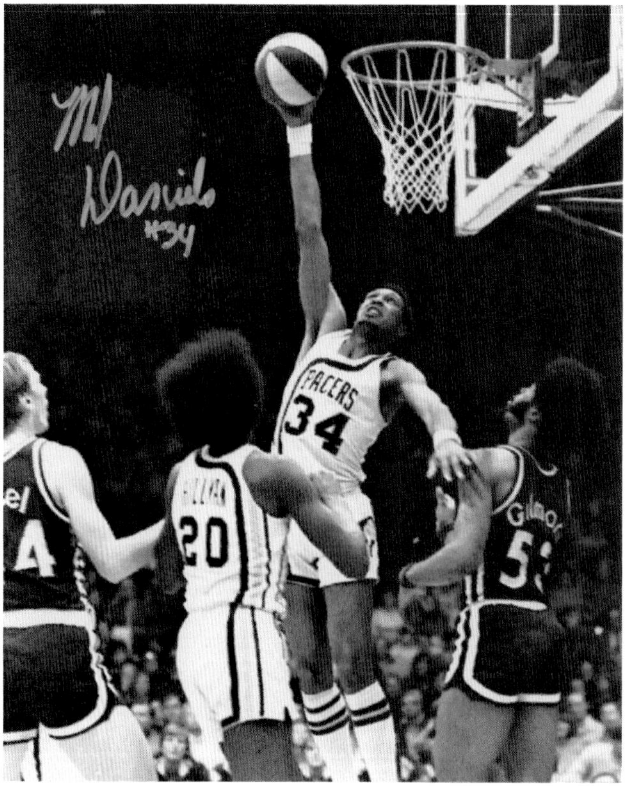

Mel Daniels (b. 1944)
One of the first black basketball players at UNM, Mel Daniels played for the Lobos squad from 1964 to 1967. The six-foot, nine-inch center led the Lobos in scoring in each of his three seasons at UNM. Not even a freak injury (requiring 352 stitches) slowed Daniels down. He was UNM's first All-American basketball player. He entered the new American Basketball Association and played on seven ABA all-star teams.

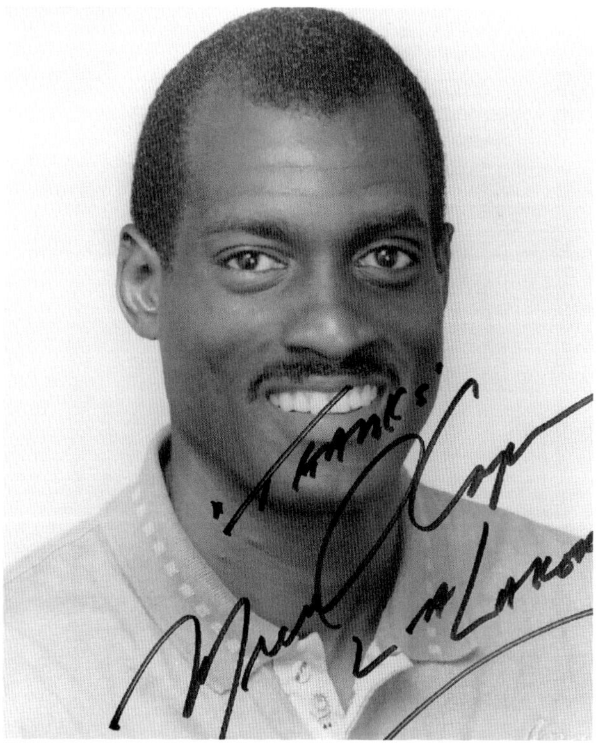

Michael Cooper (b. 1956)
Standing six feet, five inches, Michael Cooper arrived on the UNM campus to play basketball at the peak of the Lobos' success in the mid-1970s. "Coop" scored well, but he was especially effective on defense. A fan favorite, Cooper played professionally for the champion Los Angeles Lakers from 1979 to 1990. He has since coached several professional basketball teams, including the Albuquerque Thunderbirds and several teams in the WNBA, the women's professional basketball league.

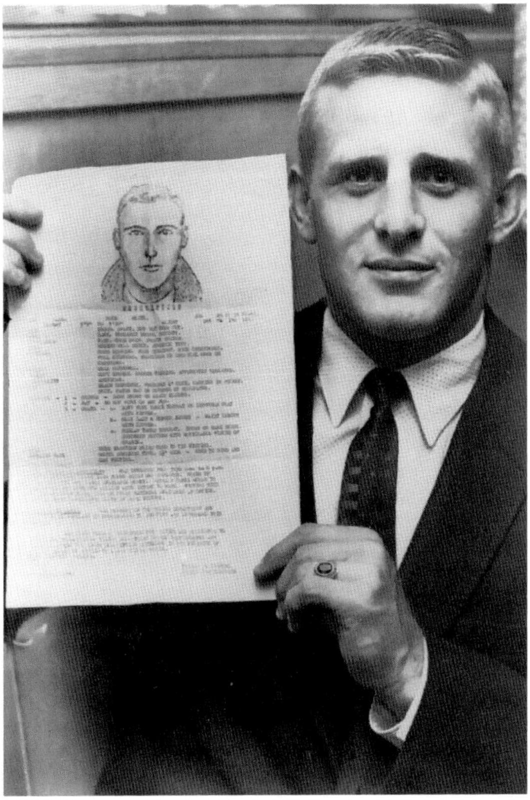

Tommy McDonald (b. 1934)
McDonald attended Albuquerque's Highland High, where he excelled in several sports, especially football. He later starred as a two-time All-American football player at the University of Oklahoma. Turning professional, he spent most of his 12-year hall-of-fame career with the Philadelphia Eagles. This 1957 press photograph shows him with a drawing of the "Lonely Heart Bandit," who looked remarkably like him. Fortunately, McDonald's image appeared in more honorable publications, including on the cover of *Sports Illustrated.*

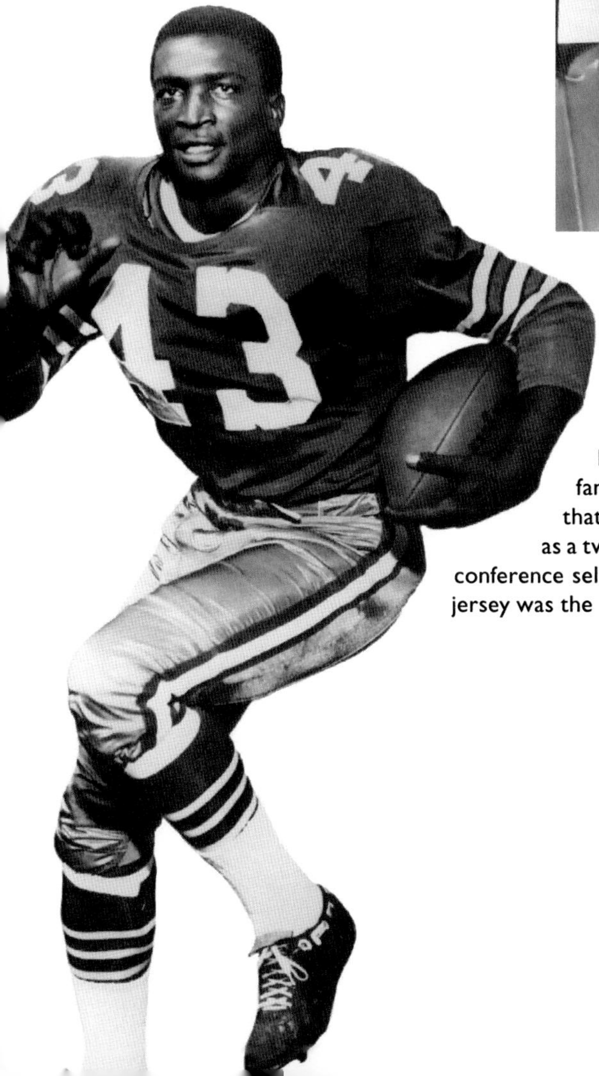

Don Perkins (b. 1938)
Perkins is remembered as one of the most famous Dallas Cowboys football players. Few recall that he first drew national attention when he starred as a two-way player for the UNM Lobos. He was an all-conference selection from 1957 to 1959, and his No. 43 UNM jersey was the first ever retired by the university.

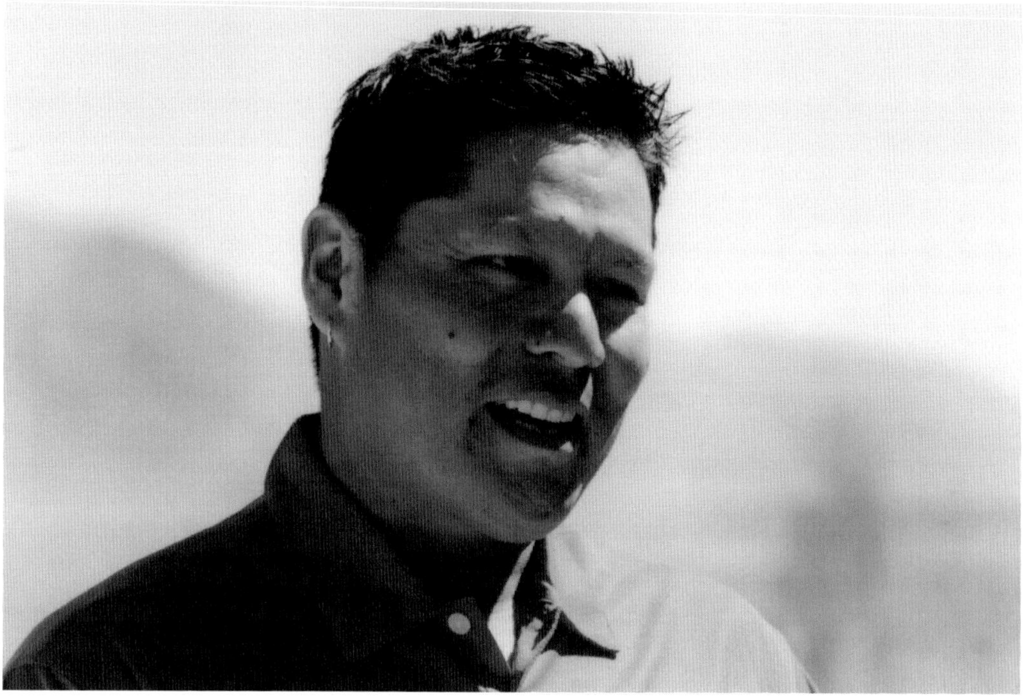

Notah Begay III (b. 1972)
The childhood home of Notah Begay was located along the 14th fairway of an Albuquerque golf course. He was named the New Mexico prep athlete of the year while playing for the Albuquerque Academy in 1990. After starring as an All-American at Stanford, he turned pro and became the first Native American to play on the professional golf tour. In 1995, Begay established a nonprofit organization to help benefit Native American youth.

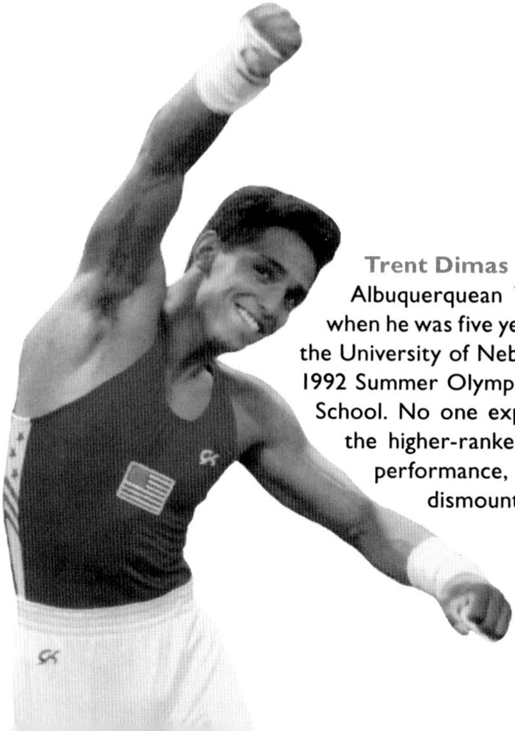

Trent Dimas (b. 1970)
Albuquerquean Trent Dimas began training as a gymnast when he was five years old. He competed as an All-American at the University of Nebraska before coming home to train for the 1992 Summer Olympics at Albuquerque's Gold Cups Gymnastic School. No one expected Dimas to win a gold medal against the higher-ranked Russian team. Dimas won with a 9.875 performance, dramatically nailing a triple-somersault dismount from the horizontal bar.

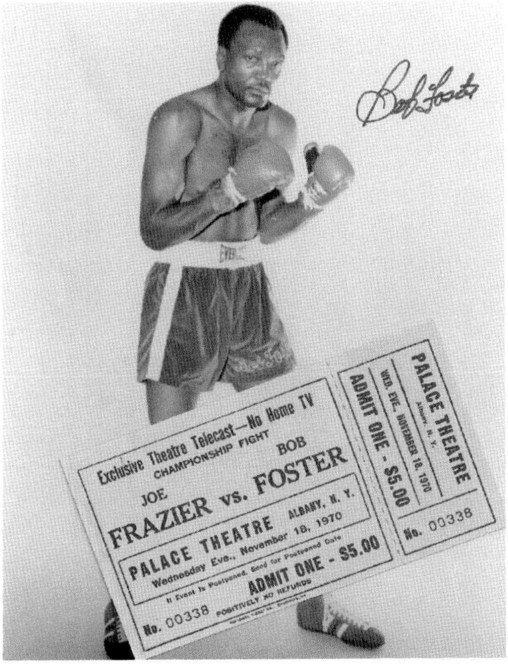

Bob Foster (b. 1938)
Born and raised in southwest Albuquerque, Bob Foster started in Golden Gloves competition when he was only 13. He became a professional boxer in 1961. Fighting as a light heavyweight, he enjoyed great success, earning the World Boxing Association championship. He fought such legends as Joe Frazier and Muhammad Ali. He retired in 1978 with a record of 56-8-1, including 46 knockouts.

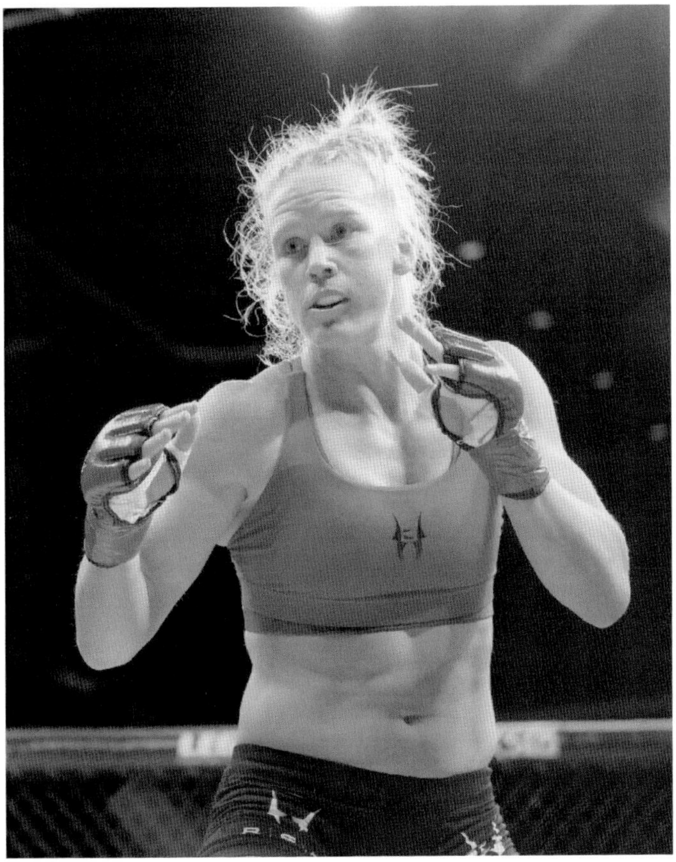

Holly Holms (b. 1981)
Growing up in Albuquerque, the only girl in a family of three children, Holly Holms was always interested in sports. She graduated from Manzano High and attended UNM before launching her professional boxing career on January 25, 2002, knocking out her opponent in three rounds. She went on to a record of 38-2. Known as the "Preacher's Daughter," the five-foot, eight-inch southpaw has enjoyed equally great success as a professional kickboxer.

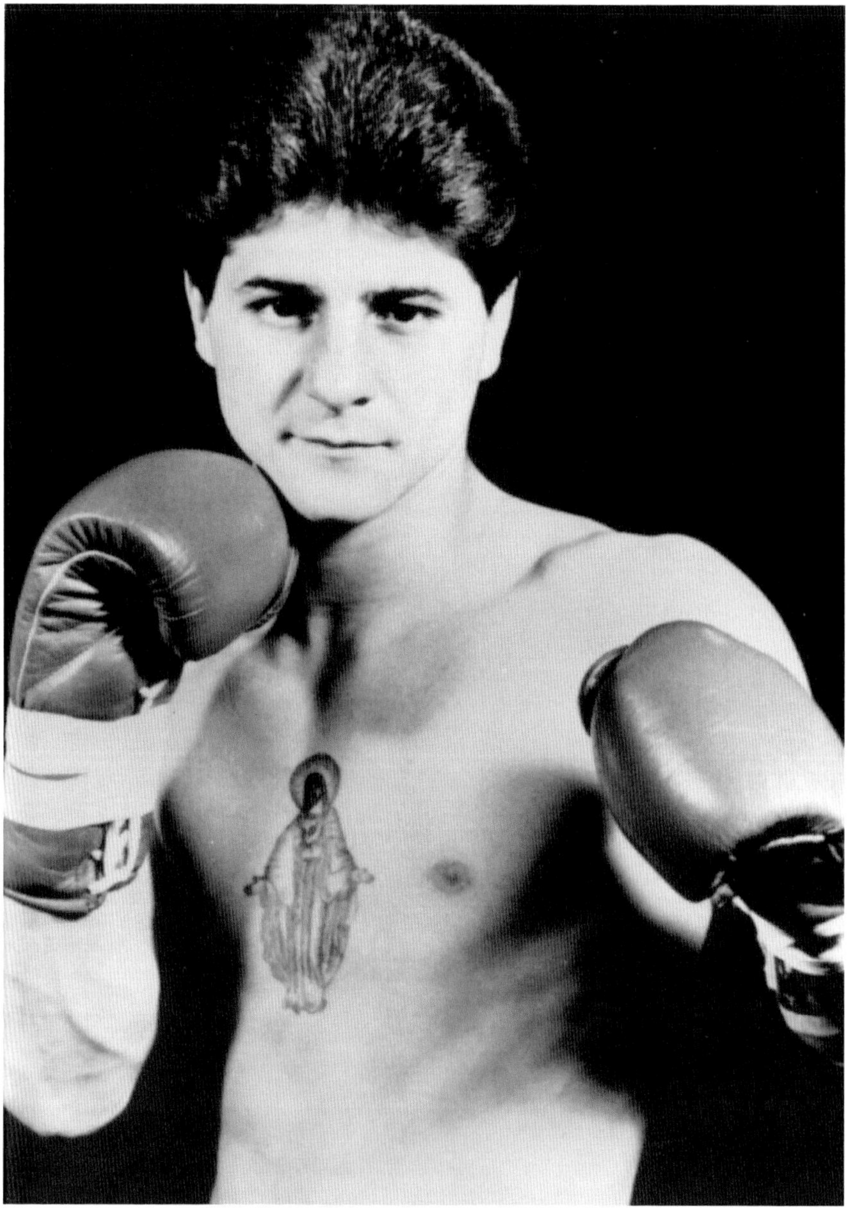

Johnny Tapia (1967–2012)

Johnny Tapia lived a short life, filled with great victories and tragic sorrows. Growing up in an Albuquerque *barrio*, he witnessed frequent violence, including his mother's murder when he was only eight. Starting to box when he was nine, he enjoyed early success, winning national Golden Gloves championships in 1983 and 1985. Turning professional in 1988, he won match after match, often by knockouts. He won five world boxing championships and was famous for his rivalry with fellow Albuquerque boxer Danny Romero. At the end of his fights in Albuquerque, Tapia often yelled, "I love you, Albuquerque," to thunderous applause by his devoted fans. But tragedy continued to haunt Tapia, as he lived what he called his *vida loca* (crazy life), a saying later tattooed on his chest. He died of heart failure in his Albuquerque home in 2012. He was 45. Beloved by thousands, his many acts of kindness were recalled in local newspapers for many days after his passing.

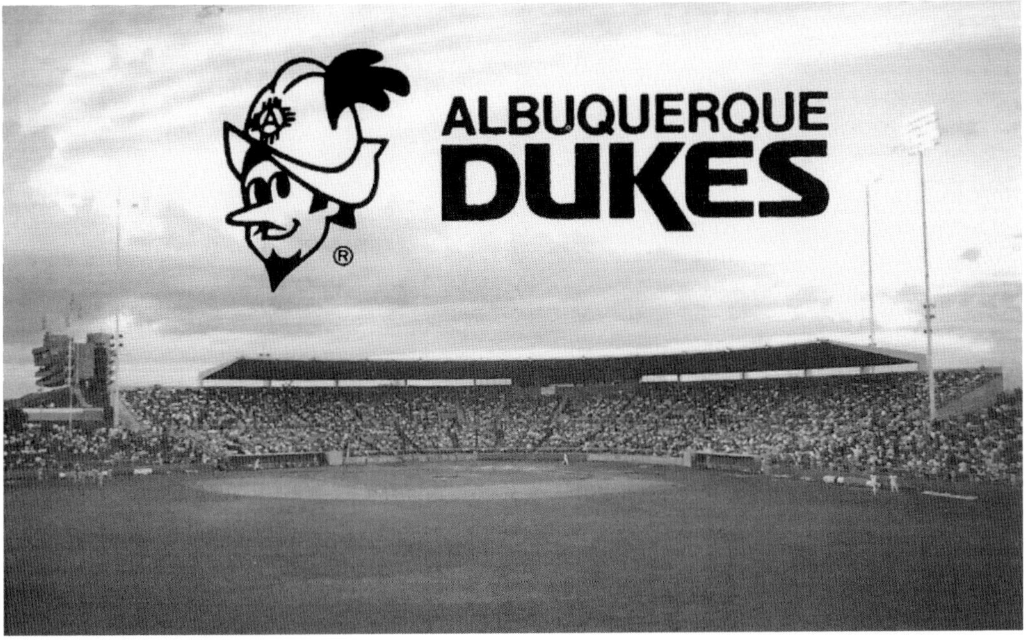

Albuquerque Dukes

The Los Angeles Dodgers transferred its top minor-league team to Albuquerque in 1972. Local readers were polled to see if they preferred to call the new team the "Dodgers" or the "Dukes," in honor of the Duke of Alburquerque. The "Dukes" won by a wide margin. Artist Dick Moots designed the team's logo. Dressed as the team's mascot, Leroi Otero played "Mr. Duke" at Dukes games for 15 seasons.

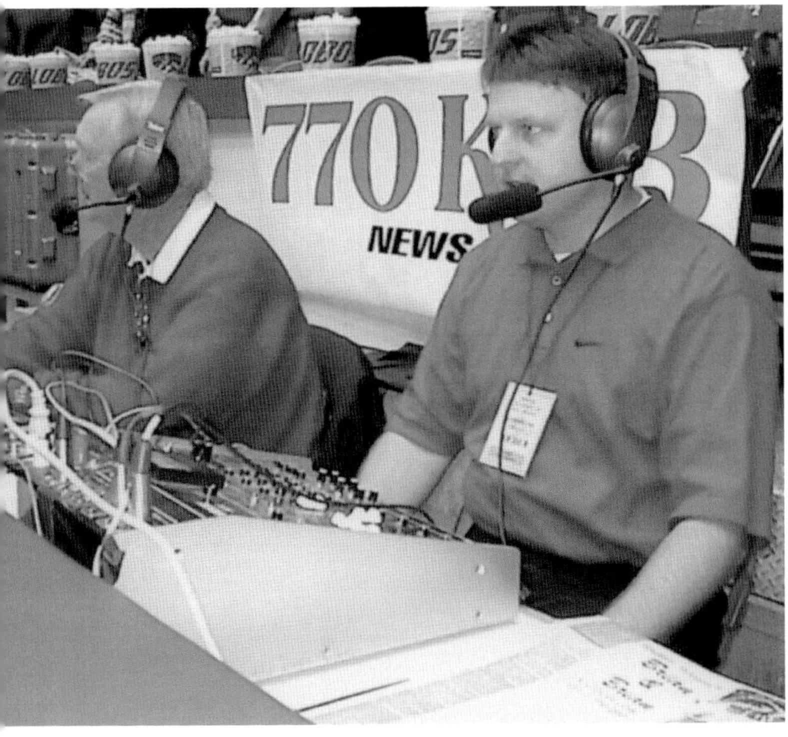

Mike Roberts (b. 1933)

Long known as "the voice of the Lobos," Mike Roberts (left) began calling UNM basketball games in 1966. Two years later, he began doing play-by-play radio broadcasts of UNM football games. If that were not enough, Roberts called Albuquerque Dukes baseball games from 1982 to 1999 and local football games until 2013. He is in both the New Mexico Broadcasters Hall of Fame and the Albuquerque Professional Baseball Hall of Fame. (Courtesy of Gary Herron.)

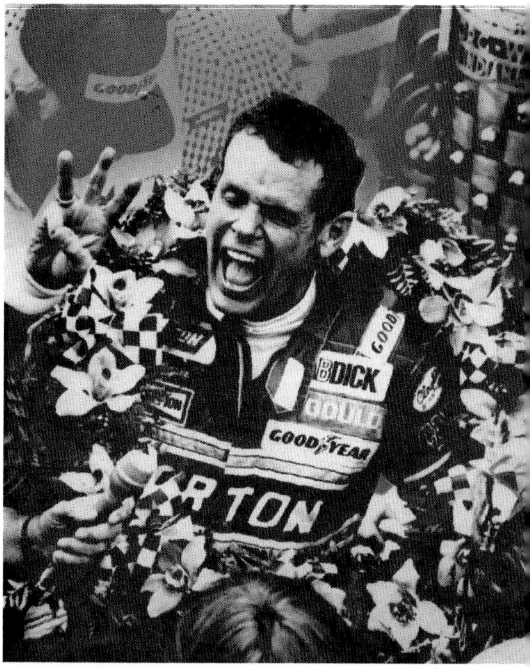

Al, Mary, and Bobby Unser

The Unser family is synonymous with racing in Albuquerque and across the nation. The Unsers opened a garage on Central Avenue in 1936. Family members were among the first Pike's Peak racers and stockcar drivers, but they are most famous for their Indianapolis 500 victories, winning nine races from 1968 to 1994. In all, six Unsers have raced at Indianapolis, and three have won: Bobby (right) in 1968, 1975, and 1981; "Big Al" in 1970, 1971, 1978, and 1987; and "Little Al" in 1991 and 1994. Their mother, Mary, became famous as well, bringing as much as 75 gallons of her popular New Mexico chili to every race until her death in 1975. Below, Bobby and Big Al help celebrate Mary's 65th birthday. Sadly, racing is a terribly dangerous sport; Joe and Jerry Unser were killed in 1929 and 1959, respectively. The Unser Racing Museum, at 1776 Montano Road Northwest, opened in 2005.

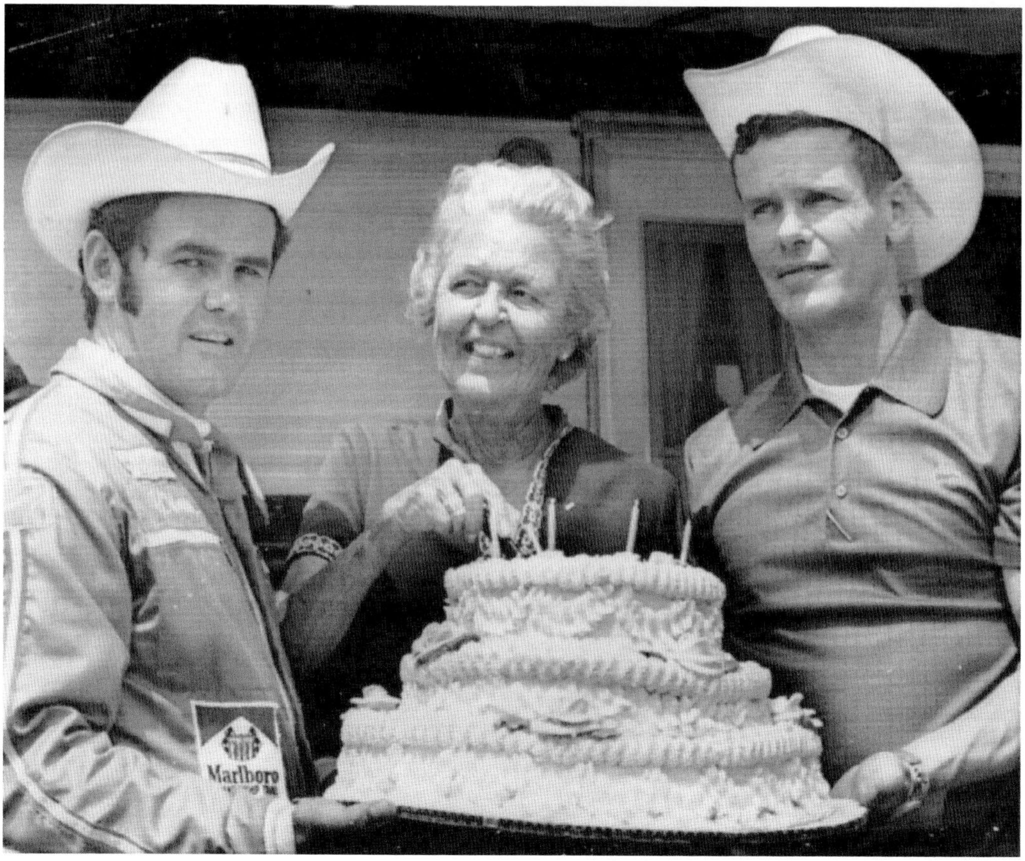

INDEX